Islamophobia in Britain

Leonie B. Jackson

Islamophobia in Britain

The Making of a Muslim Enemy

palgrave
macmillan

Leonie B. Jackson
University of Huddersfield
Huddersfield, UK

ISBN 978-3-319-58349-5   ISBN 978-3-319-58350-1   (eBook)
DOI 10.1007/978-3-319-58350-1

Library of Congress Control Number: 2017940832

Cover design by Tjaša Krivec

Printed on acid-free paper

This Palgrave Macmillan imprint is published by Springer Nature
The registered company is Springer International Publishing AG
The registered company address is: Gewerbestrasse 11, 6330 Cham, Switzerland

This book is dedicated to my mother, Mandy Jackson,
who taught me to read, question, struggle and survive.

ACKNOWLEDGEMENTS

My deepest gratitude goes to George Kassimeris, who has patiently taught me how to be a scholar through numerous ups and downs, and who has sifted through endless drafts of this manuscript with a stamina that is truly remarkable. I would also like to thank Richard Jackson, Eammon O'Kane and Mike Cunningham for their insightful suggestions and support as this research was being undertaken. Naturally, all mistakes are my own.

Earlier versions of chapters three and four first appeared as articles in *Critical Studies on Terrorism* (5:2, 2012) and *The British Journal of Politics and International Relations* (17:1, 2015) and I am grateful to the editors of both for permission to reproduce sections here.

I would also like to extend my deep thanks and love to my extended family. Daniel Koczy, whose love of learning has inspired and excited me for more than a decade, and who never fails to make me laugh. Sian Jackson, who is an endlessly patient tower of love, support and encouragement. Dal Nijjar, whose belief and understanding has been astonishing. Thanks also to Dan Bolton, Rob Endean, Mick Jackson, Colin Fuller and the Haywards. I have been blessed with an army of strong women in my life, who have taught me how to tenaciously persevere against all odds, particularly Katy Mersino, Jacqueline Fuller, Kirsty Fuller, Chloe Roberts, Mary Allcock, Diane Littley and Katie Rogers. Finally, I am forever indebted to Simon Hayward, who has patiently submitted to long nights animatedly discussing, learning and living this research. This journey has been all the sweeter for having spent it with you.

CONTENTS

CHAPTER 1

Introduction: Islamophobia and Racism

In 2001 I was first year undergraduate student of politics. As we ten-tatively formed groups based on little more than seating preferences in a lecture theatre, I found myself drawn to Sofia, a local woman with a broad Birmingham accent. Ambitious and outgoing, with a fierce sense of social justice, Sofia was also visibly Muslim. She wore a headscarf (and always called it this, never *hijab*), dressed modestly, avoided alcohol and fasted at Ramadan, yet she rarely discussed her faith and when she did, always articulated it in terms of the social obligations she understood it to require.

The semester had barely started when the world was shaken by the September 11 attacks. As we meandered in the classroom, waiting for the instructor to arrive, a new polarisation formed among the class. The hijackings were on everyone's lips, and in the heated conversations sev-eral people turned to Sofia to explain them. She was Muslim, and so, the media loudly exclaimed, were the hijackers. In unease and confu-sion students looked to her for an explanation. What was it about Islam that had driven these attacks? Did she think the hijackers were right? Did all Muslims secretly share these grudges? As she tried to deal with the increasingly hostile questioning, one woman turned to me, shaking her head disapprovingly, and muttered 'how can she say this has nothing to do with Islam? This is all about Islam'.

In the fifteen years since this incident, I, like many identifiably white people, have been privy to similar whispered utterances that drew me aside as if I were an ally in the utterer's suspicion, fear and hostility

© The Author(s) 2018
L.B. Jackson, *Islamophobia in Britain*,
DOI 10.1007/978-3-319-58350-1_1

1

towards Muslims. Sofia, no doubt, like many identifiably Muslim people, has been the subject of these conversations, a proxy for the shadowy
Muslim enemy that is increasingly perceived to threaten the very civilisation in which we live. Commonly understood as Islamophobia, this fear
of, or hostility towards, Muslims is employed today to explain a plethora
of social ills. Terrorism, riots, segregated communities, lack of national
identity, child grooming and low educational achievement have all been
enfolded into a discourse that marks Muslims out as the 'other' that
threatens 'our' ideals and progress. The polarisation evident in that classroom in 2001 has become an embedded feature of British and European
society, where Muslims are at least marked out as different, and are frequently subject to suspicion, harassment, abuse and violence.

This book is the story of how Islamophobia has come to have such
explanatory power in the British (and European) imagination. Through
an analysis of Islamophobia's form and content and a theoretical exploration of its function, I argue that the key to understanding this phenomenon is an appreciation of *why* individuals and groups from across
the social strata employ these narratives. Contemporary Islamophobic
discourse is articulated at a wide variety of social sites and by differently
positioned social actors, yet the narratives it relies on are always deployed
for a purpose. This book seeks to understand that purpose, and argues
that Islamophobia upholds Eurocentrism, 'the dominant contemporary racialised system in Europe, where Western-identified subjects are
awarded a better social, economic and political 'racial contract' and seek
to defend these privileges against real and imagined Muslim demands.
Under such a system, Islamophobia is not an 'unfounded hostility', but a
rational defence of collective Eurocentric advantages.

DEFINING ISLAMOPHOBIA: A CHALLENGE FOR US ALL

It is customary to begin any writing on Islamophobia with a discussion of the controversy surrounding the term. The concept is central to
understanding the political and social struggles that mark the contemporary world, yet it is highly contested and its definition, social meaning
and analytical use is fraught with conflict. Everyday conversational use
of the term ranges from uncritical acceptance to virulent denial, making
the lack of an agreed upon definition a central controversy. But the issue
is not merely semantic. The debate over whether there is such a thing as
Islamophobia and what it might comprise is a political struggle, over the

recognition, articulation and protection of identities, and the incorpora-
tion, and limits, of difference.

There is some dispute about when the expression 'Islamophobia' was
first used in English. AbdoolKarim Vakil has noted that Edward Said
used it in his article 'Orientalism reconsidered', published in three different print contexts in 1985, and thus reaching both an academic and a
wider activist readership (Vakil 2008, 43). Most other scholars date the
term to the early 1990s. Chris Allen (2007, 148–149) placed the first
usage around December 1991, when it appeared in both the American
journal *Insight*, and Tariq Modood's book review in *The Independent*,
while others have dated its first appearance in the UK media to 1994,
indicating that the term had gained popular traction, likely because of
the first Gulf War and increased perceptions that Muslims were being targeted on the basis of their religious identity in both global and local contexts (Hopkins and Kahani-Hopkins 2006, 249; Cole 2009, 1681).

The Runnymede Trust's 1997 report, *Islamophobia: A challenge for us all*, however, has come to form the starting point for discussions regarding the movement of the term into the mainstream.
Labelled as a shorthand way of referring to the dread or hatred of
Islam, the Commission on British Muslims and Islamophobia defined
it as unfounded hostility towards Islam, and the practical consequences
of this for Muslims. Foreseeing potential objections to this definition,
it was disambiguated by an attempt to clarify the point at which legitimate criticism ended and unfounded hostility began. To this end a list
of eight views about Islam and Muslims was submitted, with 'closed'
and 'open' positions attached to them, comprising whether Islam was
seen as: monolithic or diverse; separate or interacting; inferior or different; whether Muslims were considered enemies or partners; manipula-
tive or sincere; whether Muslim criticisms of the West were rejected or
considered; whether discrimination against Muslims was defended or
criticised; and whether Islamophobia was seen as natural or problematic.
Legitimate criticism, the Commission claimed, was the province of open
views, while Islamophobia was 'the recurring characteristic of closed
views' (Commission on British Muslims and Islamphobia 1997, 4).
Islamophobia could therefore be challenged by the proliferation of open,
and the challenge of closed, views.

The report was groundbreaking in its assertion that Muslims were
experiencing specific targeting on the basis of their faith and represents
the first attempt to comprehensively define this phenomenon. It has also

been hugely influential on the conceptualisation of Islamophobia for policy makers, and a number of organisations have incorporated similar definitions (for example, the Council of Europe). However, it has drawn criticism for its procedural approach to Islamophobic discourse and practice, as well as the essentialisation of identities that follows from such a conceptualisation.

The first criticism foregrounds the procedural manner in which Islamophobia was defined. Because the report was intended as guidelines for equalities and anti-racist practitioners, it overemphasised a checklist style approach, which gave rise to a reductionist and dualistic conceptualisation of the phenomenon. This is embodied in the central focus on Islamophobia as the recurrence of 'closed views', a focus that Chris Allen notes took on a life of its own, becoming so central to Runnymede's understanding of Islamophobia that the immediately preceding definition was changed only a page later, from fear or hostility towards Muslims and Islam, to the recurring characteristic of closed views and nothing more (Allen 2008, 31). Although this tick-box approach may be useful to discern routine and overt cases of Islamophobia, it is severely limited when considering more complex and subtle articulations.

This was exacerbated by the Commission's suggestion that closed views could be challenged by the proliferation of open views, a position that might be termed Islamophilia (Allen 2010, 168). If Islamophobia is an abnormal and pathological dislike of Muslims and Islam, then Islamophilia is the equally abnormal love of Muslims and Islam, and is no less reductionist or essentialist with regard to Muslim identities. Defending the neologism, the report stated that the coining of a new word and the identification of a growing danger could 'play a valuable part in the long endeavour of correcting perceptions and improving relationships' (Commission on British Muslims and Islamphobia 1997, 4). The very terms used in this passage point to a profound problem with the way the Commission conceived Muslim identities and the status of Islamophobia. To correct a perception implies an essence that can be uncovered, a correct Islam that could be endorsed through open views, and an incorrect Islam that individuals had been mistakenly promoting. What makes this notion so deeply problematic is its assumption of some form of collective responsibility among Muslims for the circulation of this 'incorrect' Islam. In its reliance on the notion of a right way to be Muslim, identities were restricted and existing power relations reinforced through a dualism which conferred on outside observers the right to decide whether particular Islamic expression fell into the realm of open or closed. Such essentialising, especially when backed up by the power of the state to legitimise particular versions of Islam, has the potential to silence and delegitimise individuals outside of these traditions. This dualism rears itself again in the form of 'good' and 'bad' Muslims; those who conform to the correct Islam and those who do not.

The Commission's understanding of what constituted Islamophobia not only implicated Muslims as collectively responsible for the circulation of this 'incorrect Islam', but also intimated that 'bad', 'extremist' Muslims bore some responsibility for the Islamophobia directed towards them. By this logic, Islamophobia is only illegitimate when directed at 'good', 'moderate' Muslims, while 'bad', 'extremist' Muslims bear some responsibility for Islamophobic sentiment and may therefore be legitimately targeted with 'closed' views. In his Oxford University Press blog, Walter Laqueur made exactly this point, stating that people subscribe to such 'closed views' (that Islam is a political ideology, separate and 'other', and profoundly aggressive) because this is precisely what Iranian leaders had preached to the world for more than three decades (Laqueur 2006). For Laqueur, these closed views had some legitimacy because of the behaviour of some Muslims, and this view is widely shared. Ed Husain, writing in the *London Evening Standard*, stated 'If there is anti-Muslim sentiment, we Muslims have to ask what some of us have done to provoke such feelings in a country that is proudly multi-cultural' (Husain 2008). Such statements would be inconceivable for any other racialised group, yet it is precisely this type of thinking that the Runnymede Report encouraged. Until 'bad' Muslims stop saying and doing what 'bad' Muslims say and do, Islamophobia is (at least when addressed to these Muslims) in some sense legitimate, and 'closed' views justified.

The Runnymede Report's conceptualisation of Islamophobia is profoundly problematic. Its reductionist approach meant that Islamophobic expression was dualistically sorted into categories of legitimate and illegitimate, and Muslims were subsequently reduced to 'good' and 'bad', undeserving or deserving of Islamophobic sentiment. What is most troubling, however, is its failure to recognise the power dynamics inherent in Islamophobia. By reducing it to a question of perceptions that can be corrected, this understanding fails to significantly challenge most Islamophobic discourse and practice, which is predicated not on closed minded 'views', but ideological currents and shared social narratives that are perceived to have a great deal of explanatory power.

More sophisticated conceptualisations have compared it to other discourses of exclusion. Historical approaches to the phenomenon have identified contemporary Islamophobia as rooted in imperial and colonial discourses, particularly Orientalism. Scholars adopting this understanding have foregrounded the historical antecedents of Islamophobia and argued that its manifestation today involves the recycling and rearticulation of older tropes for similar exclusionary purposes and with analogous effects. Another approach considers that Islamophobia can be most usefully understood through comparison with similar exclusionary discourses. Proponents of this position have made use of the vast theoretical literature on racism and anti-Semitism to aid understanding of the contemporary situation of Muslims. While the historical approach tells us something about *where* Islamophobia comes from, the comparative approach attempts to explain *what* it is and *how* it works.

Imperialism, Colonialism and Orientalism

Tracing the historical antecedents of Islamophobia, a number of scholars have drawn attention to the way in which imperial, colonial and Orientalist discourses are rearticulated for the social and political needs of the present period, and in doing so have foregrounded the constitutive role that Islam and Muslims have played as the other against which European and Western identity has defined itself.

Imperialistic understandings of Islam have shaped and formed the identity of Europeans since the fifteenth century, when the expulsion of the Moors and Jews from Spain at the same historical moment as the discovery of the Americas involved a confrontation with (and eventually a conquest of) both the religious internal others of Europe and the racial external 'others' of the New World (Geisser 2010). In this geopolitical environment, Christian European identity increasingly defined itself in contradistinction to rival civilisations, the most imposing of which were the Islamic empires of the East.

As Europeans conquered Muslim territory, imperial understandings of Muslims as religious and geopolitical rivals gave way to colonial management strategies, which viewed Islam as a dying civilisation and sought to replace theological power with European secularised nationalism by imposing Western control (Grosfoguel and Mielants 2006). Colonial strategies of governance understood Islam as the foundation of life for these populations and attempted to discipline them by harnessing religious authority to repress rebellion and keep order. The continued contemporary relevance of these understandings has led some scholars to argue that Islamophobia is a neo-colonial discourse. As Tariq Ramadan has noted, colonial literature was explicit in its binarism marking out 'good' Muslims who collaborated and 'bad' Muslims who resisted the colonial enterprise (Ramadan 2010), a division that endures through contemporary state funding, or sanction, of particular theological traditions.

Deeply connected to imperialism and colonialism is Orientalism. As Edward Said (1978) conceptualised it, Orientalism is a cultural discourse of power that posits a unified 'West' against an imagined 'Orient' that is dehumanised and sensualised as exotic, barbaric and despotic. Orientalism legitimised domination by Western powers through its representation of Islam as timelessly static and resistant to change and rationalism. Understanding Islamophobia as neo-Orientalism, several scholars have pointed to the way images of barbarism, primitive violence, and fundamental threat have become the mainstay of contemporary Islamophobic discourse (Love 2009; Gingrich 2005; Kaya 2011). The notion that Muslims are centrally constituted by their (timeless) Islamic identity is contemporarily articulated through the assertion that people's politics can be read from their religion, and the tendency to look to the Qur'an in order to understand contemporary political and social struggles. This idea is central to Samuel Huntington's (1993) clash of civilisations narrative, which rejuvenated Orientalism for the present international relations environment, constructing Muslim societies (or civilisations in Huntington's parlance) as weak and primitive and thus requiring Western intervention.

Islam's effortless transformation from religious rival, to imperial contender, to rival superpower, has made it a perennial enemy-outsider, capable of being altered and distorted to meet the social realities and necessities of any given historical moment. In a mediaeval Europe divided by war, anti-Muhammadism played a cohesive role, while the religious threat that Islam represented was in the fifteenth century rearticulated into geopolitical danger. Understanding Islamophobia as the heir to these discourses centres the constitutive centrality of imperial, colonial and Orientalist worldviews that have historically constructed Muslims as antithetically other to Western subjects and legitimised the domination of the former by the latter.

The tendency to see contemporary Islamophobia as merely a 'neo' form of these discourses, however, obscures important characteristics. In contrast to the historical discourses discussed above, which were directed at geographically distant imperial or colonial subjects, contemporary European Islamophobia is largely directed at the Muslim residents or citizens of European states. This has led some to argue that Islamophobia, as an assimilative state discourse which aims to manage and domesticate internal Muslim populations, should be contrasted with these discourses (Birt 2008). The usefulness of Orientalism to understanding this phenomenon is also questionable. As Yasmin Hussain and Paul Bagguley (2012, 719) have noted, Orientalism is usually identified with the Middle East and the racialisation of Arabs, while the majority of British Muslims, and certainly those considered the most 'troublesome', have heritage in the Indian subcontinent. Nonetheless, the contemporary period may be understood to have produced its own internal Orientalism directed at European Muslims and developed according to the political and social needs of the 'War on Terror' (Fekete 2009, 193). The Orient, in the present period, is not treated as a separate geographical region, but as an essence located within Europe's Muslim population

Perhaps a more pressing concern with focusing on these historical discourses is the possibility of reifying Islamophobia as something ancient, naturalised and ineradicable. Although historical representations of Muslims and their contemporary rearticulation are important to note, Islamophobia in the present period is clearly shaped by contemporary events and the novel discourses that have sought to explain them. The challenge for this approach is to explain why these discourses remain coherent for explaining Muslim behaviour in the current period. Islamophobia is not just the modern incarnation of these old discourses. It has very specific instrumental uses, and viewing it as a transcendent discourse, whose incarnations are merely reformulations of older dominations, runs the risk of submerging important aspects under an umbrella explanation that understands European societies as inescapably Occidentalist without explaining *why* and *how* Islamophobia today performs the role that was historically accomplished by these older discourses. In order to attend to these concerns, some of the most useful studies of Islamophobia have approached the phenomenon through a comparison with the discourses and strategies of racism.

Islamophobia and Racism

A key debate underpins the use of racism as a theoretical framework to understand Islamophobia. On one side of this debate stand those who argue that Islamophobia, which targets a heterogeneous racial group because of their religious identification, is analytically distinct from racism and cannot be collapsed into the category. On the other side stand those who argue that since Islamophobia includes fear, prejudice and discrimination towards an out-group demarcated largely by physical appearance, it should be considered a particular type of racism. Proponents of this position argue that Muslims have come to occupy the position of racialised other in the contemporary period, and the example of anti-Semitism has been used to demonstrate how religious identities can be and have been racialised according to the needs of particular historical, political and cultural contexts.

In the second edition of their classic study of racism, Robert Miles and Malcolm Brown (2003, 164) argued that although there are parallels, Islamophobia should not be considered a form of racism, since the alleged distinctiveness of Muslims is not biological. This distinction between biological and religious difference is one of the most important debates surrounding Islamophobia, and the contention that Islam is a religion, not a race, has become central to this position as articulated by the populist right and various 'muscular liberal' commentators. These arguments are usually based on the assertion of a fundamental difference between religion and race, where the former is constructed as something voluntary, while the latter is considered innate.

Employing this perspective, Kenan Malik (2005) has argued: 'you can't choose your skin colour; you can choose your beliefs. Religion is a set of beliefs. I can be hateful about other beliefs, such as conservatism or communism. So why can't I be hateful about religion too?' Others have also articulated themselves using this distinction. For example, militant atheist Richard Dawkins deflected accusations of racism by stating: 'if you can *convert* to something (or convert or apostatize out of it) it is not a race… Islam is a religion and you can choose to leave it or join it' (Dawkins 2013). This argument has become central to the arguments of those who reserve the right to criticise Islam and Muslims, and may be seen to operate within Islamophobic discourse in the same way as the 'disclaimer' (I'm not racist, but…) in racist discourse (van Dijk 1993a, 77–84). The position that Islam is not a race also has some academic credibility. Henk Dekker and Jvander Noll (2011, 15), for example, have argued that Islamophobia is only a form of racism if it is believed that Islam is in the blood of Muslims and cannot be removed. In the absence of this biological determinism, and if it is believed that assimilation is a possibility, they argue that Islamophobia cannot be considered racism. There are two problems with this position. First, the race concept has always been intermingled with religion, and second, the distinction between voluntary, chosen religious identities and involuntary, externally assigned racial identities fails to take into account processes of racialisation.

On the first point, contrary to the contemporary belief that racial and religious differences are separate and distinct, several scholars have demonstrated not only that religion has historically been essential to the race concept, but that the contemporary understanding of race as a purely somatic and biological category is a relatively recent historical development. Religious difference formed the first mark of 'Otherness' in the modern world, differentiating Europeans from the people they expelled and conquered, and the privileging of biological difference as natural was largely a product of the secularisation of the race concept in the eighteenth and nineteenth centuries (Mignolo 2006; Rana 2007).

On the second point, the 'voluntary' nature of religious identity has been discussed in detail by Nasar Meer (2008, 76–77), who has argued that this supposed (voluntary religious/involuntary racial) dichotomy leads logically to the position that only involuntary identities deserve protection from discrimination or hostility. Meer points out that even if an individual could distance herself from a racialised identity (by passing for a non-Muslim) in order to avoid stereotyping, hostility or discrimination, this would not destabilise the racialisation of such identities. Avoiding racial targeting by changing one's identity does not make the racial targeting any less real, it merely protects one against its immediate effects, while the racialised system remains in place. Islamophobia relies on a rationalisation and justification that claims that it is nothing more than criticism of a belief system, but this is undermined by the fact that religious belonging has come to act as a symbol of racial difference(Kundnani 2007, 30).

The symbolic nature of racialised belonging, and the role of perception, is fundamental. Since racial assignment is usually something allocated from outside on to the racialised body of the 'other', the actual Muslimness of the individual targeted with Islamophobic discourse and practice is largely irrelevant. For example, in the aftermath of the 11 September 2001 hijackings, Sikhs were attacked because their assailants believed them to be Muslim. In the contemporary climate of Islamophobic hostility the possession of a 'Muslim sounding' name, a particular ethnic or national heritage (particularly, in the British context, Pakistani), or clothes that are identified as 'Islamic', is enough to assign individuals a 'Muslim' identity, and religiosity, or lack thereof, has little to do with perceived belonging in the racialised group. The example of Islamophobic hate crimes is instructive here. Such crimes usually incorporate violence against the body of the Muslim subject, a phenomenon that is typical of racist violence, however, empirical studies suggest that individuals are not targeted on the basis of their race. Rather, perpetrators are moved to act against symbolic somatic features such as headscarves, turbans, or 'Islamic clothing', precisely because these symbols have come to have racial meaning(Carland 2011).

The above arguments bring us to the notion of racialisation and cultural racism, concepts that emphasise the historically flexible social construction of race and the way it has been adapted according to the particular needs of specific social, political, economic and historical conditions. Racialisation refers to the process by which 'others' are created that can contain the economic and social fears of a society by acting as a body onto which these fears may be projected. For the study of Islamophobia it also bridges the arguments of the two positions described above, by detailing the way in which phenotypical and cultural signifiers have come to have racial meaning. In this sense it provides a rejoinder to the argument that Islam is not a race, by demonstrating how Muslims have been and are contemporarily racialised.

As those who are uncomfortable with the concept of Islamophobia have pointed out, Muslims are neither racially nor culturally homogenous (Lorente 2010, 119; Etienne 2007, 239). Islamophobia, which implies that Muslims are racialised and 'othered' as a *group*, is therefore controversial. To the charge that Islam is not a race, and that the analytical tools of racism are not appropriate, scholars have responded that Muslim culture has been racialised to the extent that it is now widely considered to be innate, something from which Muslims cannot escape. This position holds that Islamophobia should be understood as an instance of new racism.

Within the new racism thesis, religion is not viewed as a matter of private contemplation, but a public, externally assigned identity that cannot be simply disengaged from (Erdenir 2010, 35). New racism focuses on the challenge that difference presents to 'our way of life', and Islamophobia exemplifies this in its unrelenting focus on the unacceptable and incompatible nature of Muslims' cultural difference. It is the cultural turn of new racism that has allowed overtly Islamophobic groups to explicitly reject traditional racism, while at the same time using its frames and discourses in order to exclude culturally defined out-groups.

That religious signifiers can come to take on racial significance is, of course, nothing new. Anti-Semitism provides a classic example of how religious and cultural differences have been historically racialised to designate a religiously defined group as a racial other. European anti-Semitic thought has over time, and according to differing historical circumstances, marked Jewish people out as an unassimilable racial other; inherently different and deliberately aloof self-segregating fifth columnists who were loyal to a nation outside the one in which they resided (Meer and Noorani 2008). Anti-Semitism's focus on the danger that Jews posed to the unity and cohesion of the national community bears direct comparison with contemporary national questioning of Muslims across Europe. Additionally, conspiracy theories have played an important role in both of these discourses. The 'Sharia conspiracy' and the 'Eurabia thesis' have come to dominate right-wing Islamophobic discourse, and hold that through stealth jihad and demographic challenges to democracy in Europe, Muslim political activity represents a secret plan to impose totalitarian government on the world(Kundnani 2014, 249; Lean 2012, 8). What both anti-Semitic and Islamophobic conspiracy theories have in common is the fantasy that a group with little power has the ability to impose its (unified) will onto society, and the corresponding rationalisation and justification of discrimination and hostility as a means to protect the institutions that the nation holds dear.

Although the comparison is appealing, there exist important differences in the racialisation of Muslims and Jews that largely stem from the different historical functions of the two. Traditional nineteenth and early twentieth-century anti-Semitism was designed to exclude Jews from the national body, based on the notion that they represented a racial threat to an ethnically pure nation. Contemporary anti-Semitism, however, has no comparable agenda; there is simply no mainstream contemporary debate on the legitimacy of the Jewish presence in Europe. Islamophobia, in contrast, is a genuine political issue in Europe and as a phenomenon of the current age it is not mobilised to protect the ethnic purity of the nation, as was traditional anti-Semitism, but to safeguard European civilisation(Bunzl 2005, 506).

Understanding the history of Islamophobia and comparable strategies of religio-cultural othering is vital to understanding the way contemporary Islamophobia works, and more importantly why it exists. By considering the usefulness of racisms for human societies at particular historical moments, theories of racism potentially provide an explanation for why Islamophobia should have traction and resonance at this particular moment. Notwithstanding the advantages of this approach, there remain reasons to be cautious. First, by conceptualising Islamophobia as a form of racism, its specificities may be lost and subsumed within a larger, more universal explanation. Should Islamophobia be approached as just another type of racism, the uses and purposes of this specific phenomenon may be obscured. As the discussion of historical antecedents of Islamophobia demonstrated, specific histories and contexts must be considered in order to understand the particular tropes that make up contemporary Islamophobic expression.

This raises an important issue central to the debate on Islamophobia: namely, whether there is such a thing as 'Islamophobia' and whether it is more analytically correct to consider 'Islamophobias'. While there is growing sympathy with this position (Iqbal 2010, 174; Miles and Brown 2003, 165; Allen 2010, 34), owing to the sheer complexity of Islamophobia and the contingent nature of each utterance, analyses that compartmentalise in this way may lose sight of the bigger picture. And this bigger picture is clearly important. Islamophobia is always expressed in a local context, but it draws upon and adds to a larger collection of narratives that are both temporally and spatially formed: historical narratives that cherry pick from older discourses of exclusion, and geographical contexts that place certain racialised 'others' in an adversarial relationship with national, European and Western social collectives. While there are certainly differences between and within contemporary expressions of Islamophobia it is important not to lose sight of what binds them together and makes them coherent for a large proportion of contemporary 'Western' populations.

Islamophobia has many layers; historical antecedents that are recycled, theories of 'otherness' that draw boundaries between in-groups and out-groups, and strategies of essentialisation and exclusion that mark Muslims out as 'them', intrinsically different to 'us'. Without an understanding of the historical context, the tropes that are recycled and the identities that are incorporated are meaningless. Similarly, a theoretical understanding of what Islamophobia might be is essential in order to consider the discursive strategies employed by actors. On the whole I find the insights of the comparative approach to be most useful in explaining Islamophobia and the mechanisms by which it works. By encompassing both theological and cultural hostility, and highlighting the way Muslims have been racialised as a group, this explanation builds on the new racism thesis developed by scholars in the 1970s and 80s, which sought to explain novel articulations of prejudice, and turns on the emphasis of cultural signifiers that are believed to condition human behaviour. This 'new racism' has variously been conceptualised as: 'subtle' (Pettigrew 1998; Pettigrew and Meertens 1995); 'covert' (Augoustinos et al. 1999; Durrheim and Dixon 2000; Omi and Winant 1994); 'symbolic' (McConahay and Hough 1976; Berry and Bonilla-Silva 2008, 217); and 'differentialist' (Rattansi 1994; Taguieff 2001, 4–5), but refers to an observed change in discourse from overt expressions of superiority to an emphasis on the intrinsic and inescapable role of culture. Scholars of new racism stress that although the language of biological or genetic race may have receded, a particular pseudo-biological understanding of culture has come to take its place, which holds that human behaviour and aptitudes are determined by belonging to particular historical cultures (Barker 1981, 20–23; Balibar 2007, 85).

For those who employ Islamophobia, Muslims are the living bearers of an immutable 'Islamic culture', which conditions their psychology, behaviour and actions in a fundamentally different way to members of other cultures. This essentialisation of culture not only provides an explanatory framework for human difference, but also theorises that tension will be a natural result if cultures are mixed. To regulate social tension, members of differing cultural groups are thus required to renounce their cultural belonging and assimilate into the (culturally different) societies in which they reside in order to forestall the inevitable backlash and social strife that will occur.

Although new racism shares with its 'old' counterpart the essentialisation of human groups (through sociological rather than biological signifiers), there is no necessity within this ideological framework for proponents to regard culturally different groups as inferior. Islamophobia is not dependent on the notion that non-Muslim cultures are better, but turns on the idea that cultural mixing leads to social tension and it is thus in the interests of Muslims to assimilate in order to avoid discrimination or violence.

The new racism thesis is not without its detractors. Some scholars have argued that it is not 'new' at all, and covert and indirect expressions of racism were the norm even prior to *de jure* racial equality (Leach 2005, 434). Others have pointed out that cultural difference has always been implicitly tied up with racial discourse even when biological racism enjoyed widespread scientific support, the classic example of which is anti-Semitism.(Meer and Noorani 2008; Schiffer and Wagner 2011, 77–84). These points have implications for the study of contemporary Islamophobia. Although the new racism thesis suggests that covert and subtle racialised expression will be more prominent, historical biological racism towards Muslims (particularly based on national or ethnic origins) has not disappeared and any study of Islamophobia must consider how these 'old' racisms are rearticulated within culturally racist discourse.

This conceptualisation of Islamophobia suggests that old forms of understanding the world as structured by discrete human groups have found a new articulation, where culture is represented as a determining and relevant human classification. Although the new racism thesis alerts us to the subtle ways race takes on cultural inflections, its ambiguity on hierarchy leaves open the question of why actors choose racialised representations of the world. In order to understanding the appeal of Islamophobia, its purpose, and the benefits it provides its adherents, must be interrogated. The insights of critical race theory (CRT) and whiteness studies help to situate the phenomenon by foregrounding racism as a central organising principle of society.

A CONCEPTUAL FRAMEWORK FOR ISLAMOPHOBIA

The contribution of CRT to the theoretical framework I am developing here lies in its understanding of social relations as centrally constituted by racism and the distributed group privileges and benefits that this gives rise to.

Although its status as a theory has been questioned and its perspectives are far from universally accepted, CRT nevertheless rests on several central tenets. Critical race theorists broadly agree on the centrality of racism in social organisation and its intersectionality with other forms of subordination (class, gender, etc.), and seek to challenge dominant ideology and its claims to neutrality through a commitment to social justice, a transdisciplinary perspective and the centring of the experiential knowledge of those subordinated by racism (Gillborn 2008, 26–30; Leonardo 2004, 137–152).

Three theoretical insights of CRT are particularly pertinent for this book, and concern the nature of race, the character of racism, and the purpose it serves.

The Nature of Race

Critical race theory rests on the constructivist position that the concept of race has no objective, material or fixed reality, and should be approached as a complex and shifting social construction that changes over time according to the needs of certain historical and political moments. As products of human thought and relations, races are never fixed categories, but are always subject to change when it is politically convenient to do so. A much cited example of this process of racialisation is the 'whitening' of the Irish, whereby racialised representations of Irish people, politically useful in a period of British colonial control, became less pronounced as historical conditions changed and political necessity retreated. Noel Ignatiev (2009) specifically connects this process in America to the deliberate accumulation by Irish immigrants of cultural capital, the prevailing strain of which was white supremacy, in order to establish themselves as part of the dominant (white) group. Although this particular example is controversial (Arnesen 2001), the notion that racial categories and the groups that belong to them have changed over time finds strong support (Winant 1994; Bonilla-Silva 1996; Goldberg 1993). Understanding the ebb and flow of racism and racial progress, then, requires a careful consideration of the conditions prevailing at different times and the collective attitudes developed to justify the subjugation and dominance of racialised groups.

CRT implies a broader focus than most popular understandings of racism allow. Borrowing from whiteness studies, it holds that any analysis of racism must take into account not only the representation of minorities, but also the ways in which whiteness is constructed through racist discourse. This foregrounds the invisible character of dominant (white) racial identities, and the need to unveil what Henry A. Giroux (1997, 382) has called the 'rhetorical, political, cultural and social mechanisms through which whiteness is both invented and used to mask its power and privilege'.

These observations attend to the ambiguity around hierarchy within new racism. Rather than overt expressions of cultural dominance or superiority, contemporary expressions of racist ideology often articulate power in covert, subtle and de-racialised ways.

The Character of Racism

In its focus on the racialised social system, CRT emphasises the difference between white people, a socially constructed identity, and whiteness, a racial discourse. This distinction between actors and structure is important in that it moves analytical focus away from the utterances and attitudes of individuals to an understanding of social dominance. In such a system dominance need not be explicitly uttered, rather it is enacted through the collective routine actions that shape people's life chances according to their place in the racialised system. As a mundane and everyday practice, racism is reproduced by covert and invisible structures and actions. Accordingly, we should not be focusing on the actions of a few racists, but on the way actors belonging to the dominant racial group utilise and articulate social representations that seek to explain and justify the racialised world as it is or ought to be.

The concept of white supremacy is of paramount importance here, understood as an all-encompassing system in which white-identified people receive benefits, while those constructed as non-white do not. White supremacy is not, as it is often understood, limited to the actions and discourse of extremist groups, such as the Ku Klux Klan and the British National Party, who mobilise on the basis of hatred. Rather, white supremacy represents:

> … a political, economic and cultural system in which whites overwhelmingly control power and material resources, conscious and unconscious ideas of white superiority and entitlement are widespread, and relations of white dominance and non-white subordination are daily re-enacted across a broad array of institutions and social settings. (Frances Lee Ansley, quoted in Mills 2003, 37)

White supremacy does not even need to express itself as such, existing instead as the patterned and enduring treatment of social groups, secured through a series of actions whose meaning may be obscured, and shaping the world in the interests of the dominant group. Of course, whiteness in such a system is neither an essence nor a reality, but something that can be accumulated by identifying with white interests (Riley 2009; Hage 2000).

The Purpose of Racism

This conceptualisation of a system of racial dominance brings us closer to an understanding of the purpose of racism. White supremacy, understood from the CRT perspective, implies a much broader understanding than is normally denoted by the term. Chiefly, it highlights the investment that white-identified people have in this system, which implicates all white people as benefitting from the advantages bequeathed to them by the racialised system. The notion that white people accrue unearned advantages in the current racial structure has been theorised as white privilege, but the language of privilege can obscure the process of appropriation and the centrality of agency to domination (Leonardo 2004, 137–138; Feagin et al. 2001, 5–7). White supremacy is the system that secures the privileges enjoyed by white people because they have created a structure of domination under which they can thrive.

The notion that white people universally benefit from a system of racial domination has been the subject of much controversy. Marxist scholars in particular have criticised this conceptualisation of racism's function for its homogenisation of white people in positions of power and privilege, as well as preventing a rational analysis of racism by equating far-right movements with institutional racism (Cole and Maisuria 2007). In addressing these criticisms it is important to keep in mind the understanding of white supremacy as a scale of domination, in which mobilisation on the basis of race hatred is at the most extreme and visible end, while everyday practices that uphold white supremacy (discrimination, institutional racism) are less extreme and often invisible. All of these activities, however, contribute to the exclusion and marginalisation of non-whites, and uphold a system which benefits white-identified people. As David Gillborn has emphasised, not all white-identified people benefit in the same way, but they do all benefit: 'even with the most extreme forms of poverty and exclusion, Whiteness matters. CRT does not assume that all White people are the same—that would be ludicrous; but CRT does argue that all White people are implicated in White Supremacy' (Gillborn 2008, 34).

This position draws upon the understanding that while some white people receive material benefits in their monopolisation of economic, social and state resources, even those on the margins are rewarded a social-psychological wage that grants them social status and deference from non-whites. Understanding white privilege as secured through white supremacy offers some clues as to why differently situated actors might invest in this ideology. As a social construction, whiteness is something that can be accumulated, by identifying with and articulating the norms of white society.

Critical Race Theory and Islamophobia

What does all this mean for the study of Islamophobia? First, the insights of the new racism thesis and CRT on the nature of racism highlight the constructed nature of all racialised identities. If race has no objective or fixed meaning, but is rather a category subject to constant change, then sociological signifiers can have as much importance as biological signifiers. Muslims can be culturally racialised through Islamophobic discourses which represent them as behaviourally conditioned by their belonging to a particular culture. The understanding and analysis of Islamophobia thus requires a consideration of the signifiers that come to have meaning when individuals and groups discuss Muslims, and a tracing of the ways in which Muslims are racialised through repetition and emphasis of those signifiers that are believed to mark their essential difference.

Second, the CRT conceptualisation of racism draws attention to its role as a central organising principle of society and its routine, unremarkable and unrecognised character. This observation foregrounds the invisible and unnoticed aspects of Islamophobia, as the 'business as usual' discourses and social relations that structure society. Analytical attention therefore must be focused on how certain representations come to have a 'common sense' character and the way these narratives are drawn upon and rearticulated in everyday and mundane ways that serve to present Muslims as culturally different to non-Muslims.

Finally, and most important to the argument I am developing here, is the understanding that racism serves an important purpose for actors in contemporary society, sustaining a hierarchy of benefits and serving important psychic and material functions for the dominant group. Understanding the ebb and flow of racism requires a careful look at the conditions prevailing at different times and the collective attitudes developed to justify subjugation and the dominance of one group over another. The notion of racism as a human construct that distributes privileges draws our attention to the function it serves for those employing it, and contrary to the ambiguity of the new racism thesis, centres the notion of hierarchy. This focus on the hierarchical distribution of material and psychic goods relies on an understanding that racialised social systems require an ideology of dominance which functions to distribute these privileges. It is not enough to consider only what Islamophobia is. We must also consider the ideological effects of its articulation, the social system it sustains and the purpose it serves.

The social construction of races, the character of racism and the purpose it serves all lead to an emphasis on the importance of discourse as the vehicle through which racist ideology and practices are transmitted. In order to understand and challenge cultural racism, we must approach it at the level of discourse, while keeping in mind the fact that racialised discourses have real social effects and are the means by which societal privileges, status and resources are allocated.

DISCOURSE AND IDEOLOGY

Teun A. van Dijk (1993, 249) has argued that new racism is primarily discursive; enacted through text and talk and having a central role in the reproduction (and challenge) of dominance. As a racist discourse, I understand Islamophobia as the means by which ideological understandings of Muslims and their position in society are transmitted, shared, and resisted by individuals acting as group members. It is the nature of these ideological understandings that the present study seeks to determine.

The racialised understandings of Muslims that are central to Islamophobic discourse can be understood as the broad mental frameworks that social groups use to make sense of the world (Bonilla-Silva 2001, 62). Since these frameworks are a sum of the ideas, prejudices and myths that are used by individuals to understand and justify the way the world is, they can be interrogated for representations of race. The approaches to analysing these frameworks vary slightly in each chapter of this book; however, the methodology is guided by the understanding that, as a culturally racist discourse, Islamophobia involves the marking of boundaries of identity, where Muslims are represented as different and discursive work serves to construct them as antithetical to local, national and civilisational identities.

From this perspective, understanding the ideology of Islamophobia requires careful attention to the content of text and talk identified as (potentially) Islamophobic. Representations of Muslims and Islam may be isolated through predicate analysis, which focuses on collocates of these nouns. Predicates establish what sort of thing a subject is, and direct analytical attention to particular representations and the ways they come to have social significance. The nature of Islamophobia can thus be revealed through an analysis of the discourse's content: the common topics and frames that recur, the style and rhetorical structure of the discourse, and the repeated narratives that seek to explain the different positions of Muslims and non-Muslims in contemporary society.

Simply pointing out that certain narratives are Islamophobic, however, tells us little about its purpose. The critical method can bridge this gap, by explicitly linking discourse with broader social forces. Foregrounding the inherent instability of all ideological discourse, critical methodology aims first to uncover the internal contradictions and myths drawn upon to sustain particular ideological understandings, and second to make explicit the ideological effects of employing particular representations. Critical methodology makes clear the relationship between discursive choices and their social consequences, and maintains a broader critical project which aims to equip individuals and groups for resistance to these discourses.

Aims of the Book

This book has three central aims. First, I want to understand what Islamophobic discourse is. This concerns the nature of Islamophobia, the representations that are central to it and the way in which Muslims are socially constructed as having cultural aptitudes that guide their behaviour. By focusing attention on the discursive work undertaken to construct Muslim identity as discrete, culturally determined and essentially different, a greater understanding may be attained of what constitutes Islamophobia. Second, I want to understand how Islamophobia constructs boundaries. This is related to the observation above that, understood as a racist discourse, analytical attention must focus on the way in which particular representations of Muslims serve to construct and maintain group boundaries of inside and outside. Finally, I want to understand the purpose of Islamophobia. If Islamophobia is understood as a racial ideology, it must perform some function for its adherents. In order to understand why it has such salience at the present historical moment, the benefits that this racialised understanding of the world offers to those employing it must therefore be considered. This is a question that has been largely ignored by scholars seeking to understand the phenomenon, either because Islamophobia is conceptualised as a continuation of older colonial, imperial and/or Orientalist discourse, whose purpose is domination, or because Islamophobia is theorised as racism, which is considered to have clear hierarchical purposes for its proponents. Although both of these propositions offer partial explanation of why Islamophobia is drawn upon by social actors, they fail to fully comprehend the reality of contemporary Islamophobia.

On the first point, although historical antecedents mark its contemporary configuration, conceptualising Islamophobia as merely a continuation of these discourses does not fully explain the current form of the discourse. Why would ordinary British people invest in propagating colonial and imperial interests at a time when these things are a distant memory? Similarly, if Islamophobia is merely neo-Orientalism then why are Muslims represented in almost exclusively negative terms? Where is the exoticism and fascination that marks Orientalist thought? On the second point, how can the understanding of Islamophobia as racism be reconciled with the clear articulation, even by staunch anti-Muslim commentators, that they do not consider Muslims in hierarchical terms? Current theories of Islamophobia are lacking in explanatory power because they do not adequately deal with why individuals and groups would choose to interpret and represent the world in these ideological terms.

In order to understand the widespread appeal of contemporary Islamophobia, I am primarily concerned with the British context. However, even a cursory glance at British Islamophobia reveals that it is deeply entwined with more widely shared social narratives that situate Britain within 'the West' as a bearer of Enlightenment rationality and sharing in a history of civilisational glory. These narratives are essential to British Islamophobia's story of itself, and of the dangers and threats Muslims are believed to pose. For this reason the analysis, although focused on Britain, does not ignore the importance of broader discourses with European and global resonance.

The conceptual framework adopted in this book conceives of Islamophobia as a culturally racist discourse and employs the insights of CRT in order to guide methodology and interpretation. I understand discourse as social representation, enacted and interpreted through text, talk, and visual symbols. I am also interested in the ideological effects of such representations and the ways in which particular representations advantage some groups over others. Critical methodology is employed to determine this, by applying first- and second-order critiques to the particular narratives in order to understand the identity constructions and boundaries they create. Finally, I am centrally concerned with why Islamophobic discourse appears across diverse social and political sites, and employ the theoretical insights of CRT in order to understand how identities are created relationally through racialised discourse and the ways in which invisible racial identities may be brought to visibility through critical approaches to racialised discourse. The book aims to answer three central research questions that attend to the nature, character and function of Islamophobia: What is Islamophobic discourse? How does it work to mark boundaries of identity? What is its purpose for those employing it?

In order to understand Islamophobic discourse, careful attention must be paid to the contextual settings in which it is articulated. Chapter 2 sets out the context by considering discourses of national prominence that have constructed Muslim identity in Britain since 2001. In this chapter, I trace the way that key construction moments (the Northern Uprisings of summer 2001 and the September 11, 2001 and July 7, 2005 terrorist attacks) opened up space for new conceptualisations of Muslim identity and argue that the discourses which emerged have provided the central frames through which British Muslims were subsequently understood and represented. Considering the community cohesion and counterterrorism discourses, this chapter traces the social construction of a racialised Muslim identity, by foregrounding the central discursive frame of good/bad Muslims and the de-emphasis of salient aspects of Muslim identity within these dominant discourses, such that culture became the primary prism through which Muslims in Britain were understood in the post-2001 period.

Chapters 3 and 4 are concerned with the frames and themes of Islamophobic representation and the central narratives that make up this discourse. These case studies highlight the ways in which Islamophobic understandings created group boundaries, and are analysed using the critical method in order to highlight the internal inconsistencies in the discourses as well as the ideological effects of such representations.

Chapter 3 considers Islamophobia at the local level, tracing how particular representations of Muslims were employed to argue against construction of a mosque in the West Midlands town of Dudley. By considering the argumentative strategies used by correspondents to local newspaper *Dudley News*, this chapter identifies how Muslims were constructed, and foregrounds the way dominant national representations were recycled and rearticulated in a local context to prevent Muslim action and change to the locality.

Chapter 4 considers the way group boundaries were created and maintained through Islamophobia by considering the discourse of overtly 'anti-Islamist' group, the English Defence League (EDL). Concentrating on the group's central assertion that it is not racist, this chapter demonstrates how Islamophobia functions stylistically, through an analysis of the way Muslims and Islam were represented on the group's website *EDL News*. This chapter is concerned with both the narratives and the discursive strategies of Islamophobia, and considers the way (culturally) racist discourse is constructed, focusing on the role of denials, diminutives, and positive self and negative other representations have in legitimising and rationalising Islamophobic discourse.

Chapter 5 considers how Islamophobia was used to draw national boundaries in four European states. Through an analysis of construction moments in Switzerland, Denmark, the Netherlands and France, I demonstrate how Islamophobic representations created and maintained national boundaries by presenting Muslims as antithetical to a particular cherished national value. A content analysis of the types of discourses brought to fore during these controversies highlights the similarities in the ways actors in a number of European states utilised Islamophobic narratives in order to construct national boundaries which implicitly excluded Muslims as national subjects. This chapter also considers how Islamophobic discourse is reliant on appeals to a larger discourse of civilisation.

Chapter 6 draws together all of these analyses to interpret and explain the reasons why these constructions might have salience and relevance in such varied social spaces and for differently situated people. Although Islamophobia undoubtedly plays a role in constructing national boundaries, even a cursory glance at nationalistic Islamophobic discourse reveals that larger shared narratives are employed which incorporate continental and civilisational imagined communities. Even when instrumentalised for very specific purposes, such as the building of a mosque in a small post-industrial town, Islamophobia draws upon extra-national social and cultural discourses and identities that are believed to be pertinent. The civilisational thrust of the discourse is indisputable, yet has been only sparsely addressed in the literature. Why does Islamophobia so often address itself to existential angst about the imagined civilisational community of the West? And why do local and national discourses of Islamophobia so readily incorporate the idea of the West even when they are specifically directed towards local or national issues?

In other words, if Islamophobia is socially constructed, what is it socially constructed *for*? Drawing on the work of Ghassan Hage, Chap. 6 demonstrates how Islamophobia relies on the idea of spatial management, and attempts to construct stable identities as a way to resolve identity crises brought on by the perception that Muslims are trying to change particular spaces. By considering both inclusive Islamophobia and exclusionary discourses, this chapter demonstrates how they rely on the same identity constructions. I argue that the varied articulations of Islamophobia are best understood as Eurocentric discourse, a shared social narrative of the West, which attempts to control the Muslims in its midst by constructing them as antithetical and requiring management before Islamic will gets out of control.

Understanding Islamophobia means not only delineating what it is, but also questioning what it is for. *Islamophobia in Britain* seeks to answer these questions through an analysis of the various representations of Muslims that have come to have salience in British discourse. However, the proliferation of Islamophobia in the contemporary period is not just confined to Britain. At the present historical moment there is a widespread acceptance that there is something *different* about Muslims that accounts for many of the social problems and issues confronting Western societies. For a large segment of the contemporary West, Islamophobia explains the world and provides an ideological blueprint of how to fix it. Social narratives of such power do not materialise spontaneously. The question that scholars have failed to adequately address is the central consideration of the present book: Why is Islamophobia increasingly seen to have explanatory potential for the social world? And, more importantly, why now?

REFERENCES

Allen, Chris. 2007. Islamophobia and Its Consequences. In *European Islam: Challenges for Society and Public Policy*, ed. Samir Amghar, Amel Boubekeur, and Michael Emerson, 67–144. Brussels: Centre for European Policy Studies.
———. 2008. K.I.S.S. Islamophobia (Keeping It Simple and Stupid). In *Thinking Thru' Islamophobia, Symposium Papers*, March, ed. Bobby S. Sayyid and Abdoolkarim Vakil, 30–33. Leeds: University of Leeds.
———. 2010. *Islamophobia*. Surrey: Ashgate.
Arnesen, Eric. 2001. Whiteness and the Historians' Imagination. *International Labor and Working-Class History* 60 (Fall): 3–32.
Augoustinos, M., K. Tuffin, and M. Rapley. 1999. Genocide or a Failure to Gel? Racism, History and Nationalism in Australian Talk. *Discourse & Society* 10: 351–378.
Balibar, Etienne. 2007. Is There a 'Neo-Racism'? In *Race and Racialization: Essential Readings*, ed. Tanya Das Gupta, 83–88. Toronto: Canadian Scholars' Press.
Barker, Martin. 1981. *The New Racism: Conservatives and the Ideology of the Tribe*. Frederick, MD: University Publications of America.
Berry, Brent, and Eduardo Bonilla-Silva. 2008. 'They Should Hire the One with the Best Score': White Sensitivity to Qualification Differences in Affirmative Action Hiring Decisions. *Ethnic and Racial Studies* 31 (2): 215–242.
Birt, Yahya. 2008. Governing Muslims After 9/11. In *Thinking Thru' Islamophobia, Symposium Papers*, ed. Bobby S. Sayyid, and Abdoolkarim Vakil, 26–29. Leeds: University of Leeds.
Bonilla-Silva, Eduardo. 1996. Rethinking Racism: Toward a Structural Interpretation. *American Sociological Review* 62 (June): 465–480.
———. 2001. *White Supremacy and Racism in the Post-Civil Rights Era*. London: Lynne Rienner.
Bunzl, Matti. 2005. Between Anti-Semitism and Islamophobia: Some Thoughts on the New Europe. *American Ethnologist* 32 (4): 499–508.
Carland, Susan. 2011. Islamophobia, Fear of Loss of Freedom, and the Muslim Woman. *Islam and Christian-Muslim Relations* 22 (4): 469–473.
Cole, Mike. 2009. A Plethora of 'Suitable Enemies': British Racism at the Dawn of the Twenty-First Century. *Ethnic and Racial Studies* 32 (9): 1671–1685.
Cole, Mike, and Alpesh Maisuria. 2007. 'Shut the F*** up', 'You Have No Rights Here': Critical Race Theory and Racialisation in Post-7/7 Racist Britain. *Journal for Critical Education Policy Studies* 5 (1).
Commission on British Muslims and Islamphobia. 1997. *Islamophobia: A Challenge for Us All*. London: Runnymede Trust. http://www.runnymede-trust.org/publications/17/32.html. Retrieved 20 Jun 2010.
Dawkins, Richard. 2013. Calm Reflections after a Storm in a Tea Cup. The Richard Dawkins Foundation, 26 August. https://richarddawkins.

net/2013/08/calm-reflections-after-a-storm-in-a-teacup-polish-translation-below/. Retrieved 1 Dec 2014.

Dekker, Henk, and Jolanda van der Noll. 2011. Islamophobia and Anti-Semitism and Their Explanations. In *6th General Conference of the European Consortium for Political Research (ECPR)*, August 25–27, in Reykjavik.

Durrheim, Kevin, and John Dixon. 2000. Theories of Culture in Racist Discourse. *Race and Society* 3 (2): 93–109.

Erdenir, Burak. 2010. Islamophobia qua Racial Discrimination. In *Muslims in 21st Century Europe: Structural and Cultural Perspectives*, ed. Anna Triandafyllidou, 27–44. Oxon: Routledge.

Etienne, Bruno. 2007. Islam and Violence. *History and Anthropology* 18 (3): 237–248.

Feagin, Joe R., Hernan Vera, and Pinar Batur. 2001. *White Racism*. New York: Routledge.

Fekete, Liz. 2009. *A Suitable Enemy: Racism, Migration and Islamophobia in Europe*. London: Pluto Press.

Geisser, Vincent. 2010. Islamophobia: A 'French Specificity' in Europe? *Human Architecture* VIII (2): 39–46.

Gillborn, David. 2008. *Racism and Education: Coincidence or Conspiracy?* London: Routledge.

Gingrich, Andre. 2005. Anthropological Analyses of Islamophobia and Anti-Semitism in Europe. *American Ethnologist* 32 (4): 513–515.

Giroux, Henry A. 1997. White Squall: Resistance and the Pedagogy of Whiteness. *Cultural Studies* 11 (3): 376–389.

Goldberg, David Theo. 1993. *Racist Culture: The Philosophy and the Politics of Meaning*. Oxford: Blackwell.

Grosfoguel, Ramon, and Eric Mielants. 2006. The Long-Durée Entanglement Between Islamophobia and Racism in the Modern/Colonial Capitalist/Patriarchal World-System: An Introduction. *Human Architecture* V (1): 1–12.

Hage, Ghassan. 2000. *White Nation: Fantasies of White Supremacy in a Multicultural Society*. New York: Routledge.

Hopkins, Nick, and Vered Kahani-Hopkins. 2006. Minority Group Members' Theories of Intergroup Contact: A Case Study of British Muslims' Conceptualizations of 'Islamophobia' and Social Change. *The British Journal of Social Psychology* 45 (Pt 2): 245–264.

Huntington, S.P. 1993. The Clash of Civilizations? *Foreign Affairs* 72 (3): 22–49.

Husain (ed.). 2008. Stop Pandering to the Islamist Extremists. *London Evening Standard*, July 7. http://www.standard.co.uk/news/stop-pandering-to-the-islamist-extremists-6912982.html. Retrieved 12 Nov 2014.

Hussain, Yasmin, and Paul Bagguley. 2012. Securitized Citizens: Islamophobia, Racism and the 7/7 London Bombings. *The Sociological Review* 60 (4): 715–734.

Ignatiev, Noel. 2009. *How the Irish Became White*. New York: Routledge.

Iqbal, Zafar. 2010. Understanding Islamophobia: Conceptualizing and Measuring the Construct. *European Journal of Social Sciences* 13 (4): 574–590.

Kaya, Ayhan. 2011. *Islamophobia as a Form of Governmentality: Unbearable Weightiness of the Politics of Fear*. Malmo: Malmo Institute for Studies of Migration, Diversity and Welfare (MIM). http://muep.mah.se/handle/2043/12704. Retrieved 2 Sep 2012.

Kundnani, Arun. 2007. *The End of Tolerance: Racism in 21st Century Britain*. London: Pluto Press.

———. 2014. *The Muslims Are Coming!* London: Verso.

Laqueur, Walter. 2006. The Origins of Facism: Islamic Facism, Islamophobia, Antisemitism. Oxford University Press Blog. http://blog.oup.com/2006/10/the_origins_of_2/. Retrieved 20 Apr 2011.

Leach, Colin Wayne. 2005. Against the Notion of a 'new Racism'. *Journal of Community & Applied Social Psychology* 15 (6): 432–445.

Lean, Nathan. 2012. *The Islamophobia Industry: How the Right Manufactures Fear of Muslims*. London: Pluto Press.

Leonardo, Zeus. 2004. The Color of Supremacy: Beyond the Discourse of 'white Privilege'. *Educational Philosophy and Theory* 36 (2): 137–152.

Lorente, Javier Rosón. 2010. Discrepancies around the Use of the Term 'Islamophobia'. *Human Architecture VIII* 2: 115–128.

Love, Erik. 2009. Confronting Islamophobia in the United States: Framing Civil Rights Activism among Middle Eastern Americans. *Patterns of Prejudice* 43 (3–4): 401–425.

Malik, Kennan. 2005. The Islamophobia Myth. *Propsect Magazine*, February 20. http://www.prospectmagazine.co.uk/features/islamophobiamyth. Retrieved 28 Nov 2014.

McConahay, John B., and Joseph C. Hough. 1976. Symbolic Racism. *Journal of Social Issues* 32 (2): 23–45.

Meer, Nasar. 2008. The Politics of Voluntary and Involuntary Identities: Are Muslims in Britain an Ethnic, Racial or Religious Minority? *Patterns of Prejudice* 42 (1): 61–81.

Meer, Nasar, and Tehseen Noorani. 2008. A Sociological Comparison of Anti-Semitism and Anti-Muslim Sentiment in Britain. *The Sociological Review* 56 (2): 195–219.

Mignolo, W. D. 2006. Islamophobia/Hispanophobia: The (re) Configuration of the Racial Imperial/Colonial Matrix. *Human Architecture* 5 (1): 13–28.

Miles, Robert, and Malcolm Brown. 2003. *Racism*, 2nd ed. London: Routledge.

Mills, Charles W. 2003. White Supremcy as a Sociopolitical System: A Philosophical Perspective. In *White Out: The Continuing Significance of Racism*, ed. Ashley Doane, and Eduardo Bonilla-Silva, 35–48. London: Routledge.

Omi, Michael, and Howard Winant. 1994. *Racial Formation in the United States: From the 1960s to the 1990s*, 2nd ed. New York: Routledge.
Pettigrew, Thomas F. 1998. Reactions Toward the New Minorities of Western Europe. *Annual Review of Sociology* 24: 77–103.
Pettigrew, Thomas F., and R.W. Meertens. 1995. Subtle and Blatant Prejudice in Western Europe. *European Journal of Social Psychology* 25: 57–75.
Ramadan, Tariq. 2010. Good Muslim, Bad Muslim. *New Statesman*. http://www.newstatesman.com/religion/2010/02/muslim-religious-moderation. Retrieved 30 Nov 2010.
Rana, Junaid. 2007. The Story of Islamophobia. *Souls* 9 (2): 148–161.
Rattansi, Ali. 1994. 'Western' Racisms, Ethnicities and Identities in a 'Postmodern' Frame. In *Racism, Modernity and Identity: On the Western Front*, ed. Ali Rattansi, and Sallie Westwood, 15–88. Cambridge: Polity Press.
Riley, Krista Melanie. 2009. How to Accumulate National Capital: The Case of the 'Good' Muslim. *Global Media Journal – Canadian Edition* 2 (2): 57–71.
Said, Edward. 1978. *Orientalism*. New York: Vintage.
Schiffer, S., and C. Wagner. 2011. Anti-Semitism and Islamophobia – New Enemies, Old Patterns. *Race & Class* 52 (3): 77–84.
Taguieff, Pierre-Andre. 2001. *The Force of Prejudice: On Racism and Its Doubles*, ed. Hassan Melehy. Minneapolis: University of Minnesota Press.
Vakil, AbdoolKarim. 2008. Is the Islam in Islamophobia the Same as the Islam in Anti-Islam; Or, When Is It Islamophobia Time? In *Thinking Thru' Islamophobia, Symposium Papers*, ed. Bobby S. Sayyid and Abdoolkarim Vakil. Leeds: University of Leeds.
van Dijk, T.A. 1993. *Elite Discourse and Racism*. London: Sage.
———. 1993b. Principles of Critical Discourse Analysis. *Discourse & Society* 4 (2): 249–283.
Winant, Howard. 1994. Racial Formation and Hegemony: Global and Local Developments. In *Racism, Modernity and Identity: On the Western Front*, ed. Ali Rattansi, and Sallie Westwood, 266–289. Cambridge: Polity Press.

CHAPTER 2

Good and Bad Muslims in Britain: Community Cohesion and Counterterrorism Discourse

INTRODUCTION

The summer of 2001 saw widespread and sustained confrontations between British Asian youths and police in several Northern towns of England. In Oldham, heightened tensions were generated by several local incidents, including skirmishes between visiting football supporters and local Asians and the framing by local and national newspapers of an attack on an elderly white war veteran, who was mugged and beaten by three Asian men, as racially motivated. In response to this, the far-right National Front marched on Oldham in May, triggering three nights of confrontation between riot-gear clad police and Asian youths determined to defend their neighbourhoods. Similar scenes played out in Burnley that June and Bradford a month later. Hearsay and rumour that racist gangs were planning to march led hundreds of young Asian men on to the streets to defend their communities, and the heavy-handed tactics of the authorities led to escalation and prolonged confrontation between youths and the police. Two months later, the planes crashed into the twin towers of the World Trade Center and ignited the 'global war on terror'.

From these violent events emerged two discourses, which entwined with one another to construct Muslims as both domestically and internationally threatening. The first was community cohesion, which understood the 'riots' as caused by a lack of empathy between self-segregating, culturally defined communities who lived side by side but with little contact or understanding of one another. The second was counterterrorism

© The Author(s) 2018
L.B. Jackson, *Islamophobia in Britain*,
DOI 10.1007/978-3-319-58350-1_2

discourse, which sought to respond to terrorist attacks by dismantling the ideology believed to underpin them. As foreign extremism was understood to be the cause of Islamist terrorist attacks, a value-driven British Islam was stressed as its solution. Both community cohesion and counterterrorism discourses relied on a culturalised explanation of violence and unrest, in which Islam was singled out as determining, dangerous and threatening.

The present chapter demonstrates how these discourses converged to construct a post-2001 Muslim subject in opposition to British national identity. This construction pivoted on the splitting of the category 'Muslim' into good and bad, where 'good Muslims' could be integrated and embraced, while 'bad Muslims' represented everything the nation was not.

Community cohesion discourse performed this function by producing a bad un-integratable Muslim subject whose tendency towards self-segregation threatened British values and social cohesion. Bad Muslims were targeted through initiatives which admonished them for speaking native languages at home, tightened immigration controls to make transnational marriages and the importation of foreign cultures more difficult, and compulsory citizenship courses for established migrants, all of which sought to coerce them into being 'good'. At the same time, counterterrorism discourse constructed 'bad Muslims' as those who existentially threatened the nation through their adherence to violent jihadist ideology. The 'home-grown' nature of the July 2005 London transport bombings and the subsequent understanding that terrorism required the tacit support of communities led to a reorientation towards the domestic Muslim population. Muslims were now presumed 'bad' until proven otherwise, and counterterrorism discourse and practice sought to prevent terrorism through the promotion of 'good' Islamic organisations whose values were endorsed by the state.

These twin discourses performed two interrelated functions. First, in the post-2001 British context 'bad Muslims' were blamed for the central problems of the day, exteriorising threats of social unrest and terrorism. Second, since the blame for these problems was thought to lie with 'others', the remedy was an explicit restatement of British values. Both community cohesion and counterterrorism discourse served to bolster British nationalism through a focus on national identity as the solution to Muslim cultural dysfunction.

MAKING AN INTERNAL MUSLIM ENEMY: THE NORTHERN UPRISINGS AND COMMUNITY COHESION DISCOURSE

The summer of 2001 saw a number of confrontations between youths and police in former mill towns of the North of England. Oldham, Burnley and Bradford had in common huge levels of long-term unemployment, social deprivation and low educational achievement, and all contained large Asian communities residentially segregated from white areas and in fierce competition for scarce resources. Despite the significance of the socio-economic problems of the affected areas and the immediate threat from racist gangs that had triggered the uprisings, the popular press, community leaders, and official government inquiries all chose to highlight culture, and specifically Muslim culture, as the essential cause of the Northern disturbances.

The scale and intensity of the uprising in Bradford, as well as its construction in the national imaginary as the archetypal polarised city, meant that this area came to be the focus of much of the post-uprising discussion. The disturbances in Bradford were officially categorised as a riot, resulting in an estimated £27 million worth of damage and injuring more than 300 police officers (McGhee 2003, 397). The shock engendered by the images of the Bradford riot played a large part in cementing the representations that later gained currency. Among a British public used to seeing Asians as placid, the spectacle of burned out cars and buildings, and young Asian men hurling missiles at police was incredibly powerful. This very visible, and apparently racial, aspect of the disturbances led to them being categorised in the media as 'race riots', yet this initial interpretation was swiftly overtaken by a culturalised understanding of the causes of the violence.

The Bradford District Race Review (BDRR), known as the Ouseley Report, was commissioned prior to the riots; however, its publication coincided with the uprising and its central conclusions were therefore taken to provide some explanation for the violence. Despite its title, the Review focused on 'cultural communities', indicating that a culturalisation of political issues in Bradford was taking place before violence broke out. The Ouseley Report highlighted as its key concern the notion that cultural communities were fragmenting and relationships deteriorating along racial, ethnic and faith lines:

Rather than seeing the emergence of a confident multicultural District, where people are respectful and have understanding and tolerance for differences, people's attitudes appear to be hardening and intolerance towards differences is growing. This situation is hindering people's understanding of each other and preventing positive contact between people from different cultural communities (Ouseley 2001, 6).

The Ouseley Report's concern with respect, understanding and tolerance of cultural difference gives an insight into the ideological underpinnings of the community cohesion agenda. Culture was seized upon to the detriment of other explanations, and this was mirrored in the later (Cantle and Denham) reports that specifically aimed to explain the uprisings. Both of these echoed Ouseley's conclusions, emphasising segregated communities that had retreated into themselves at the expense of meaningful cross-cultural contact.

Community Cohesion: Report of the Independent Review Team (the Cantle Report) analysed the causes of the disturbances by concentrating on the conditions and relationships in those towns and cities affected, and comparing them with similar large multicultural areas that had not experienced violent uprisings. Highlighting cross-community suspicion and distrust as the tinderbox conditions for riot, the Report arrived at similar conclusions to the BDRR, arguing that the thing most lacking in those areas that had experienced violence was pride in the community and a positive approach to diversity (Community Cohesion Review Team 2001, 15). Although the Cantle Report was nuanced in its understanding of the varied social conditions governing the lives of people in differing multicultural contexts across the UK, its emphasis on segregated communities retreating into themselves at the expense of meaningful cross-cultural contact echoed the conclusions of the Ouseley Report. This understanding of life in the Northern towns and cities that experienced unrest as taking place in the context of 'parallel lives' was seized upon by both government and media as the starting point for addressing the causes of the violence (Community Cohesion Review Team 2001, 9).

The Ministerial Group on Public Order and Community Cohesion (chaired by John Denham) was convened to identify what help the government could offer to communities to begin addressing the problems manifested by the uprisings, and its conclusions followed a similar logic. The Denham Report, *Building Cohesive Communities*, aimed to identify the issues that had created the conditions for the disturbances, and, building on the work of Cantle and Ouseley, noted among its most important contributory factors the lack of a strong civic identity or shared social values and 'the fragmentation and polarisation of com-munities – on economic, geographical, racial and cultural lines – on a scale which amounts to segregation, *albeit to an extent by choice*' (Home Office 2001, 11, Emphasis added).

By understanding the uprisings as centrally caused by a lack of cross-community communication and shared values, the unrest became cultur-alised; viewed as the result of segregation and distrust, at the expense of other causal factors. Arguably, the two most important of these are the deteriorated socio-economic conditions of the areas affected and the immediate racist contexts in which the disturbances took place. In proposing community cohesion as the policy response to the problems of the affected areas, these contexts were de-emphasised and the class and racial identities attached to them subordinated to an understand-ing which considered diverse cultures problematic unless contained by an overarching and superordinate set of common (British) values. As the Cantle report stated, 'It is easy to focus on systems, processes and insti-tutions and to forget that community cohesion fundamentally depends on people and their values. Indeed, many of the present problems seem to owe a great deal to the failure to communicate and agree a set of clear values that can govern behaviour' (Community Cohesion Review Team 2001, 18).

Community cohesion aimed to prevent further outbreaks of vio-lence by promoting understanding and communication between dis-parate communities and articulating a clear set of values to unite them. But this conceptualisation of the violence as resulting from ignorance, suspicion and hostility among culturally defined communities not only overlooked important contributory factors, but also shifted focus to the cultural practices of problematic communities. Through community cohesion discourse, Muslims came to be viewed as particularly difficult to integrate, chiefly responsible for the parallel lives being lived, and in need of state intervention to coerce them out of their tendency to self-segregation.

Community Cohesion and the Culturalisation of Social Problems

After the disturbances, community cohesion became the central strand of the government's approach to preventing social unrest. The policy aimed to counter future outbreaks of violence through a preventative programme that would promote understanding and communication between disparate communities, and at the same time articulate a clear set of values to unite them. In 2002, the Local Government Association report, *Guidance on Community Cohesion*, defined a cohesive community as one which had a common vision and sense of belonging, where people's diverse backgrounds and circumstances were positively valued, and where strong and positive relationships were developed (Local Government Association 2002, 6).

By emphasising culture as the single most important feature of the 2001 uprisings, community cohesion discourse played a fundamental role in the racialisation of British Muslims in the early twenty-first century. Through a concerted de-emphasis of class, race and ethnic identities, and a corresponding culturalisation of political issues, Muslims were singled out as uniquely problematic and the uprisings interpreted as symptomatic of a larger, nationwide problem of excessive Muslim cultural diversity. From this discourse emerged a 'bad' Muslim subject who threatened British values and cohesive communities, and whose influence and power could be tempered by state support of 'good' Muslims and the vociferous articulation of uniting national values.

Culturalizing Class

All three of the summer 2001 disturbances took place in economically deteriorated areas of multiple deprivation, previously dominated by thriving textile industries which had experienced dramatic decline. Having met frequently in the labour market, the opportunities for meaningful contact between communities was dramatically reduced with the collapse of industry (Amin 2003, 461). And although the material disadvantage that followed from deindustrialisation impacted on all communities, inner city areas populated largely by Muslims of Pakistani and Bangladeshi descent were particularly affected and working-class people of Muslim heritage suffered disproportionately from the deprivation that followed. In the case of Bradford, for example, 53.2% of Pakistanis and 81% of Bangladeshi residents lived in multiple stress areas, compared to 19.5% of the general population (Singh 2001).

That material disadvantage and working-class frustration might have contributed to the uprisings, however, was largely overlooked within community cohesion discourse. Instead, cultural explanations laid the socio-economic condition of working-class Muslims at Islam's door, blaming low educational achievement on the time spent at mosques, *statistics?*

long stays in Pakistan and hours spent in Islamic education after school (Lewis 2002). The cultural pressures on Muslim children were believed to lead them to neglect their homework, perform poorly in exams and perpetuate the problem of unemployment (Tweedie 2001). In this way, low educational attainment and high levels of unemployment were accounted for through a focus on culture.

This culturalisation of class was exemplified by both local and national media. Neil Darbyshire, writing in *The Telegraph*, contrasted the acceptable socio-economic frustrations of the youth involved in the 1981 Brixton riots with unacceptable participation in the 2001 Bradford riots. Disregarding the specifically local economic conditions of the areas affected, he claimed that the 2001 riots took place in a healthy economy with low unemployment and inflation, implying that the youths involved had no claim to being economically marginalised (Darbyshire 2001). Assertions such as this were part of a genre of contemporary texts that sought to delegitimise the uprisings in the context of a nation coming to terms with its racist past.

The MacPherson Report into the murder of black teenager Stephen Lawrence had been published 2 years earlier, and among its revelations was the claim that institutional racism was rife within British society. As the government accepted the Report's recommendations, a period of reflection commenced, with media discourse on race moving to a markedly more empathetic and remorseful tone (Neal 2003). While there was widespread acceptance that the uprisings of the past could be excused to some extent by the racist culture in which they took place, for writers such as Darbyshire, the MacPherson Report had absolved the present moment of its racism and appeals to the 'acceptable' riots of the past to help explain the uprisings of the present were met with incredulity. Specifically, local economic conditions and uneven regional development were discounted in media reports of the Northern uprisings, and the frustrations of participants excluded by local circumstances from the benefits of a healthy national economy were overlooked. This reluctance to consider economic marginalisation as a causal factor was a notable feature of much of the discussion around the violence and served to sustain the discourse of cultural blame that thrived in the aftermath of the uprisings.

Class was further culturalised through the focus on parallel lives and segregation as value-driven and a product of choice, rather than the result of socio-economic factors. Propelled by the implicit understanding that divided, morally fragmented communities were characterised by structural economic deprivation, community cohesion was an instrument targeted to very specific groups. Working-class Muslims of Pakistani and Bangladeshi descent were those for whom community cohesion was considered a necessary instrument of social control. The professional, middle-class Egyptian Muslims of the Southeast of England, in contrast, were not targeted with state intervention to ensure their integration, any more than the self-segregating inhabitants of gated communities were admonished for the societal effects of their wealth social exclusion (Phillips 2006, 29).

Class played an important part in how the riots, and the subsequent community cohesion discourse was constructed, but this was culturalised (and racialised) by the reports and particularly by the media. White participants in the violence were presented as being justifiably angry about perceived unfair government hand-outs to Asian communities. Contrastingly, young Asian Muslim participants were consistently aligned with criminality, drug dealing and gangs (Alexander 2004). The cultural racialisation of the riots ensured that while working-class whites were granted a socio-economic explanation for their anger, working-class Muslims were assigned a cultural explanation for their socio-economic position.

The de-Emphasis of Race

An initial separation was made in the media between the white and Asian youths that participated in the uprisings. Where white perpetrators of violence were represented as exceptional extremists, Asian youths were considered representative of a generation of discontent. Yet, as the uprisings were increasingly portrayed as the violent expression of inherently dangerous alien culture, this 'Asian' subject was culturalised and de-racialised.

As the conceptualisation of Muslims came to be shaped by the discourses emerging in the context of the September 11, 2001 attacks, Asian rioters were *a posteriori* cast within the terms of a good/bad dichotomy. As their identities shifted from 'Asian', to 'Muslim', participants were presented as trapped between the values of the (good) law-abiding Asian community, rooted in tradition, and a new generation of (bad) macho, masculine defiance fed specifically by Muslim culture's tendencies towards isolation, misogyny and violence.

كراهية السا_ـ

misogynistic

A series of articles by Amit Roy in *The Telegraph* illustrates how Muslims were isolated as the root of unrest. Reporting on the response to the Oldham uprisings, Roy described Manchester's Asian community as growing increasingly uneasy with the term 'Asian', because it placed them 'in the same category as rioting Muslim youths of Bangladeshi and Pakistani origin in nearby Oldham' (Roy 2001a). Non-Muslim Asians reacted to the violence by emphasising Pakistani parents' lack of control over their children, a culture of criminality and drug dealing, the radicalisation of Muslim youth over international issues like Kashmir, and the mosques; described as training grounds for the Taliban (Roy 2001b).

Having isolated out of control Muslim youth as the instigators of violence, local non-Muslim Asians went on to dismiss the notion that the riots were reactions to economic exclusion. Hashmukh Shah, spokesman for the World Council of Hindus, argued that deprivation and discrimination were excuses: 'When Indians came to Britain, they suffered from the same conditions. They had a level playing field. Because of our hard work, perseverance and keeping our youth under control, Indian children are leading in the field of education today. The responsibility for taking control of Pakistani youths lies with their parents and community leaders' (Quoted in Roy 2001b). The need to dissociate Indians from 'Muslim violence' can be understood as an example of national capital accumulation (Riley 2009). Shah's argument culturalised the uprisings at the same time as claiming for non-Muslim Asians a stake in the nation. His argument highlighted that since all Asians started from the same position, the poor performance of Muslims must have something to do with their culture, namely feckless Pakistani parenting and lack of a work ethic. Through associating Indians with values of hard work and good parenting, Shah was able to identify with the nation while isolating Muslims as possessing culturally determined values that impeded their integration. Roy's articles illustrate how the category of Asian was split following the uprisings, in order that non-Muslims could distance themselves from risky identities and align with British values, while Muslims were further problematised as culturally dysfunctional.

The Problematisation of Muslim Identities

One of the central concerns of the community cohesion agenda was to redefine and rearticulate an inclusive Britishness which would unite disparate communities across the nation. The focus on the need to speak

English, the 'Britishness test' and the tightening of immigration laws to make marriage to foreign spouses more difficult underlined a concern with the transnational loyalties of targeted communities.

Those communities perceived to be most in need of civic re-education were never explicitly named, but the cultural practices thought to exemplify failed integration made clear that Muslims were considered most lacking in Britishness and in need of state intervention. The debate on the need to speak English, for example, focused on non-economically active Muslim mothers who disadvantaged their children educationally and contributed to intergenerational schizophrenia by not speaking English at home (Fekete 2008, 46). Attention was particularly focused on the language skills of those spouses from Pakistan and Bangladesh who married via transnational networks of clan and caste, and through which Muslims in Britain were perceived to be importing foreign cultures intent on remaining isolated.

The debate on intolerable cultural practices further emphasised that Muslims were the primary focus of community cohesion. Gender relations were highlighted as one of the most important indicators of integration and were central to community cohesion discourse's articulation of the values which defined Britishness. Home Secretary David Blunkett, highlighting the publication of the government reports into the disturbances, spoke of the need to 'protect the rights and duties of all citizens, and confront practices and beliefs that hold them back, particularly women', and argued that British norms of acceptability meant that practices of female genital mutilation and forced marriages could not be tolerated (Blunkett 2001). Michael Wills, minister responsible for defining Britishness in the context of the newly formed community cohesion discourse, similarly cited supposedly Islamic cultural practices to draw the line of tolerance: 'some things are absolutely clear. We don't accept forced marriages, genital mutilation or discrimination on any grounds' (Sylvester 2001).

The cultural practices held up as exemplifying non-British values were those associated with Muslim communities, and Muslims therefore came to be associated with a particularly un-British value system. The practices in question are clearly not 'Islamic', in the sense that they are in any way sanctioned by religious authority or carried out by Muslim communities across the globe (they are more correctly associated with particular ethnic or national traditions). However, the factual accuracy of these associations is not what is at issue. More important is that they were attached, in the public imagination, to Islam and through repetition called up Muslims every time they were mentioned.

The positioning of intolerable 'Islamic' cultural practices as the values against which British identity was articulated made Muslim masculinities deeply problematic. A gendered good/bad division emerged through community cohesion discourse, where Muslim women were portrayed as victims in need of state intervention, and men's adherence to such practices became a litmus test of Britishness. Blunkett stated in 2002: 'Respect for cultural difference has limits, marked out by fundamental human rights and duties. Some of these boundaries are very clear, such as in the examples of forced marriage or female circumcision (more accurately described as female genital mutilation, for that is what it is). These practices are clearly incompatible with our basic values' (Blunkett 2002). It should be noted that these practices were already illegal at this time, and thus not 'accepted'. The oppressive patriarchy of Muslim culture had, however, taken on a larger significance. Intertwined with discourses surrounding the invasion of Afghanistan, and the rescuing of Muslim women from the tyranny of the Taliban, the community cohesion's reliance on this dichotomy of good oppressed women and bad patriarchal men, and the necessity of state intervention to correct it, found a great deal of support.

Emerging from the context of Home Office reports into the 'riots', it is difficult to escape the conclusion that these community cohesion measures were primarily aimed at Britain's Muslim communities. David Blunkett's announcement of a test of national allegiance while discussing the uprisings served to link domestic civil disorder with excesses of cultural diversity and transnational attachments. Although he emphasised that lack of English language skills were not the cause of 2001 riots, he nevertheless pathologised those who did not speak English at home, claiming that fluency helped 'overcome the schizophrenia which bedevils generational relationships' (Blunkett 2002). Legislation which tightened immigration controls and impeded family reunification, announced in the context of press conferences about the riots, further emphasised the conviction that foreign spouses and imported cultures were thought to endanger British social cohesion (Yuval-Davis et al. 2005, 518–519).

The debate engendered by the Northern uprisings led to an attempt to reaffirm the values that bound the national community. Multiculturalism, with its celebration of diversity, was problematised for creating segregated communities and failing to provide a unifying social vision, and community cohesion aimed to repair this damage through an explicit celebration of Britishness. Yet the culturalisation of communities and their problems helped to give this discourse a decidedly anti-Muslim spin. Through the de-emphasis of class and race, and the emphasis on problematic transnational attachments, a bad Muslim subject was produced, detached from other salient identifications, pathologised as culturally dysfunctional and held up as marking the limits of British tolerance.

At the same time as community cohesion discourse was carving out this bad Muslim subject as responsible for domestic unrest and social strife, a global discourse was emerging which held Muslims responsible for violence and tyranny on an international scale. It is impossible to artificially separate the anti-Muslim elements of community cohesion from the influence of the 'war on terror' discourse which was being formulated and articulated simultaneously. The following section considers how the representation of Muslims in counterterrorism discourse contributed to the construction of the 'bad Muslim'.

MAKING AN EXTERNAL MUSLIM ENEMY: BRITISH COUNTERTERRORISM DISCOURSE

While community cohesion discourse culturalised politics to produce a bad Muslim subject against which British identity could be articulated, counterterrorism discourse performed a similar function by constructing an 'Islamic terrorist' enemy as a foreign threat that endangered the integrity and existence of the nation.

Following the September 11, 2001 attacks, this discourse of foreign threat was employed relatively unproblematically. Britain was portrayed by Prime Minister Tony Blair as one of the US's staunchest allies, sharing in its mourning and loss, and committed to freedom, increasingly represented as the central value for which the 'war on terror' would be waged. By committing troops to campaigns in Afghanistan and Iraq, Britain became intimately involved with the military aspect of the 'war on terror', and the discourse employed to justify this involvement made liberal use of binary logic. British counterterrorism discourse focused on the need to dissociate 'good' patriotic British Muslims from their 'bad' foreign co-religionists.

The 'home-grown' nature of the 7 July, 2005 London transport bombings and the foiled plots two weeks later, however, dislocated this construction. Following July 2005, the domestication of the foreign threat led to renewed government focus on 'bad' British Muslims and an emphasis on the promotion of a British Islam that would provide a robust counter-narrative to jihadist doctrine. The following section considers the employment of the good/bad Muslim binary in the 'war on terror' discourse, before moving on to consider how British counterterrorism discourse responded to the July 2005 attacks through the Prevent strategy.

The September 11, 2001 Attacks and the Discourse of the 'War on Terror'

It has been noted that the September 11, 2001 attacks on the World Trade Center and the Pentagon created a 'void of meaning' (Nabers 2009), which was swiftly filled by a particular construction of what the terrorist attacks meant, for the US and for the world. President George W. Bush sought, in numerous speeches, to draw the 'civilised world' into America's pain by representing September 11, 2001 as more than localised strikes on the USA, but an attack on freedom itself, a global tragedy, and the concern of every 'freedom loving nation'. Splitting the entire global system into a moral order in which a choice between good and evil must be made, Bush famously stated: 'Every nation in every region now has a decision to make: Either you are with us or you are with the terrorists' (Bush 2001).

In formulating the 'war on terror' discourse, he employed a central us/them binary to represent the attacks and those responsible. Binarism is a useful rhetorical device for leaders because of its simplification of complex issues into an easily identifiable cast of heroes and villains, which may be faithfully echoed by mass media. The us/them categorisation, and the signifiers attached to each side of the binary, operates as a standard relational pair; using one always invokes the other, and the consistent repetition of this binary conditioned both the response to the hijackings and the identities of actors in the global terrain being carved out.

The fact that the attacks were justified in religious language by Osama bin Laden, and that this was mirrored and echoed by Bush's rhetoric of militant evangelism, meant that from the outset there was a religious dimension to the attacks (and thus the subsequent 'war on terror') that simply could not be denied. As bin Laden constantly asserted in his communications, the perpetrators of the attacks were Muslim. Therefore, it followed that the enemy was Muslim. The enemy was also 'evil', 'terrorists', 'uncivilised', and 'barbaric'. Once such a binary has been instituted invocation of any of its terms evokes the whole range of subject positions and characteristics attached to it. Each description of the enemy conjured up all aspects of his identity, and the central aspect was Islam. It is for this reason that the good/bad Muslim dichotomy became central to both 'war on terror' and British counterterrorism discourse.

Leaders were careful to qualify any reference to Islam in the context of the 'war on terror' with disclaimers that emphasised that the *majority* of Muslims were peaceful and the fight was not with Islam. Both Bush and Blair (2001b) stated that the *true* followers of Islam were brothers and sisters in the struggle against those who had hijacked the faith. Bush assured Muslims, 'We respect your faith... Its teachings are good and peaceful, and those who commit evil in the name of Allah blaspheme the name of Allah' (Bush 2001). This differentialisation was based partly on the need to dissociate the terrorists' actions from religion in order to delegitimise bin Laden's pronunciations of a holy war, as well as the very real need to reassure Western Muslims and maintain civil peace by not appearing to give rhetorical support to possible retaliations. Bush and Blair therefore divided the category 'Muslim' into 'good Muslims', whose faith they respected, and 'bad Muslims', who were traitors, blasphemers, and hijackers of Islam. Bin Laden's claim to be acting in the name of Islam was thus delegitimised by assertions that his interpretation of Islamic justification for his actions was misguided, cynical, or 'evil'. However, the good/bad divide served further functions. Through their assertions that *true* Islam was peaceful and good, speakers demonstrated their own broadmindedness and tolerance, their knowledge of Islam, and, in speaking for their country, their nation's place on the righteous side of the us/them binary.

British Counterterrorism Discourse

Prime Minister Tony Blair sought to stake Britain's place on the virtuous side of the conflict from a very early point. Parliament was recalled on 14 September 2001, and Britain was entreated to see itself as sharing in the pain and grief caused by the attacks. He stated that the attacks were 'not just attacks upon people and buildings; nor even merely upon the USA; these were attacks on the basic democratic values in which we all believe so passionately and on the civilised world' (Blair 2001a). Blair drew Britain into America's pain (and its subsequent fight) by insisting that the civilised world and democratic values had been attacked. The implication was inescapable: Britain was part of the in-group—the civilised world—and should consider its own values brutally assailed and itself a direct victim.

The September 11 attacks required an explanation of both the identity and demands of the perpetrators and a reaffirmation of national ideals to reassure the public that order would be restored. Blair's rhetoric to this effect was not as overtly religious as Bush's and was notable for its attempts to move away from the discourse of evil. The religious discourse employed by Bush had relatively little purchase in a religiously ambivalent 'Christian Britain', meaning that Blair could not capitalise on this powerful rhetorical mode to the same extent. His discourse instead concentrated on a civilisational rather than a religious dichotomy, and this was readily echoed by other MPs in the Commons debate on 14 September 2001, as well as the media. Yet, despite Blair's attempts to distance himself from the good/evil binary, the dominant construction of the September 11 attacks meant that the articulation of any one of the relational pairs that formed the discourse effectively invoked the whole binary. In the British context, this necessitated the institution of the good/bad Muslim binary.

Good/Bad Muslims in British Counterterrorism Discourse

Tony Blair made an early distinction between 'good' and 'bad' Muslims. In his speech to the Commons, three days after the September 11 attacks, he stated that if Islamic fundamentalists had been responsible for the attacks:

> we know they do not speak or act for the vast majority of decent law-abiding Muslims throughout the world. I say to our Arab and Muslim friends: neither you nor Islam is responsible for this; on the contrary, we know you share our shock at this terrorism; and we ask you as friends to make common cause with us in defeating this barbarism that is totally foreign to the true spirit and teachings of Islam. (Blair 2001a)

The category of 'Muslim' was divided into those evil, barbaric, terrorist Islamic fundamentalists who had been responsible on one side, and the vast majority of decent, law-abiding, shocked 'friends' on the other. More tellingly, he placed those in the former category on the 'foreign' side of the inside/outside binary.

Several MPs were similarly keen to stress that they did not hold Muslims *en masse* responsible for the attacks and underlined that Muslims in their community had experienced the same dismay as the rest of the nation. Jean Corston (Bristol, East) highlighted the widespread shock after the attacks, stating that her Muslim constituents had been 'just as appalled as anyone else. They feel their Britishness just as strongly as many of us and they have been horrified at what has happened' (House of Commons 2001, col. 646). Others sought to emphasise that Islamic scripture had no part in the violence: 'the Muslim communities–those who believe in the Qur'an–in our country are settled, integrated and positively horrified by what they have seen on television' [Stuart Bell, Middlesbrough] (House of Commons 2001, col. 657). From a very early point, as the 'war on terror' discourse was developing, elite speakers were careful to emphasise the un-Islamic nature of the attacks, that bore no relation to the beliefs and values of those who truly followed Islam. But it was the Britishness of 'good' Muslims that was most forcefully stressed.

This emphasis on settled, integrated British Muslims who were 'like us', may appear contradictory to community cohesion discourse's emphasis on the segregated, parallel and un-British lives of Muslims. Yet despite this apparent reformulation of community cohesion discourse, there was continuity in the need to establish and nurture a particularly British Islam. By stressing British Muslims' horror at the attacks, counterterrorism discourse reformulated the good/bad binary around (good) British and (bad) foreign Muslims. Although the September 11 attacks were represented as an assault on civilisation, the danger was exteriorised. Good Muslims were 'our' Muslims, and the challenge lay in the need to distinguish between those good, law-abiding Muslims who must be protected and bad foreign Muslims who must be prevented from preparing terrorist attacks.

The 2005 London bombings dramatically dislocated this understanding of terrorism and both intensified and focused the good/bad Muslim divide. The bombers were British and apparently integrated, dispersing the stable construction of 'Islamic terrorism' as a largely foreign threat. The 'goodness' of British Muslims could no longer be assumed, rather, it had to be tirelessly promoted through state intervention in Islamic practice itself. The Prevent portion of the CONTEST counterterrorism strategy represented the government's attempt to support and promote a British Islam that would counter extremism and radicalism in Muslim communities, yet it was predicated on the articulation of Britishness as a remedy for terrorism and the notion that Muslims were dangerous, suspicious, and particularly susceptible to violent extremism.

The London Bombings and Good/Bad Muslims in the Prevent Strategy

The London bombings of 7 July 2005, and the attempted bombings two weeks later, dislocated the hitherto stable construction of terrorism as an exterior threat to Britain. The Britishness of the bombers lent a new focus to the good/bad Muslim discourse, and the realisation that 'home-grown' terrorism required a circle of tacit support led to a greater emphasis on the domestication of a threat that had previously been represented as largely foreign. Government focus in turn shifted to prevention strategies and the necessity of disrupting sympathy for the objectives and motives of terrorism.

The central policy consequence of the July 2005 attacks was renewed focus on the Prevent element of the CONTEST anti-terrorism framework. Created in 2003 and made public in 2006, CONTEST was based on four broad strands: pursuing terrorists and those who sponsored them; preventing terrorism by tackling radicalisation; protecting the public, key national services and UK interests overseas; and preparing for the consequences of terrorist attacks (Briggs et al. 2007, 24). Prevent represented an attempt to win the 'hearts and minds' of Muslims in the UK who might be susceptible to violent extremism. Focusing on the challenging of extremist ideology and government funding for the voices of 'moderate Islam', it came to form the central pillar of state engagement with Muslim communities.

What is important about the renewed focus on Prevent for the purpose of this chapter is the way in which this strategy internalised and reproduced the good/bad Muslim divide. Through a monocultural focus on Muslims alone, the linking of funding to certain accepted ideas, social engineering of Muslim organisations and leaders to align them with state-sanctioned doctrinal stances, and the targeting of particular Muslim communities as especially susceptible to violent extremism (chiefly Salafis and Islamists), Prevent internalised the good/bad Muslim binary as an integral part of policy.

IMP

Prevent

The announcement of the Prevent programme in October 2006 created the impression that it was a response to the July 2005 attacks. However, the key elements of the strategy had been mapped long before, in response to the September 11 attacks, the Northern uprisings of summer 2001 and intelligence that indicated British men were present in jihadist training camps in Afghanistan (Thomas 2010).

British Muslim radicalisation

The first manifestation of this approach emerged from the Preventing Extremism Together taskforce in August 2005, which consisted of ministerial visits to areas with large Muslim populations and discussions with more than 1000 Muslims. Building on the recommendations of the taskforce, a limited scheme, the Preventing Violent Extremism (PVE) pathfinder fund, was introduced in October 2006 with a £6 million budget for priority local authorities (those with Muslim populations greater than 5%). In June 2008, PVE was rolled out nationally as the largest domestic funding strand under Prevent with a budget of £45 million (HM Government 2008, 49).

The revised Prevent strategy had the overall aim of stopping people becoming violent extremists or supporting terrorism and was comprised of five core strands which aimed to challenge violent extremist ideology and support mainstream voices; to disrupt those who promoted violent extremism and support the institutions where they were active; to support individuals who were being targeted and recruited to violent extremism; to increase the resilience of communities to violent extremism; and to address grievances being exploited by ideologues; to develop understanding, analysis and evaluation; and strategic communications (HM Government 2008, 6). Prevent aimed to tackle support for violent extremism at the local level through the funding of 'moderate' mosques, Muslim community organisations and initiatives, youth groups, forums against extremism, anti-extremism road shows and the training of imams.

From its inception, Prevent focused solely on Muslims as particularly susceptible to violent extremism. Local funding was allocated according to the size of Muslim communities, apparently based on the (unsubstantiated) belief that dense Muslim communities were more likely to breed terrorism. This monocultural focus on Muslims within Prevent served to indicate that only 'Islamic extremism' was dangerous in a national security context, and since funding was linked to an explicitly anti-terrorism agenda this had blanket connotations for the entire faith community, implying that all British Muslim communities potentially had a problem with terrorism and must therefore be closely watched by their local authorities.

These aspects of Prevent would seem to suggest that all Muslims in Britain were considered (potentially) 'bad'. However, a closer analysis of the strategy reveals the implementation of binarism through the linking of Prevent funding to particular doctrinal understandings of Islam. By sponsoring 'moderate' organisations in order to create a dominant leadership which would contest radical expressions, the government targeted funding towards the influencing of religious ideas and practice, and in this way explicitly subsidised 'good' Muslims, while withdrawing funding for and engagement with 'bad' Muslims.

The Implementation of the Good/Bad Muslim Divide in the Prevent Strategy

Through the funding and promotion of certain organisations as the voice of moderation, the Prevent strategy implemented the good/bad Muslim divide based on the values of organisations rather than their effectiveness in reaching 'at risk' individuals. Predicated on the understanding that violent Islamist terrorism was best understood as gross theological error, this approach held that ideological contestation, theological counter-narrative, and the formation of a moderate, modern and progressive British Islam represented the best way to tackle terrorism. Government funding was targeted towards organisations that were considered to have a robust approach towards tackling extremism, such as the Quilliam Foundation, which received more than £1 million, the Radical Middle Way (£400,000) and the Sufi Muslim Council (£200,000) (Kundnani 2009, 36). At the same time as promoting 'good' Muslim organisations and initiatives, the government announced its intention to retract funding and support from organisations whose values did not meet its expectations. This change of direction was underlined by the withdrawal of government engagement with the Muslim Council of Britain, which was not considered to have a sufficiently anti-extremist position, as well as the proscription of avowedly non-violent Islamist groups such as Hizb-ut-Tahir.

In October 2006, then Communities Secretary Ruth Kelly announced that Muslim organisations that did not explicitly defend core British values and or take a proactive role in the fight against extremism would lose access to funding. Highlighting that grants would be targeted towards those organisations that accepted and promoted 'non-negotiable values', Kelly stated: 'It is only by defending our values that we will prevent extremists radicalising future generations of terrorists' (quoted in Helm 2006). Funded organisations were expected to uphold shared values, including the respect for law, freedom of speech, and equality of opportunity, as well as actively condemning and working to tackle violent extremism, and *The Prevent Strategy* outlined a number of indicators of organisational commitment to these values, including

> whether the organisation: publicly rejects and condemns violent extremism and terrorist acts, clearly and consistently; can show evidence of steps taken to tackle violent extremism and support for violent extremism; can point to preventing violent extremism events it has supported, spoken at or attended; can show that its actions are consistent with its public statements; and can show that its affiliated members or groups to which it is affiliated meet these criteria. (HM Government 2008, 60)

The enormous emphasis on the values of Muslim organisations indicates that the Prevent strategy's concern was with shaping the practice of British Islam, rather than working with groups that were more likely to be effective in reaching individuals at risk of radicalisation. Linking funding to values meant that those organisations which potentially had the most credibility with such individuals would be sidelined by Prevent. Similarly, the likelihood of individuals committed to violent Islamism attending government-backed roadshows and anti-extremism conferences is questionable. As one member of a prominent Muslim grassroots organisation, interviewed by Suraj Lakhani, stated: '...you wouldn't get Germaine Lindsay [one of the 7 July 2005 bombers] going to a [Prevent] community day...' (Lakhani 2012, 195). Through concentrating on the values of an organisation, Prevent may have misdirected resources and effort away from those groups who shared an interest in PVE, yet were uncomfortable with the overtly pro-Government agenda that funding demanded.

Prevent's tactic of attempting to reduce the influence of radical Islam by funding 'moderate' organisations may in fact have been based on an overinflated perception of the importance of Islamic doctrine in motivating terrorist acts. The assumption underpinning Prevent's values-based strategy is that ideological factors are the prime motivation driving individuals to join radical groups. Yet, as David Stevens has demonstrated, spiritual or religious principles rarely constitute primary incentives for those who join such groups. Rather, individuals engage in complex cost/benefit calculations about the goods provided by membership, and social benefits such as group solidarity have a higher value than theological principles (Stevens 2011, 169–171).

Prevent's values-based approach to engagement with British Muslim organisations represents, according to Basia Spalek and Robert Lambert (2008, 261), a form of identity building, where 'moderates' were seen to be allies in the prevention of terrorism while those who did not meet the stringent conditions set by the Government in terms of values were viewed as a threat to social cohesion and national security. The good/bad divide as implemented in the Prevent agenda viewed legitimate Muslims as those who engaged with the government on its own terms, while those who refused such an engagement, irrespective of their motives, were perceived as radical, not sufficiently 'anti-extremist', and a potential terrorist threat. This had profound implications for recipients of Prevent funding, many of whom were uncomfortable with its overt anti-terrorism focus and feared that it could cause backlash within Muslim communities and undermine local solidarity. This was reflected in Lakhani's interviews with Muslim grassroots groups. A number of respondents were concerned that Prevent-funded projects were viewed with suspicion by mass society and strengthened assumptions that Islam and terrorism were intimately associated. As one respondent noted 'when the government gives money to other community organisations to open up the youth centre... nobody bats an eyelid... [but] if the money came from Prevent and the youth centre is geared for Muslims then all of a sudden it has different connotations' (Quoted in Lakhani 2012, 197–198).

Lakhani's data further suggest that Prevent project leaders were viewed with suspicion *within* their communities as government puppets and spies. Around half of respondents admitted they either regretted receiving Prevent funding, subsequently refused it, or attempted to conceal acceptance from their communities, and several were concerned that the negative connotations of the strategy would damage their credibility. Such studies suggest that Prevent's overt attempt to encourage 'good' and disengage from 'bad' Muslims actually had the effect of fracturing Muslim communities, intensifying the view of wider society that Islam was intractably connected with terrorismand increasing suspicion and distrust within those communities that Prevent's work was most needed.

There is ample evidence that Prevent created real divisions within Muslim communities, but also between Muslim communities and others, including: non-Muslim ethnic and faith groups who resented the monocultural focus of funding; local authorities, who were increasingly viewed as colluding with the police and security services in the surveillance of their Muslim communities; and wider society, for whom Prevent funding intensified the connection between Islam and terrorism. Its early work with *only* Muslims gave the impression that religious identification was the only identification and experience for Muslims, and its concentration on promoting a convivial British Islam that would challenge extremist narratives implied that British Muslims had hitherto failed to understand their faith or had been practising it incorrectly. Overall, by treating Muslims in Britain as a generalised 'suspect community', Prevent entrenched the good/bad divide that had been instituted by both community cohesion and counterterrorism discourse.

Conclusion: Good/Bad Muslims and British National Identity

Since 2001, identity in Britain has become a central concept and the dominant discourses of community cohesion and counterterrorism were pivotal in the construction of British Muslim identity. By focusing almost exclusively on Muslims, these discourses subordinated other identifications to religious identity and projected a state-sanctioned 'correct' way to be Muslim in Britain.

This chapter has demonstrated how dominant national discourses consistently identified Muslims out as dangerous and threatening. Yet, Muslims as the community to be targeted were rarely, if ever, named, with speakers relying on cultural practices and common-sense understandings that implicitly referred to Muslims without ever explicitly singling them out. There are at least two reasons for this. First, racialised discourses in liberal democratic societies are bound by convention to not appear to target a particular racial, ethnic or cultural group. There are strong social injunctions that govern the way in which people, and particularly elites such as ministers and the media, speak about minority groups. Even when Muslims were clearly the community being targeted, linguistic strategies such as hedging, disclaimers and diminutives were used by speakers to make clear that they didn't consider *all* Muslims to be dangerous. These strategies served to present a positive self-image of speakers as broad-minded, while at the same time deflecting accusations of the illegitimate targeting of Muslims. Second, the simple self-evident fact that the vast majority of British Muslims were not engaged in anti-social activity or terrorism meant that the targeting of Muslims as a group was obviously illegitimate. Sweeping powers which primarily targeted Muslims could therefore not be justified under a discourse that overtly constructed them all as dangerously other, since most Muslims were clearly peaceful British citizens. This tension between the need to single out Muslims as a problematic group and the necessity to avoid charges of Islamophobia goes some way to explaining the omnipresence of the good/bad Muslim binary in post-2001 British discourse.

The good/bad dichotomy that was central to both community cohesion and counterterrorism discourse was crucial to the development of British Islamophobia. 'Good' Muslims were represented as those who could be drawn into the national community, while 'bad' Muslims were to be isolated and delegitimised. Yet, despite their focus on Muslims, these discourses were simultaneously instrumental in bolstering British national identity.

The discursive work of national identity lies in its need to mark difference in order to demarcate an area of belonging. As an imagined community, the nation sustains itself by consistently representing 'others' who affirm the nation by existing as something the community is not. David Campbell (1992, 3) famously noted that these 'others' are integral to the construction of national identity, and are usually represented as dangerous to the integrity of the national community. National identity by necessity induces a dichotomous discourse, whereby the recognition of those who belong to the nation is predicated on the construction of those who do not.

British discourse since 2001 has engaged national identity in a way that is predicated on the representation of Muslims as the nation's 'significant others'. As Anna Triandafyllidou has argued, significant national others can be internal or external; while the former threaten the unity and authenticity of a nation, the latter threaten to wipe it out (Triandafyllidou 1998, 602–603). Community cohesion discourse worked to represent Muslims as this internal significant other, a community within the national community whose excessive cultural diversity was deemed threatening. 'Self-segregation' and 'parallel lives' were the watchwords, and served to represent Muslims as withdrawing from the nation in a way that increased suspicion and mistrust among communities, and had the potential to cause rioting and violence on the streets. The fact that a remedial programme of civic education in British values was posited as the antidote to urban unrest indicates the centrality of national identity discourse to the community cohesion agenda. By forcefully articulating Britishness, it was believed that Muslims would feel they had more of a stake in the national community, and would thus be less likely to riot.

At the same time, British counterterrorism discourse represented Muslims as the nation's external significant other. Following the terrorist attacks of September 2001, Islamist terrorism was identified as a threat to civilisation itself, while the London bombings of July 2005 brought terrorism home as an existential threat to Britain. National identity discourse was employed to respond to both international and domestic terrorist attacks. In the former case, the exteriorisation of Islamist terrorism as 'foreign' marked British Muslims out as 'our' Muslims, sharing in the nation's horror and not to be 'tarred with the same brush' as the hijackers. In the latter, the home-grown nature of the attacks led to a concerted state effort to shape a nationally defined Islam that would promote British values and provide a counter-narrative to radical Islamist ideologies. The articulation of national identity was considered a central remedy for terrorism, and counterterrorism discourse was premised on the idea that if religious authorities could promote Britishness in an Islamic way, extremism could be quelled.

National identity is an ideological concept that requires constant articulation to be meaningful. To sustain the imagined community of the nation, the state must consistently communicate what it is; and like all discursive identity work, this requires difference. We can only understand what we are by understanding what we are not. In this sense, both community cohesion and counterterrorism were the expressions of national identity discourse. Both considered the national community threatened by Muslim difference, and both articulated Britishness as a remedy to the problems believed to be caused by excessive Muslim cultural diversity.

As this chapter has demonstrated, the dichotomy of good/bad Muslims was integral to both discourses but was at its heart an expression of national identity. The 'good' Muslim figure was constructed as secular, liberal, English-speaking and integrated, and with strong national attachments, while the 'bad' Muslim was its opposite; overtly religious and foreign in language, dress and ideology, with overriding attachment to the *ummah*, and a strong link with terrorism and extremism. Good Muslims were part of the nation, to be embraced and nurtured out of their cultural exclusivism, while bad Muslims were deeply threatening to national cohesion and national security. The latter figure played the role of the national 'folk devil' after 2001, threatening the nation internally and externally, and thus became the nation's 'significant other'. While community cohesion discourse and practice aimed to contain the 'bad' Muslim internally through coercive civic education practices that targeted Muslim communities as insufficiently integrated, counterterrorism discourse and practice responded to the external threat by attempting to shape and promote a particularly British Islam that would delegitimise violent Islamist extremism at the ideological level. Both were sustained by the central premise that a strong articulation of Britishness could remedy the problems believed to be caused by excessive attachment to Islam, and it is in this way that British national identity crystallised as dependent upon, and articulated in opposition to, the 'bad' Muslim figure.

Yet, a larger narrative was also articulated through this discourse of national identity. The post-2001 world was a global landscape of binaries, and the invocation of any one implicitly summoned its oppositional other. While 'we' represented freedom, civilisation and pluralism, 'they' represented despotism, barbarism and fanaticism. The community cohesion discourse's need to integrate Muslims into the nation and the counterterrorism discourse's desire to promote a British Islam both produced an archetypal 'bad' Muslim figure that frustrated these desires and had to be overcome in order to fix national identity, and Muslim identity within it. Yet this figure was the same spectre that haunted the international order in the guise of the Taliban and al-Qaeda. The community cohesion's folk devil was the self-segregating Muslim more attached to transnational kinship networks and the international Muslim community than Britain. The 'unacceptable' patriarchal cultural practices (female genital mutilation and forced marriage) of those Muslims targeted by community cohesion were immediately recognisable as those of the Taliban regime that Britain was bombing. Similarly, the folk devil of counterterrorism discourse was the raging Muslim fanatic whose international twin was al-Qaeda. Asserting Britishness as a remedy to problematic Muslims within the nation was thus analogous to asserting global belonging to the 'right' side of the international order.

British discourse on Muslims after 2001 was, like nationalist discourse in many other European countries, infused with Islamophobic dimensions. In targeting Muslims as culturally problematic, the community cohesion and counterterrorism discourses reified Islam as the primary identification of Muslims. Yet the apparently parochial domestic dimensions of these discourses were saturated with an understanding of British values as Western and universal. When Blair stated in a 2003 speech to Congress 'ours are not Western values, they are the universal values of the human spirit' (Blair 2003), he was explicitly articulating the Eurocentric assumptions implicit in community cohesion and counter-terrorism discourse.

As a domestic expression of a global narrative that identified Muslims as the West's cultural 'other', post-2001 British discourse articulated Islamophobia through consistent binary representation of the 'bad' Muslim as the nation's 'significant other' that threatened both internal cohesion and national security. It is little wonder that this discourse, with its easily identifiable cast of heroes and villains, was readily consumed and rearticulated by the British public in its understanding of Muslims.

REFERENCES

Alexander, C. 2004. Imagining the Asian Gang: Ethnicity, Masculinity and Youth after 'The Riots'. *Critical Social Policy* 24 (4): 526–549.

Amin, Ash. 2003. Unruly Strangers? The 2001 Urban Riots in Britain. *International Journal of Urban and Regional Research* 27 (2): 460–463.

Blair, Tony. 2001a. Full Text of Blair's Speech to the Commons. *The Guardian*, September 14. http://www.theguardian.com/politics/2001/sep/14/house-ofcommons.uk1. Retrieved 8 Dec 2013.

———. 2001b. Tony Blair's Speech: Full Text. *Independent*, October 1. http://www.independent.co.uk/news/uk/politics/tony-blairs-speech-full-text-9269196.html. Retrieved 8 Dec 2013.

———. 2003. Text of Blair's Speech. *BBC*, July 17. http://news.bbc.co.uk/1/hi/uk_politics/3076253.stm. Retrieved 8 Jan 2014.

Blunkett, David. 2001. Full Text of David Blunkett's Speech. *The Guardian*, December 11. http://www.theguardian.com/politics/2001/dec/11/immigrationpolicy.race. Retrieved 6 Nov 2011.

———. 2002. What Does Citizenship Mean Today? *The Guardian*, December 15. http://www.theguardian.com/world/2002/sep/15/race.thinktanks. Retrieved 23 Aug 2013.

Briggs, Rachel, Catherine Fieschi, and Hannah Lownsbrough. 2007. *Bringing It Home: Community-Based Approaches to Counter-Terrorism*. London: Demos.

Bush, George W. 2001. Transcript of President Bush's Address. *CNN*, September 21. http://edition.cnn.com/2001/US/09/20/gen.bush.transcript/. Retrieved 2 Dec 2013.

Campbell, David. 1992. *Writing Security*. Manchester: University of Manchester Press.

Community Cohesion Review Team. 2001. *Community Cohesion: A Report of the Independent Review Team (Chaired by Ted Cantle)*. London: Home

Office. http://resources.cohesioninstitute.org.uk/Publications/Documents/ Document/Default.aspx?recordId=96. Retrieved 20 Dec 2011.

Darbyshire, Neil. 2001. These Riots Are Not the Same as Brixton 20 Years Ago. *Telegraph*, July 10. http://www.telegraph.co.uk/comment/4263753/These-riots-are-not-the-same-as-Brixton-20-years-ago.html. Retrieved 21 Aug 2013.

Fekete, Liz. 2008. *Islamophobia and Civil Rights in Europe*. London: Institue of Race Relations.

Helm, Toby. 2006. Back British Values or Lose Grants, Kelly Tells Muslim Groups. *Telegraph*, October 12. http://www.telegraph.co.uk/news/ uknews/1531226/Back-British-values-or-lose-grants-Kelly-tells-Muslim-groups.html. Retrieved 5 Jan 2015.

HM Government. 2008. *The Prevent Strategy: A Guide for Local Partners in England*. London: Home Office. http://webarchive.nationalarchives.gov. uk/20130401151715/https://www.education.gov.uk/publications/ eOrderingDownload/Prevent_Strategy.pdf. Retrieved 3 Jan 2014.

Home Office. 2001. *Building Cohesive Communities: A Report of the Ministerial Group on Public Order and Community Cohesion*. London: Home Office. http://resources.cohesioninstitute.org.uk/Publications/Documents/ Document/DownloadDocumentsFile.aspx?recordId=94&file=PDFversion. Retrieved 11 Oct 2011.

House of Commons. 2001. Hansard Debate 14 September 2001. http://www.publications.parliament.uk/pa/cm200102/cmhansrd/vo010914/debtext/10914-01. htm. Retrieved 10 Dec 2013.

Kundnani, Arun. 2009. *Spooked!: How Not to Prevent Violent Extremism*. London: Institute of Race Relations.

Lakhani, Suraj. 2012. Preventing Violent Extremism: Perceptions of Policy from Grassroots and Communities. *The Howard Journal of Criminal Justice* 51 (2): 190–206.

Lewis, Phillp. 2002. Between Lord Ahmed and Ali G: Which Future for British Muslims. *Bradford Race Review: Supplementary Reports*. www.bradford2020. com/pride/docs/section6.doc. Retrieved 14 Feb 2014.

Local Government Association. 2002. *Guidance on Community Cohesion*. London: LGA Publications. http://resources.cohesioninstitute.org.uk/ Publications/Documents/Document/Default.aspx?recordId=93. Retrieved 14 Feb 2015.

McGhee, Derek. 2003. Moving to 'our' Common Ground—A Critical Examination of Community Cohesion Discourse in Twenty-First Century Britain. *The Sociological Review* 51 (3): 376–404.

Nabers, Dirk. 2009. Filling the Void of Meaning: Identity Construction in U.S. Foreign Policy After September 11, 2001. *Foreign Policy Analysis* 5 (2): 191–214.

Neal, Sarah. 2003. The Scarman Report, the Macpherson Report and the Media: How Newspapers Respond to Race-Centred Social Policy Interventions.

Journal of Social Policy 32 (1): 55–74. http://www.journals.cambridge.org/abstract_S004727940200689X.

Ouseley, Herman. 2001. *Community Pride Not Prejudice—Making Diversity Work in Bradford.* London: Institute of Community Cohesion. http://resources.cohesioninstitute.org.uk/Publications/Documents/Document/DownloadDocumentsFile.aspx?recordId=98&file=PDFversion. Retrieved 20 Oct 2011.

Phillips, Deborah. 2006. Parallel Lives? Challenging Discourses of British Muslim Self-Segregation. *Environment and Planning D: Society and Space* 24 (1): 25–40.

Riley, Krista Melanie. 2009. How to Accumulate National Capital: The Case of the 'Good' Muslim. *Global Media Journal—Canadian Edition* 2 (2): 57–71.

Roy, Amit. 2001a. Indians Try to Escape Catch-All 'Asian' Tag. *Telegraph*, June 19. http://www.telegraph.co.uk/news/uknews/1309153/Indians-try-to-escape-catch-all-Asian-tag.html. Retrieved 21 Aug 2013.

———. 2001b. Muslim Parents and Mosques Are to Blame, Says Hindu Leader. *Telegraph*, July 9. http://www.telegraph.co.uk/news/uknews/1333287/Muslim-parents-and-mosques-are-to-blame-says-Hindu-leader.html. Retrieved 21 Aug 2013.

Singh, Ramindar. 2001. Future Race Relations in Bradford: Factors That Matter. www.bradford2020.com/pride/docs/Section8.doc. Retrieved 22 Aug 2013.

Spalek, Basia, and Robert Lambert. 2008. Muslim Communities, Counter-Terrorism and Counter-Radicalisation: A Critically Reflective Approach to Engagement. *International Journal of Law, Crime and Justice* 36 (4): 257–270.

Stevens, David. 2011. Reasons to Be Fearful, One, Two, Three: The 'Preventing Violent Extremism' Agenda. *The British Journal of Politics & International Relations* 13 (2): 165–188.

Sylvester, Rachel. 2001. Getting to Grips with the National Identity Crisis. *Telegraph*, December 15. http://www.telegraph.co.uk/news/uknews/1365383/Getting-to-grips-with-the-national-identity-crisis.html. Retrieved 21 Aug 2013.

Thomas, Paul. 2010. Failed and Friendless: The UK's 'Preventing Violent Extremism' Programme. *The British Journal of Politics & International Relations* 12 (3): 442–458.

Triandafyllidou, Anna. 1998. National Identity and the 'Other'. *Ethnic and Racial Studies* 21 (4): 593–612.

Tweedie, Neil. 2001. Frightened Whites in Bradford's 'Two Worlds.' *Telegraph*, November 2. http://www.telegraph.co.uk/news/uknews/1361206/Frightened-whites-in-Bradfords-two-worlds.html. Retrieved 21 Aug 2013.

Yuval-Davis, Nira, Floya Anthias, and Eleonore Kofman. 2005. Secure Borders and Safe Haven and the Gendered Politics of Belonging: Beyond Social Cohesion. *Ethnic and Racial Studies* 28 (3): 513–535.

CHAPTER 3

Islamophobia at the Local Level: The Case of Dudley Mosque

INTRODUCTION

For more than a decade the West Midlands town of Dudley was embroiled in a heated debate. In pubs, cafes, shops, the council chamber and the mosque, the community was polarised over the issue of the 'Pride of Dudley', a planned mosque and community centre that was on and off the local agenda from 1999. Although the construction of mosques has become contentious in both Britain and Europe, no saga has lasted as long, or arguably been as contentious, as the case of Dudley mosque. The subject of angry petitions, several far-right protests, innumerable local debates and increasingly hostile legal battles between Dudley Muslim Association (DMA) and the local council, the mosque issue was finally settled in the council's favour in November 2015 when the Court of Appeal ruled that the council could buy back land it had swapped with DMA in 1999, and the mosque plan was finally defeated.

The case of Dudley mosque is noteworthy not just because of the length and intensity of the dispute, but also because of the presence of specifically local inflections of the themes discussed in the previous chapter. British discourse has, since 2001, represented Muslims as deeply problematic, focusing on their perceived lack of integration and the security danger that 'Islamic extremism' presented. The narratives central to the community cohesion and counterterrorism discourses worked to represent all Muslims as responsible for and dangerous to the internal cohesion and external security of British society. The Dudley mosque case is a

© The Author(s) 2018
L.B. Jackson, *Islamophobia in Britain*,
DOI 10.1007/978-3-319-58350-1_3

stark illustration of the appeal and use of such discourses for those seeking to prevent change in local areas.

In order to demonstrate the structure, character and purpose of these discourses, the present chapter considers how writers to local newspaper *Dudley News* represented Muslims in their arguments for or against the proposed mosque. Between 2006 and 2010 more than 160 letters were published on this topic, with the vast majority opposing the mosque and employing the national themes discussed in the previous chapter to do so. Community cohesion's focus on the threat that Muslim segregation posed to unified 'British identity', and counterterrorism discourse's emphasis on Muslim culture as existentially threatening the nation's security, were locally rearticulated by correspondents in order to represent Muslims as posing integration and security threats to Dudley.

Considering the local representation of Muslims is advantageous for our understanding of what constitutes Islamophobia. When speakers employ such discourse, consciously or (more often) not, they are appealing to a set of narratives and stereotypes that are considered to have multi-context explanatory power. Analysis of the representations that were prevalent during the mosque controversy enables a deeper understanding of how ordinary people interpret and rearticulate national discourses for local circumstances.

Threat and blame were the two most frequent frames through which Muslims in the locality were understood, and this had long-lasting consequences for Muslims in Dudley and their claims for religious and civic rights. It is doubtful that the controversy would have lasted so long had there not been such opposition in the town. And without the legitimacy that the national discourses provided, the campaign against the mosque may well have lost its momentum. The locality proved a remarkably receptive audience for national discourses, with their central representations of Muslims as unwilling to integrate and prone to violent extremism, and by appealing to these discourses, those opposing the mosque portrayed local Muslims as exemplary of this cultural dysfunction in order to prevent change in the area. These discourses thus served an ideological purpose to maintain things as they were, despite justified Muslim objections that their existing mosque was not fit for purpose.

The case discussed here is by no means unique; however, it does provide a window into the way Islamophobia functions not only as a discourse, but also as a practice of exclusion. When national discourses, with a legitimacy furnished through elite approval and an emphasis on the danger posed by Muslims, were interpreted and articulated by non-Muslims in Dudley, the effect was discriminatory. Muslims were denied access to a new mosque at least in part because of the opposition of their fellow Dudleians, and this opposition was driven to a large extent by the narratives of threat and blame that were central to the community cohesion and counterterrorism. Reinterpreted for a local context, these discourses allowed the drawing and policing of group boundaries that have proven difficult to demolish.

DUDLEY AND *DUDLEY NEWS*

Dudley

Dudley is an urban borough in the West Midlands with a Muslim population of almost 13,000 (4.1%) (Office for National Statistics 2013). Established in the town since the 1970s, Dudley Central Mosque has had traditionally strong relations with other faith groups and the population in general, through interfaith networks and community events. The government's Preventing Violent Extremism Pathfinder Fund, set up in 2007 as part of its counterterrorism strategy, positively highlighted DMA as an example of good practice, citing its work in engaging the local community through conferences, seminars, and exhibitions which aimed to discourage the radicalisation of young Muslims and promote community cohesion (Department for Communities and Local Government 2007, 12).

Standing on Castle Hill, in the centre of town, Central Mosque is a quaint but ageing building which operates well beyond its capacity, especially during festivals when three separate prayer services have often had to be held, and is well known to cause congestion and parking problems. Seeking to expand, in 1999, DMA embarked upon a series of land swaps with the council and acquired derelict land in Hall Street for the purpose of building a mosque and community centre. The agreement stipulated that the building must be iconic and of good quality and that substantial progress towards completion must have been made before 2008 (Reeves 2009, 92–93).

As a direct result of the September 11 attacks, DMA decided to detach the community centre from the mosque so that it could be used by all sections of the community in an effort to promote integration and understanding. Plans for the project were launched in February

2005, and a series of consultations with locals followed, which aimed
to accommodate objections and ensure that the project was in accord-
ance with the character of the area. Accordingly, the mosque's minaret
was scaled down to 65 feet and Christian arches were incorporated into
the design. Khurshid Ahmed, chairman of DMA, stated "It is meant to
be a celebration of our heritage and Christianity and Judaism are part
of that heritage. We believe this will be the first mosque in the world
to have half-Christian and half-Muslim architecture. We are very proud
of that" (quoted in Bright 2003). Despite this outreach work, the project received escalating local opposition, chiefly as a result of campaigns
by the United Kingdom Independence Party (UKIP) and the British
National Party (BNP) both of whom made the mosque a central issue in
local election campaigns.

The area has historically been a site of far-right activity. Simon Darby,
the BNP's former Deputy National Chairman, stood in six elections during the decade as a candidate in Dudley's Castle and Priory ward, receiving consistent support, and on one occasion polling more than 40% of
the vote. However, although the BNP exploited local concerns in their
election literature, the initiative was seized by UKIP's St James's ward
councillor, Malcolm Davis.

Davis (who defected to UKIP from the Liberal Democrats) spear-
headed the anti-mosque campaign, organising a 22,000 strong petition
against it, and was among the first to express opposition in a 2006 letter
to *Dudley News*. Stressing the Christian heritage of Dudley, Davis argued
in this letter that the mosque was unnecessary given the small number of
Muslims in the town, and suggested that its true purpose, and the reason Labour councillors had supported it, was to attract mass immigration
into the town and thus greater revenue for the locality from central government (Letter to the Editor, *Dudley News*, 15 September 2006).

Although some of these themes were taken up by correspondents,
particularly the notion that Dudley's heritage would be endangered
and, to a lesser extent, the idea that the mosque was unnecessary, public
discourse remained remarkably resistant to the local political agenda of
either UKIP or the BNP. Both parties centrally focused on the notion
that the mosque would increase Muslim presence in Dudley by attracting
migration to the area, a theme that was disregarded by correspondents to
Dudley News. Election records show that support for these parties dramatically increased during the decade, and there is little doubt that the
mosque issue galvanised this. However, the reasoning and justifications

of correspondents reflected mainstream national discourses to a far greater extent.

Other local issues should also be noted when considering the context of community relations in Dudley, particularly in relation to counterterrorism discourse. The 2001 capture and subsequent internment in Guantanamo Bay of the 'Tipton three', local men caught allegedly fighting against allied troops in Afghanistan, significantly affected the perception of Muslims in the area. Similarly, the arrest of two local men (one of whom was the son of Dudley Central Mosque Chairman Ghulam Choudhary) in a December 2003 nationwide anti-terrorism sweep added further fuel to rumours that Central Mosque was under the influence of extremists. These men were later released without charge; however, these incidents, along with the 2007 revelation of a Birmingham-based plot to behead a British soldier, served to give national counterterrorism discourses a local focus, and increased suspicion and distrust within the locality (Lambert and Githens-Mazer 2010, 150–151). Alongside a national context of dramatically heightened coverage of Muslim-related issues, this served as the backdrop against which the mosque was debated.

Dudley News

Dudley News is a free weekly regional newspaper with a circulation of more than 30,000 and a web presence at dudleynews.co.uk. During the mosque debate, the newspaper became a central site of local opinion making, and as events such as protests and court cases were reported on, the newspaper regularly solicited opinions from its readers. As such the letters column may be understood as a site of voluntary political participation, where writers could voice their concerns about the future of the community and engage in the exchange and discussion of ideas, while attempting to convince others of the acceptability of a point of view and provoke them to action (Atkin and Richardson 2007, 2). More than 160 letters about the mosque were published between 2006 and 2010, and the vast majority were opposed to the building. This opposition rested on two central themes: threat and blame. Shoring up arguments against the mosque, these discourses overlapped, intertwined and were used in a circular way to support the contentions of one another, but ultimately culminated in a remarkably hostile depiction of Muslims in Dudley.

THE DISCOURSES OF DYSFUNCTION: THREAT AND BLAME IN *DUDLEY NEWS* LETTERS

For correspondents to *Dudley News*, Muslims represented both a violent and particularly a terrorist threat and, due to their antagonistic and inassimilable culture, a threat to local and national identity. The discourse of blame similarly took two forms. Muslims were considered collectively responsible for the (violent) actions of other Muslims, as well as being blamed for not wanting to integrate, choosing to self-segregate within their communities and holding themselves apart from the majority Dudley community. These narratives relied on conceptions that were pervasive in the dominant national representations of Muslims discussed in the previous chapter. But it is the specifically local inflection of these discourses that is of interest for the purpose of this chapter.

The Threat of Violence

Arguments against the construction of Dudley mosque coalesced centrally around the threat of violence that Muslims were believed to represent. Presenting their opposition to the mosque through a fear-laden discourse, correspondents relentlessly highlighted Muslim culture as dangerously predisposed to violence and these themes were used to present resistance to the mosque as legitimate. As one correspondent stated, "Is it no wonder the people of Dudley do not want this mosque and community centre? We are living in an era where so called Muslims will commit mass murder and suicide in order to make this world Islamic using whatever means they can get hold of" (Letter to the Editor, *Dudley News*, 22 February 2007). This conflation of 'extremists' and Muslims in general was articulated as rational opposition, and drew upon common-sense background understandings that Muslims and violence were intrinsically and irredeemably connected. Repetition across the published letters served to cement this representation, to the extent that it became the dominant reason invoked to support the anti-mosque position: "If a church was built in Pakistan it would be bombed the next day. The Muslims would go mad before it was even built" (Letter to the Editor, *Dudley News*, 22 February 2007).

This narrative was the most common argumentative strand against construction of the mosque, and rested heavily upon the national discourses that had risen to prominence after 2001. The counterterrorism discourse's contention that Muslims were particularly inclined to violence was readily repeated in the pages of *Dudley News,* and the fear that local Muslims were ripe for violent radicalisation served to underline the arguments of those opposed. Significantly, there was an underlying understanding within the letters that however unlikely it may be that local Muslims would suddenly turn to violence, the *possibility* was enough to prevent the building. This association between Muslims and terrorism, and more crucially mosques and terrorism, was central to local opposition, and this link was sustained by the very same relations of equivalence articulated in national counterterrorism discourse.

Correspondents drew upon this national understanding that mosques were a breeding ground for 'Islamic terrorism' in order to rationalise their opposition to Dudley mosque. As one correspondent argued: "... some Muslims are indeed bogey men, who use mosques to train and indoctrinate less informed Muslims to walk alongside decent members of society, including fellow Muslims, and detonate their bombs..." (Letter to the Editor, *Dudley News,* 7 March 2007). This uncritical acceptance that mosques and terrorism were linked was pervasive throughout the letters. Since the link between Muslims and terrorism was well established, the authors had no need to substantiate claims such as these. Correspondents accepted that mosques *had* been used for breeding terrorism, and the possibility that this one could potentially be used for radical indoctrination was enough for most of the writers to oppose it. The connections were considered so self-evident that few writers felt the need to explain their position. Since some mosques had trained violent terrorists, it followed that all mosques were suspect and this mosque must therefore be opposed.

Repetition of these themes helped to cement the idea that Muslims represented a danger to Dudley, and the relationship believed to exist between Muslims and violence allowed correspondents to present their opposition to the mosque as rational and reasonable in the face of such threat. Yet this opposition was centrally bolstered by the claims of national counterterrorism discourse, in which the threat of violence was a central feature. Relying on the central association of Islam with terrorism and extremism, Prevent, the government's counterterrorism programme, fixed its gaze solely on Muslim communities and in this way worked to construct Muslims as particularly prone to violent extremism. As several studies have demonstrated, government language (Allen 2004; Jackson 2007), legislation (F. Ansari 2005; Pantazis and Pemberton 2009), and the media (Allen 2001; Fekete 2004) drew upon and sustained this link between Islam and violence. This was the context in which the correspondents to *Dudley News* were ideologically operating their opposition to the mosque, and they drew upon the very same associations that were being constantly reiterated in British society at this time.

National counterterrorism discourse problematised mosques as the social space where radicalisation into extremist ideas occurred. The dangerous nature of these buildings was reinforced when Tony Blair, in response to the 7 July 2005 attacks, announced plans to close down 'extremist mosques' (Wintour 2005). The discursive relationship between mosques and terrorism had already been firmly established when these plans were abandoned in December 2005 amidst fears that such legislation would encourage misidentification of Islam with terrorism. By this time the notion that mosques were inherently dangerous as hotbeds of radicalism was an accepted reality in Dudley, yet the association between mosques and extremism has been destabilised by critical analysis. Marc Sageman's work on terrorist networks, for example, stressed that although a few 'fundamentalist' mosques were sites of emergent terrorism, the vast majority were conservative institutions with a strong emphasis on the *status quo* and much more likely to constrain extremism than facilitate it (Sageman 2004, 143). Muslim organisations themselves have also stressed this point. As the Muslim Council of Britain's Iqbal Sacranie stated, mosques have been "misidentified and stereotyped as incubators of violent extremism, while the social reality is that they serve as centres of moderation" (quoted in Travis 2005).

The national counterterrorism discourse's tendency to target Islam itself as particularly prone to violence found a receptive audience in Dudley. However, this 'common-sense' understanding has been problematised by numerous studies that have repeatedly refuted the perceived link between Islam and terrorism. Large-scale analysis of Gallup polling data by John Esposito and Dalia Mogahed, representative of more than a billion Muslims, for example, demonstrated that among the 7% of respondents who viewed the September 11 attacks as completely justifiable, not a single respondent employed religious justification and there was no evidence of correlation between religiosity and extremism (Esposito and Mogahed 2008, 50; see also Bloom 2005; Pape 2005).

Muslims in Dudley had in fact been at the vanguard of work to discourage radicalisation of young Muslims and promote community cohesion, long before the strategy was rolled out nationally as part of Prevent, and the government's approval of DMA's strategies demonstrates the openness with which the Association approached such matters. Although the fears articulated in *Dudley News* reflected dominant discursive representations of Muslims as linked to violence, national and local realities show this relationship to be based on flawed understandings.

The Threat to Identity

Correspondents to *Dudley News* considered Muslims to be a potentially violent threat to the locality, but this was not the only danger they were believed to pose. Beyond the narratives of terrorist threat and radicalising mosques, Muslims were represented as deeply troubling to stable local identities. The consistent focus on a person's 'Muslimness' as their primary identity encouraged the portrayal of national and religious identities as mutually exclusive, and since Muslims were considered intrinsically 'other' to both British and Dudley culture, their presence threatened national and local identity. The letters page consistently articulated the notion that religious identity, for Muslims, took precedence over every other, and conflicted with both local customs and the duty to obey British laws. As this understanding gained traction within the pages of *Dudley News,* correspondents argued that Muslims could only offer selective recognition of the law, and could therefore be conceivably expected to break the social contract should British law conflict with religious duty.

This understanding was bolstered by a number of personal stories, in which correspondents related their interactions with Muslims, who had allegedly put their faith before the requirements of good neighbourly contact. These narratives served to underline claims that Muslim culture impeded integration in the area. As one writer stated, "My wife, who was recovering from an operation at the time, was refused help in unloading crates of wine from a taxi driver's vehicle because to touch the cases would be against his religion..." (Letter to the Editor, *Dudley News,* 11 January 2007). This type of personal narrative demonstrates the way local and national concerns were entwined through anecdotal stories which sought to demonstrate cultural incompatibility. For a majority of the correspondents, Muslim culture was viewed as inflexible, and their own experiences led them to extrapolate that the uncompromising nature of Muslims meant that they would never be able to accept Dudley or the nation as it was, but would relentlessly change the world around them. For these writers, the threat to Dudley was clear; Muslims' inability to compromise meant that peaceful co-existence was impossible. Since Muslims were understood to be attempting to change Dudley's landscape and culture to be more Islamic, support for the mosque was constructed as tacit support for the cultural destruction of Dudley:

> ... [A previous correspondent] correctly stated that: "it is part of the Muslim culture to deceive and manipulate". It is also part of their culture to try to dominate and intimidate wherever they live. And that's exactly what Khurshid Ahmed and his cronies are trying to do! (Letter to the Editor, *Dudley News*, 12 August 2007)

This understanding of 'Muslim culture' as static and monolithic not only paved the way for portrayals of Muslims as responsible for the actions of their co-religionists (discussed below), but also served to present them as sharing culturally conditioned nefarious aims. Drawing on Orientalist stereotypes, this representation of the threat to Dudley relied on the on the notion that Muslims were problematic because their culture determined them to such an extent that they simply could not be any other way.

Much of the discussion about the incompatibly of Muslim culture with Dudley was based on the idea that there exists a finite amount of culture available to a person, or within an area, and that if one culture advanced, another must retreat. Correspondents were increasingly convinced that should the mosque project go ahead, Dudley would lose its identity. Through such discussions, the building became a deeply emotive symbolic threat to dominant culture. As one writer lamented: "Our Black Country heritage is the only guaranteed thing we thought we could pass on to our children. Now even that will be gone and in its place we will be known for the mosque..." (Letter to the Editor, *Dudley News*, 1 March 2007). The notion that the mosque would become the focal point of the town, somehow erasing its past, reinforced its representation as a provocative symbolic statement that placed an Islamic claim on Dudley. Such a claim was intolerable at the local level, but it was also understood as the thin end of the wedge for the nation. This allowed writers to assert that the mosque "would dominate and tell all the non-Muslim people (not just the white British) this is our area, this is our town, this is our borough and one day, this is going to be [our] country" (Letter to the Editor, *Dudley News*, 12 August 2007). As the conflict endured, correspondents represented themselves as protecting the heritage of the nation from increasing Islamic incursions.

The cumulative effect of the discourse of threat within the letters pages of *Dudley News* was to present local Muslims as deeply unsettling people, shunning both local custom and national law, intent on violence, and aiming to bring Dudley's culture, history and heritage to an end. However, most troubling for the correspondents, was that even if Dudley's Muslims were not engaged in such activities, they all had the *potential* to be so, and thus were all in some way to blame.

The representation of Muslims as a threat to national or local identities is based on the belief that Islam takes precedence over all other identities and that it is inherently oppositional to British, and Dudley, culture. This understanding was intrinsic to the discourse of community cohesion, which was predicated on the notion that Muslims were particularly resistant to national assimilation (Amin 2003, 463; Worley 2005, 483–484), as well as counterterrorism discourse, which served to position Britain as existentially threatened by Islam and its adherents (Poynting and Mason 2006, 373; Jackson 2007, 420). The central premises of these discourses were recycled and rearticulated by the correspondents, who positioned Dudley's Muslims as implicitly suspicious, potentially disloyal and dangerous.

Yet despite the reality that these representations had for the vast majority of correspondents to *Dudley News,* the notion that Islamic identity is primary for Muslims has been challenged by a number of scholars. In his historical study of Muslim presence in Britain, Humayun Ansari (2004, 4) observed that British Muslims have seldom viewed Islam as their sole form of political and social identification. Indeed, the notion that Muslim identity is statically anchored by Islam has been refuted by both qualitative and quantitative studies. Haleh Afshar et al. (2005), for example, demonstrated that hyphenated and hybrid identities were readily taken on by Muslim women in Britain, who accepted cultural, ethnic and national identities that defined them differently in different circumstances. Polling data has further problematised the notion that Muslims consider their Islamic identity to be in conflict with national identity. A 2007 Gallup poll found that 77% of British Muslims claimed to identify with the United Kingdom (compared with 50% of the general population), and 82% said that they were loyal to Britain (Gardham 2009). The emphasis on a stable Islamic identity that forms the primary self-definition for Muslims was similarly rejected by young Muslims in Luton, who emphasised the fluidity of identities: "We have multiple identity and according to mood and circumstance we call ourselves Bangladeshi,

British, Muslim or Lutonian or whatever" (Home Affairs Committee (HAC) 2005, para. 188).

Other empirical works have suggested that local identities have more salience than national identities. As Justin Gest (2010, 199) has pointed out, British separation of ethno-cultural factors from citizenship means that belonging is much more likely to be conceived in terms of passports and residence, rather than emotional attachment to the nation and British Muslims identify more strongly with local, rather than national, culture. Steve Fenton's study of young adults' conceptions of national identity supports this. Fenton found that while a small proportion embraced or enthused about English or British identity, there was a broad band of indifference and hostility towards assuming a national identity, and local identities were often cited as more important (Fenton 2007, 334–335). The prevailing assumption, so central to the narratives of opposition to Dudley mosque, that British Muslims viewed their religious and national identities as incompatible relies on a static and bounded conception of identity that finds little empirical support.

Blame for the Actions of Other Muslims

The second broad theme that ran through local representations of Muslims in Dudley was blame. This was articulated as blame for the actions of other Muslims and blame for the perceived lack of integration in the locality, and was based on the underlying premise that since all Muslims were determined by their overriding Islamic identity, Muslim behaviour was derived from an Islamic cultural imperative.

One effect of representing Muslims as inescapably culturally determined was that they were considered collectively responsible for any action undertaken by any Muslim anywhere in the world. This logic allowed correspondents to *Dudley News* to hold all Muslims responsible for the actions of some. The mosque, framed through such a lens, was understood as the thin end of an Islamic wedge that would lead, as it did in all Muslim societies, to repression. Support for the mosque was thus rearticulated as support for the repressive practices of some Muslim societies, leading one correspondent to question those who endorsed it: "You do not object to the mosque, but at what point would you object? When Islam becomes the dominant religion? When TV is banned? When freedom of speech is banned?" (Letter to the Editor, *Dudley News*, 22 February 2007). By invoking such negative practices, writers were able to conflate the characteristics of particular Muslim societies with the wishes, desires and essence of all Muslims, and in doing so the mosque was further problematised as symbolic of Muslim desires for dominance. This narrative not only assigned blame to all Muslims for the actions of some, but also implied that Muslims should apologise for the anti-dem-ocratic nature of some Muslim regimes. As one correspondent argued, "I'd ask Mr Ahmed to name one democratic multi-party, pluralistic Muslim state before he condemns the democratic decision of an elected council and the democratic voice of the people of Dudley" (Letter to the Editor, *Dudley News*, 5 April 2007). Such arguments drew directly on this notion of collective responsibility. To be hypocritical as the author suggests, Ahmed would have to share the blame for the crimes against democracy that are invoked. Such a position can only be sustained by the underlying assumption that Muslims everywhere are somehow answer-able for the actions of their co-religionists.

The notion that Muslims should take responsibility for the lack of pluralism and democracy in other Muslim societies was similarly applied to British society, where groups established to respond to discrimina-tion were charged with creating social disharmony. One correspondent argued that if the DMA chairman truly wanted to build harmony in soci-ety he should direct his efforts towards disbanding the Muslim Council of Great Britain, the Federation of Black Police Officers and the British Muslim Initiative, all of whom were accused of sowing disharmony (Letter to the Editor, *Dudley News*, 7 March 2007). Regardless of the substance of these claims, the fact that Khurshid Ahmed could be held accountable for the actions or inactions of such organisations relied on the assertion that he bore some responsibility as a Muslim. This was a prominent theme within the letters page of *Dudley News*, and essentially asserted that Muslims had no right to agitate for a mosque until they had put their own house in order.

Because culture was implicated as responsible for both the 2001 upris-ings and the September 11, 2001 and 7 July 2005 terrorist attacks, a dis-course of blame emerged within national discourse that used the notion of 'shared values' to imply that Muslims were collectively responsible for the actions of their co-religionists. The Northern uprisings had been understood as resulting from excessive cultural relativity that had weak-ened nationalistic attachment (Burnett 2004, 7; Abbas 2007, 297), while the intensive legislative focus of counterterrorism on Muslim commu-nities promoted a discourse of blame that obliged ordinary Muslims to consistently and monotonously condemn terrorism and disclaim extremism (Gest 2010, 7; Forum Against Islamophobia & Racism 2004, 19; HAC 2005, para. 171; Pantazis and Pemberton 2009, 652–654).

The discourse of collective responsibility is predicated on the essentialising of Muslims as unidimensional because of their shared adherence to Islam and the inescapable effects of 'Muslim culture'. This was regularly drawn upon by the correspondents who highlighted negative aspects of some Muslim societies in order to make broader arguments about the compatibility of Muslims with Dudley in particular and Britain in general.

It barely needs to be pointed out that, given the existence of more than a billion Muslims, settled on every continent, speaking 50 languages and innumerable variations of denomination and cultural tradition, any pronunciation on 'Muslim culture' must be treated with the utmost caution. Bruno Etienne (2007, 238–239) has argued that Islam is in fact united only in its monotheism, with every other aspect of Muslim life the object of sharp contestation between and within traditions. Contrary to the thesis that holds 'Muslim culture' as transhistorically uniting Muslims, this is precisely because the historical challenges encountered by differently socially situated Muslim societies have produced dramatically varied interpretations of the Prophetic tradition.

At a more local level, the work of Frank Reeves demonstrates the vast differences in opinion between Dudley Muslims on issues such as dietary practices, religious clothing and attitudes towards homosexuality. His survey of Dudley residents showed that 20% of Muslim respondents were prepared to relax their attitude to *halal* food at a social event out of politeness, more than a quarter (26.7%) disapproved of women wearing the *niqab* (face veil) in public places and over half (56.7%) believed that homosexuals should be treated equally (Reeves 2009, 69, 66, 62). Reeves's work demonstrates that there are significant differences of opinion even in a small sample on issues that are often articulated as evidence of Muslim cultural unidimensionalism. The notion that there exists a determinate fundamental 'Muslim culture' that shapes the behaviour of all Muslims does not bear scrutiny at the national or local level.

Blame for Lack of Integration

The final theme that found large support in the letters column was the perceived lack of integration in Dudley. Correspondents laid the blame for this with Muslims, who were accused of paying lip-service to integration while deliberately holding themselves aloof and choosing to self-segregate.

The problematic nature of Islam generally, and Dudley's Muslims in particular, was central to such arguments. One writer compared the controversy over the proposed mosque with a recently opened Hindu temple situated two miles away, at the time the largest in Europe. The fact that this had not generated such controversy was taken by the author to indicate that Hindus were more able to integrate, while Muslims were perceived to be antagonising the locality with their unreasonable demands (Letter to the Editor, *Dudley News*, 22 September 2006). Again, the determining nature of Islam was blamed for this situation. As another correspondent claimed, "Everything a Muslim thinks, says and does is governed by the will of their God with the result that compromise is impossible... Without compromise we cannot have integration" (Letter to the Editor, *Dudley News*, 10 November 2006). Through a discourse which presented Islam as completely formative of Muslim life, the discourse of the letters column worked to culturalise social realities and hold Muslims responsible for perceived lack of integration in the local area.

The writers were also pessimistic about the idea that the detached community centre would promote mixing between people of different backgrounds, primarily because Muslims were believed to be inhospitable. One writer asked "will all people irrespective of what race, religion and nationality be allowed to do 'their thing' without objections from the Muslim sector? Or will it inevitably be a case of whenever anyone else wants to use it, the place is fully booked?" (Letter to the Editor, *Dudley News*, 22 February 2007). By representing Muslims in Dudley as hostile, correspondents not only made their objections to the mosque appear rational, but also attended to potential charges of Islamophobia by marking out Muslims as the instigators of community strife. In this way, the subjects of discriminatory discourse and practice were blamed for the discrimination they received. Despite the efforts made by DMA to reach out to the local community, the overriding conceptualisation of Muslims as isolationist and inhospitable remained. By doubting the inclusiveness of the community centre, the correspondents shifted the blame for poor community relations on to Muslims.

The discourse of blame worked to hold all Muslims responsible, both for the actions of their co-religionists and for a perceived lack of local and national integration. The mosque project was represented within this imaginary as a deliberate attempt to antagonise the non-Muslim population of Dudley. All Muslims were implicated in the discourse of blame, and the correspondents held them to account by withholding support for the mosque.

Such narratives harked back to community cohesion discourse's central theme. Lack of integration was a key concern and contained the implicit understanding that Muslims were responsible for their 'parallel lives' and had chosen to self-segregate from the majority population (Ouseley 2001, 18). The Cantle Report in particular emphasised that the parallel lives of residents who lived in mixed areas but did not have contact with one another had been a major cause of the 'misunderstandings' that had led to the 2001 uprisings (Community Cohesion Review Team 2001, 9). Nationally, this was articulated as a problem of excessive cultural diversity which was managed by reversion to a monocultural ideological project that championed 'British values' and treated diversity as suspicious (McGhee 2008, 144). Correspondents to *Dudley News* rearticulated this national discourse of culture as problematic in the local context to argue that since Muslims were not willing to integrate with Dudley the mosque should not be permitted.

Self-segregation is a problematic concept, and implies a desire on the part of those suspected of it to remain aloof from the majority in order to protect their cultural identity. As Ludi Simpson's work has demonstrated, cultural explanations for segregated living patterns fail to appreciate the realities of movement, particularly in areas of deprivation. His work on Bradford, the archetypal polarised city, has demonstrated that the number of predominantly South Asian (mostly Muslim) areas did increase, but that this was due to population growth from immigration and natural increase, rather than a result of residents moving to areas of South Asian concentration (Simpson 2004, 677). Polling data on Muslims' attitudes to integration similarly throws doubt on the notion of self-segregation. A 2006 Pew Center poll found that while 64% of Britons surveyed believed that Muslims wanted to be distinct from society, only 35% of Muslims agreed with this statement, and a significant minority of British Muslims said that they believed Muslims in Britain mostly wanted to adopt national customs (Pew Research Centre 2006).

Frank Reeves's local survey similarly found little evidence that Muslims in Dudley sought to self-segregate. In fact, the overwhelming majority (93.3%) wanted the council to provide more opportunities for people of different religious backgrounds to mix. Contrastingly, only

3 ISLAMOPHOBIA AT THE LOCAL LEVEL ...   75

28.6% of non-Muslims were in favour of this, while more than a third (38.2%) were opposed (Reeves 2009, 76). Reeves's data suggests that what is perceived as self-segregation is driven more by lack of opportunity for mixing than by a deliberate drive on the part of Muslims to hold themselves apart from majority society. Indeed, the fact that the original plans for the mosque were changed in order to detach the community centre from the mosque so that it could be used by all communities undermines the idea that Muslims in Dudley did not wish to mix. On the contrary, it seems that a significant minority of non-Muslims were hostile to integrating with Dudley's Muslim communities.

CONTESTING THE DOMINANT DISCOURSES

Surprisingly few of the letters that made it into the pages of *Dudley News* contested these dominant discourses. Whether this reflects an inclusion bias on the part of the newspaper's editor, or whether it is indicative of a widespread support for these positions is not clear. What is clear is that the micro-climate of hostility made alternative positions difficult to sustain.

Those letters that did support the mosque tended to do so on the basis of the need for a new building to relieve the congestion and overcrowding problems that Central Mosque created. While this type of support was no doubt welcomed by the mosque's advocates, it did little to destabilise the dominant representations of Muslims in Dudley that were circulating. Only three letters actually engaged with these dominant discourse in order to refute their central claims. One of these contested the unidimensional portrayal of Muslims within the letters page and the dominant media representation of Muslims as linked to terrorism (Letter to the Editor, *Dudley News*, 7 March 2007). Another engaged with the fear among the correspondents that Dudley values would be corrupted, asking "Is their identity and confidence in themselves so fragile that they can't tolerate people different to themselves and instead see them as a threat? What else could be responsible for such hostile views...?" (Letter to the Editor, *Dudley News*, 28 February 2007). The final letter in this group acknowledged that Islam was viewed as threatening, but argued that the growing number of Muslims in the area needed somewhere to pray: "I think the thing that gets to people the most is that Islam is growing and that's the threat to them, not the building of the mosque. Muslims go to the mosque for a pace to worship, not to drink tea and biscuits like they do in churches" (Letter to the Editor, *Dudley News*, 22 February 2007).

The latter two letters elicited responses from others and it is worth briefly addressing the way in which those opposed to the mosque reaffirmed the dominant discourses in their counter-arguments to the points raised. A reply to the second letter, which had argued that those opposed to the mosque based their arguments on irrational fears of Muslims, was published the following week and simply refuted the central argument, maintaining that some Muslims were indeed terrorists who used mosques to plan attacks. The association between Muslims and violence, having been problematised by the original writer, was thereby restated through this response, and the link between Muslims, mosques and terrorism was reasserted.

The reply to the third letter followed a similar strategy, accepting the author's point that there was a lack of understanding between Muslims and non-Muslims, but stressing that Muslims were responsible for this because of their involvement in terrorism, arguing: "So far lessons have been dominated by the twin towers, holiday villages in Bali and the London Underground etc. Some insight into her beliefs would be more welcomed than the strident tone" (Letter to the Editor, *Dudley News*, 28 February 2007). The overall effect was that those who did engage with the dominant discourses in order to counteract them were silenced by a common-sense and widely shared understanding that Muslims, mosques and violence *were* linked and because of this the risk to Dudley, should the mosque be built, was simply too great.

In sum, correspondents to *Dudley News* held to a representation of Muslims as threatening to national security and national identity, and collectively responsible for terrorism and a lack of integration. Dominant discourses that portrayed Muslims as problematic both externally (to security) and internally (to identity), were rearticulated in the local context in order to underscore the central argument that the mosque simply could not be accepted.

THE IDEOLOGICAL EFFECTS OF THE DISCOURSES OF THREAT AND BLAME

Despite the contestable assumptions that underpinned them, the discourses of threat and blame that flourished in letters to *Dudley News* performed political and ideological functions and had real effects in the town, both on relationships and identities, and ultimately on the fate of the mosque itself.

The most conspicuous ideological effect of these discourses was the construction of a 'Muslim other', which facilitated the representation of a culturally stable Dudley threatened by the presence of Muslims. The discourses of threat and blame relied on the representation of Muslims as culturally predisposed to socially unacceptable behaviour, and this allowed correspondents to make sweeping generalisations about all Muslims in order to oppose the mosque. Predicated on the explanatory purchase of 'Muslim culture' as the primary maker and marker of behaviour, Muslims were positioned as intrinsically alien to Dudley and deeply threatening to the culture of the locality. The appeal of such representations can be understood as part of a broader contemporary trend towards the securitisation of identities. As Kinvall and Linden have highlighted, the pressures of globalisation and migration force both migrants and 'host' societies to rework their identities in response to the new realities they face, causing some to retreat into a mythical past in an attempt to 'securitise' subjectivity by clinging to one identity (Kinnvall and Linden 2010, 598–599). The anxieties about Muslims, so frequently expressed within the letters, can be understood from this perspective as an attempt to fix destabilised identities. By projecting the image of an eternal and unchanging 'Dudley culture' as threatened by culturally antagonistic Muslims, the non-Muslim community was brought together and identities could coalesce and stabilise around this perceived threat. This effect was illustrated by the self-congratulatory messages that were exchanged within the letters page every time the mosque plans were derailed. Letters that exclaimed "well done to the people of Dudley!" (Letter to the Editor, *Dudley News*, 7 March 2007) not only addressed, but also *constructed* a very specific community that implicitly excluded the Muslims within its midst.

The discourses of threat and blame also functioned to sustain existing power relations. The addition of a mosque to Dudley was consistently represented as an intolerable challenge, threatening to its history and heritage and something that could not be absorbed or accepted. Few of the correspondents were willing to entertain the notion that Dudley culture could adjust in order to accommodate the mosque. Gabriele Marranci has theorised this as fear of the 'transruptive' effects of Islam on European identities. As Islam fails to assimilate and fade within contemporary Europe, the identities of European states and peoples are changed as they come into contact with Muslims, who are also transformed by the encounter (Marranci 2004, 115–116). Marranci has argued that contemporary Islamophobia is the fear of this change, which manifests in the desire to uphold traditional identities. This was evident at the local level in Dudley, where Muslims were portrayed in negative and threatening ways as making unreasonable demands of the locality, which in turn served to justify Dudley's overwhelmingly hostile reaction. The problem of deteriorating community relations was then cast not as the result of the hostility of non-Muslims, but due to the unreasonable demands and alien values of Muslims.

At a more concrete level, discourses work to constrain and establish possibilities for action by making some actions appear inevitable and others simply implausible (Fairclough 2001, 121). The dominant discourses in Dudley worked in this way to put pressure on decision-makers to reject the proposal. Frank Reeves noted that his research team was instructed not to undertake the survey of Dudley residents prior to the outcome of the May 2008 elections lest an already volatile and contentious situation was further provoked (Reeves 2009, 81–82). The unanimous rejection of the proposal by Dudley Council's Planning Committee in February 2007 may also, arguably, be seen as a response to the dominant discourses exhibited in *Dudley News*. Of course, this is not to suggest that the letters page of a local newspaper was the only, or even primary, source of pressure on councillors. Huge public interest, the campaigns of far-right parties, sustained and hostile local media coverage and the 22,000-strong oppositional petition all coalesced to make rejection of the proposal an attractive option for councillors, who knew that should the DMA appeal the decision it would be taken out of their hands and referred to the government's planning inspector. Nonetheless, the importance of the discursive representations within the letters should not be overlooked, especially in a free newspaper delivered throughout the borough. The letters page functioned as a site of contestation and argumentation, and correspondence aimed to call others to action to reject the mosque. As such, the dominant discourses within the letters made it clear to decision-makers that the only acceptable course of action was rejection of the plans.

Related to this are longer-term effects of strained community relations and the breakdown of trust that some Muslims felt following the council's rejection of the mosque. Despite extensive remodelling of plans in the face of local objections, the proposal was unanimously rejected by councillors against the recommendations of their own planning officers. Given the efforts made to accommodate local concerns, it is not

3 ISLAMOPHOBIA AT THE LOCAL LEVEL ... 79

surprising that Muslims felt indignant at what they perceived as the discriminatory and Islamophobic nature of the council's decision to deny permission. Justin Gest has highlighted that a heightened sense of alienation among young Muslims in East London was due in large part to their perception that Muslim voices were being ignored in local struggles (Gest 2010, 192). Again, the cumulative effects of a consistently hostile discursive atmosphere in *Dudley News* should not be underestimated. As negative stereotypical representations mounted in the pages of the newspaper, the overwhelming public sentiment towards Muslims would have left few in doubt that they were unwelcome and unwanted in the area.

CONCLUSION

This chapter has critically analysed the dominant narratives expressed in opposition to the proposed Dudley mosque in order to demonstrate how the national representations of Muslims discussed in the previous chapter were employed, rearticulated and altered in local context. The purpose of the chapter is not to suggest that these were the only representations of Muslims circulating, or that these views were necessarily representative of the majority of Dudley residents. Rather, it aims to highlight how discourses with national prominence and elite approval furnished the anti-mosque position with a veneer of rationality, maintained existing power relations and served to silence alternative representations in the din of hostility, fear and threat.

The discourses of dysfunction served a clear purpose for Dudley during the mosque controversy. The national focus on Muslims as culturally responsible for the gravest contemporary ills allowed social problems such as extremism, terrorism, segregated towns and lack of social cohesion to be de-contextualised, de-historicised and repackaged as products of Muslim cultural malady. Conceived as such, reform was portrayed as the responsibility of *Muslims*, and something the state could only hope to challenge by compelling its supposedly recalcitrant subjects to assimilate. Such thinking is characteristic of a problem-solving approach to social management (Cox 1981, 128), in which the *status quo* is left secure and unscrutinised, and the historical policies, inequalities, political grievances and discrimination that have contributed to contemporary problems are dismissed in favour of an all-encompassing discourse of Muslim cultural dysfunction. The problem is with 'them', not 'us', and the solution does not require 'us' to change in any way, except to welcome Muslims out of their cultural bondage and make the transition to 'integration' as attractive and straightforward as possible.

The portrayal of the mosque as an unacceptable challenge to Dudley's history and heritage pivoted on the local articulation of dominant national representations of Muslims as dangerously opposed to an ill-defined and mythical 'British culture'. Muslims were not considered part of Dudley culture, and the idea that Dudley could itself change to include markers of Muslim faith was dismissed. The discourse demanded recognition of the eternal and unchanging heritage of Dudley, and the repeated calls for Muslims to integrate in order to be better citizens of Dudley were invested with the corresponding claim that to be a good citizen of Dudley one must respect the heritage of the town and consequently oppose the mosque as damaging to this. The demands for integration were couched in conditions that called for Muslims to abandon legitimate claims for their faith in the interests of a history from which they were excluded, and a future in which their participation was unwanted.

Muslims are clearly considered most dangerous when they are *visibly* Islamic, that is, when they make claims for their faith, in this case by calling for a new place of worship. It is at this point when anxieties about cultural incompatibilities come to dominate the discourse, and representation of Muslims as fundamentally alien to British culture becomes a key theme.

These representations support the conceptualisation of Islamophobia as cultural racism. Through an unswerving focus on 'Muslimness' and an understanding that all Muslim action and behaviour was culturally conditioned, Muslims were differentiated from non-Muslims and de-differentiated from one another through the unidimensionalising focus on the determinative nature of Muslim culture. It was this dual process that allowed Dudley's Muslims to be compared to rioters in Bradford and terrorists in Pakistan. A political conditionality was attached to Muslim interaction with society that demanded Muslims first show their willingness to integrate and repudiate terrorism before any benefits could be distributed to them. But since any claims for faith were tainted with the dangerous mark of Muslim culture, Dudley's Muslims found themselves in an impossible position.

The discourses of threat and blame and their underpinning construction of Muslims as unidimensional and culturally dysfunctional served as discursive weapons for the correspondents to argue against change in Dudley. Yet the assumptions that these discourses were based upon are vulnerable to critique at both national and local levels. Recognising the way in which these discourses serve to disguise discriminatory practices aimed at Muslims, by explaining them as the natural outcome of antithetical cultures clashing, is essential in order to challenge dominant narratives and open up spaces for contestation. As a generation of young British Muslims grows up expecting the full rights and entitlements of citizenship and making claims for their religion, discourses that exclude them as not properly belonging to the nation, while simultaneously reprimanding them for failing to integrate, serve to foster an alienation and disaffection that can all too easily be exploited.

References

Abbas, Tahir. 2007. Muslim Minorities in Britain: Integration, Multiculturalism and Radicalism in the Post-7/7 Period. *Journal of Intercultural Studies* 28 (3): 287–300.

Afshar, Haleh, Rob Aitken, and Myfanwy Franks. 2005. Feminisms, Islamophobia and Identities. *Political Studies* 53 (2): 262–283.

Allen, Christopher. 2001. Islamophobia in the Media Since September 11th. In *Conference Proceedings. Exploring Islamophobia: Deepening Our Understanding of Islam and Muslims.* London: University of Westminster. http://www.fairuk.org/docs/Islamophobia-in-the-media-since-911-ChristopherAllen.pdf. Retrieved 30 Dec 2014.

———. 2004. Justifying Islamophobia: A Post-9/11 Consideration of the European Union and British Contexts. *The American Journal of Islamic Social Sciences* 21 (3): 1–25.

Amin, Ash. 2003. Unruly Strangers? The 2001 Urban Riots in Britain. *International Journal of Urban and Regional Research* 27 (2): 460–463.

Ansari, Fahad. 2005. British Anti-Terrorism: A Modern Day Witch-Hunt. *Islamic Human Rights Commission.* London: Islamic Human Rights Commission. http://www.ihrc.org.uk/file/2005BritishANtiTerrorism.pdf. Retrieved 30 Dec 2010.

Ansari, Humayun. 2004. *The Infidel within: Muslims in Britain since 1800.* London: C. Hurst.

Atkin, Albert, and John E. Richardson. 2007. Arguing about Muslims: (Un)Reasonable Argumentation in Letters to the Editor. *Text & Talk* 27 (1): 1–25.

Bloom, Mia. 2005. *Dying to Kill: The Allure of Suicide Terror.* New York: Columbia University Press.

Bright, Martin. 2003. British Muslims Plead for Peace. *The Observer*, December 7. http://www.guardian.co.uk/uk/2003/dec/07/race.equality. Retrieved 30 Apr 2011.

Burnett, J. 2004. Community, Cohesion and the State. *Race & Class* 45 (3): 1–18.

Community Cohesion Review Team. 2001. *Community Cohesion: A Report of the Independent Review Team (Chaired by Ted Cantle)*. London: Home Office. http://resources.cohesioninstitute.org.uk/Publications/Documents/Document/Default.aspx?recordId=96. Retrieved 20 Dec 2011.

Cox, Robert W. 1981. Social Forces, States and World Orders: Beyond International Relations Theory. *Millennium: Journal of International Studies* 10 (2): 126–155.

Department for Communities and Local Government. 2007. Preventing Violent Extremism Pathfinder Fund: Guidance Notes for Government Offices and Local Authorities in England. http://www.communities.gov.uk/documents/communities/pdf/320330.pdf. Retrieved 7 May 2011.

Esposito, John L., and Dalia Mogahed. 2008. Who Will Speak for Islam? *World Policy Journal* 25 (3): 47–57.

Etienne, Bruno. 2007. Islam and Violence. *History and Anthropology* 18 (3): 237–248.

Fairclough, Norman. 2001. *Language and Power*. Harlow, UK: Pearson.

Fekete, Liz. 2004. Anti-Muslim Racism and the European Security State. *Race & Class* 46 (1): 3–29.

Fenton, Steve. 2007. Indifference Towards National Identity: What Young Adults Think About Being English and British. *Nations and Nationalism* 13 (2): 321–339.

Forum Against Islamophobia & Racism. 2004. Counter-Terrorism Powers: Reconciling Security and Liberty in an Open Society: A Discussion Paper—A Muslim Response. http://www.fairuk.org/policy12.htm. Retrieved 10 Jan 2011.

Gardham, Duncan. 2009. More Muslims Identify Themselves as British than Rest of Population. *Telegraph*. http://www.telegraph.co.uk/news/religion/5287105/More-Muslims-identify-themselves-as-British-than-rest-of-population.html. Retrieved 13 Oct 2011.

Gest, Justin. 2010. *Apart: Alienated and Engaged Muslims in the West*. London: C. Hurst.

Home Affairs Committee (HAC). 2005. *Terrorism and Community Relations, Sixth Report*. London: House of Commons. http://www.publications.parliament.uk/pa/cm200405/cmselect/cmhaff/165/16502.htm. Retrieved 8 Oct 2011.

Jackson, Richard. 2007. Constructing Enemies: 'Islamic Terrorism' in Political and Academic Discourse. *Government and Opposition* 42 (3): 394–426.

Kinnvall, C., and J. Linden. 2010. Dialogical Selves Between Security and Insecurity: Migration, Multiculturalism, and the Challenge of the Global. *Theory & Psychology* 20 (5): 595–619.

Lambert, Robert, and Jonathan Githens-Mazer. 2010. *Islamophobia and Anti-Muslim Hate Crime: UK Case Studies 2010 – An Introduction to a Ten Year*

Europe-Wide Research Project. London: European Muslim Research Centre. http://alkawni.com/wp-content/media/documents/reports_on_islam/islamophobia_and_anti-muslim_hate_crime.pdf. Retrieved 20 Oct 2011.

Marranci, Gabriele. 2004. Multiculturalism, Islam and the Clash of Civilisations Theory: Rethinking Islamophobia. *Culture and Religion* 5 (1): 105–117.

McGhee, Derek. 2008. *The End of Multiculturalism? Terrorism, Integration and Human Rights.* Berkshire: Open University Press.

Office for National Statistics. 2013. Neighbourhood Statistics: Dudley. 2011 Census. http://www.neighbourhood.statistics.gov.uk/dissemination/LeadTableView.do?a=7&b=6275081&c=DY1+1HF&d=13&e=46&g=6365166&i=1x1003x1006&k=religion&m=0&r=0&s=1466697052828&enc=1&domainId=61&dsFamilyId=2579. Retrieved 10 Oct 2011.

Ouseley, Herman. 2001. *Community Pride Not Prejudice—Making Diversity Work in Bradford.* London: Institute of Community Cohesion. http://resources.cohesioninstitute.org.uk/Publications/Documents/Document/DownloadDocumentsFile.aspx?recordId=98&file=PDFversion. Retrieved 20 Oct 2011.

Pantazis, C., and S. Pemberton. 2009. From the 'Old' to the 'New' Suspect Community: Examining the Impacts of Recent UK Counter-Terrorist Legislation. *British Journal of Criminology* 49 (5): 646–666.

Pape, Robert. 2005. *Dying to Win: The Strategic Logic of Suicide Terrorism.* New York: Random House.

Pew Research Centre. 2006. *The Great Divide: How Westerners and Muslims View Each Other.* Washington DC: The Pew Global Attitudes Project. www.pewglobal.org/files/pdf/253.pdf. Retrieved 14 Oct 2011.

Poynting, Scott, and Victoria Mason. 2006. 'Tolerance, Freedom, Justice and Peace'?: Britain, Australia and Anti-Muslim Racism since 11 September 2001. *Journal of Intercultural Studies* 27 (4): 365–391.

Reeves, Frank. 2009. Muslims and Non-Muslims in the Black Country: Relations Post 9/11. Waterhouse Consulting Group. http://www.waterhouseconsulting.co.uk/Download/Muslims&Non-MuslimsintheBlackCountryRelationsPost911.pdf. Retrieved 20 Apr 2011.

Sageman, Marc. 2004. *Understanding Terror Networks.* Philadelphia: University of Pennsylvania Press.

Simpson, Ludi. 2004. Statistics of Racial Segregation: Measures, Evidence and Policy. *Urban Studies* 41 (3): 661–681.

Travis, Alan. 2005. Reprieve for 'Extremist' Mosques. *Guardian.* http://www.guardian.co.uk/uk/2005/dec/16/terrorism.politics. Retrieved 8 Oct 2011.

Wintour, Patrick. 2005. Blair Vows to Root Out Extremism. *Guardian.* http://www.guardian.co.uk/politics/2005/aug/06/terrorism.july7. Retrieved 17 Oct 2011.

Worley, Claire. 2005. 'It's Not About Race. It's About the Community': New Labour and 'Community Cohesion'. *Critical Social Policy* 25 (4): 483–496.

CHAPTER 4

Denials of Racism and the English Defence League

INTRODUCTION

The previous chapters have demonstrated how the discourses of threat and blame worked to represent Muslims as dangerous to identity and security. At a national level this took the form of community cohesion and counterterrorism discourse, and these were rearticulated at a local level during the Dudley mosque debate for the purpose of preventing local change. My aim in these chapters has been to show how these representations were constructed and how they were able to gain enough social currency to be utilised for local struggles. As I argued in the previous chapter, these representations can be considered Islamophobic because of their unrelenting focus on Islam as the primary motivation for all Muslim behaviour.

The present chapter aims to address the question of whether Islamophobia can be considered a form of racism through an analysis of the discourse of the English Defence League (EDL), an 'anti-Islamist' street protest group that singularly focuses on Muslim activity in Britain. Despite the violence and anti-Muslim rhetoric associated with its protests, the EDL claims to be an anti-racist human rights organisation dedicated to protecting liberal freedoms and a bulwark against 'Islamic extremism,' a claim contained in their popular protest chant: 'not racist, not violent, just no longer silent.'

The EDL emerged in 2009 as a mass street protest movement able to attract supporters in the thousands to demonstrate against 'Islamic

© The Author(s) 2018
L.B. Jackson, *Islamophobia in Britain*,
DOI 10.1007/978-3-319-58350-1_4

extremism' in towns and cities across the UK. Its paradoxical combination of antagonistic, often violent, street protest and its apparently benign intellectual output has perplexed observers. The group has staged dozens of protests (including marches, static protests, and 'flash demonstrations'), which have often descended into violence as supporters broke through police lines to assault local Asians, confront counter-protesters, and attack Asian businesses and property (Copsey 2010, 26). By September 2011 the cost of policing demonstrations was estimated to be in excess of £10 million, with more than 600 arrests made in connection with EDL protest (Jackson et al. 2011, 71–73). Yet, despite the violence and virulent anti-Muslim rhetoric that has become associated with the group the EDL strongly denies Islamophobia, claiming to be only against 'Islamic extremism' and not all Muslims.

This chapter employs critical methodology to address these claims, analysing EDL literature in order to isolate the group's representation of Muslims and considering these alongside strategies identified as typical of racist discourse construction. The representations, narratives and rhetorical strategies employed by the group support the analysis of Islamophobia as a form of cultural racism which constructs opposing 'British' and 'Muslim' subjects and functions to maintain traditional ethno-cultural dominance of the former over the latter.

Studies of the group have focused primarily on the attitudes and ideology of EDL supporters. While these address an important aspect of the popular appeal of the EDL, it is remarkable the extent to which the group's own ideological position and justification for its existence has been overlooked. The present chapter is concerned with the way the EDL understands itself, and particularly how it sustains its central claim that it is not a racist movement. By analysing the publicly available texts produced by the group, the chapter aims to determine the central tenets of the EDL's ideological representation of Muslims and scrutinise its claim to be anti-racist.

The chapter first considers the extent to which the EDL can be considered a typical far-right group, before moving onto outline the central representations of Muslims employed by the EDL. I argue that despite their claims to the contrary, EDL Islamophobia is an example of (culturally) racist discourse. Through the demarcation of a non-Muslim in-group, presented as superior in culture and values, and a Muslim out-group, which threatened the privilege and position of the former, EDL discourse functioned ideologically to maintain traditional ethno-cultural privilege and exclude Muslims from the national community. An analysis of the articles published on the group's reveals three central narratives that make up the core of EDL discursive representation of Muslims; that Muslims were uniquely problematic, that 'Islamic ideology' was the source of these problems, and that Muslims were collectively responsible for the problems identified.

These narratives are critiqued in order to identify the contestable claims that they rest upon, before moving onto demonstrate how EDL Islamophobia functions as a culturally racist discourse. By essentialising Muslim culture as an immutable obstacle to integration, and through strategies typical of racist discourse construction, such as denials, projection, diminutives, and positive-self/negative-other representations, the EDL rearticulated Islamophobia as anti-racism and attempted to normalise it as the natural perspective of those committed to liberal freedom. The group may not be racist in the traditional (biological) sense, but the culturally racist discourse employed distributed privilege and laid blame along a hierarchical line through the construction of opposing and irreconcilable subjects: Muslims, who were blamed for society's ills and required to radically reform their religion, and non-Muslims, who were presented as the blameless victims of 'Islamic extremism'.

The purpose of this chapter is not to label the EDL an Islamophobic organisation, although, as will be shown, it is difficult to argue that it is not. The aim rather is to show how the group constructed all Muslims as (potentially) dangerous and proposed a culturalist explanation of Muslim inferiority to bolster the representation of superior Englishness. By representing Muslims as uniquely problematic, the EDL found explanatory value for all Muslim action within Islam, and demanded that traditional ethno-cultural dominance be maintained in the face of unacceptable Muslim challenges. As the chapter will show, the apparent gulf between the violent anti-Muslim rhetoric of those attending street protests on one hand, and the ostensibly reasonable and rational opposition to Islam that makes up the group's ideological core on the other, is in fact largely illusory. Both rest upon the notion that Muslims represent a perilous and existential threat to Britain, and both construct 'Muslim' and 'British' as opposing and ultimately irreconcilable identities. The EDL's insistence on the superiority of the latter demonstrates the fundamental similarity between racist discourse and Islamophobia.

THE ENGLISH DEFENCE LEAGUE AND THE FAR RIGHT

The English Defence League emerged in 2009 as a major 'anti-Islamist' street protest group. Formed in Luton, the group was initially comprised of a small collection of individuals on the fringes of the English football hooligan scene who objected to Islamist activity in the town. In March 2009, Ahlus Sunnah wal Jammah, an offshoot of Islamist group al-Muhajiroun, had protested at the homecoming parade of the 2nd battalion Royal Anglian Regiment, returning from a 6-month tour of Iraq. After they shouted abuse at the soldiers and held up inflammatory banners reading 'baby killers' and 'butchers', the crowd turned on them, providing the spark for the formation of United People of Luton (UPL), which later became the EDL (Copsey 2010, para. 1.8).

UPL marched through Luton in May 2009 demanding an end to Islamist presence in the town and the interest generated led to the establishment of networks of sympathisers. Tommy Robinson (Stephen Yaxley-Lennon), who emerged as the group's de facto leader, stated 'when we saw Birmingham's demonstration [organised by 'British Citizens Against Muslims Extremists'] they were using the same slogans as us: 'We want our country back', 'Terrorists off the streets', 'Extremists out', 'Rule Britannia'. From there the EDL was set up' (Booth et al. 2009).

The group grew dramatically through social networking sites and involvement with 'Casuals United', a loose association that linked 'firms' of the English football hooligan scene, and by the end of 2010 the EDL had held more than thirty protests in cities and towns across the country and attracted supporters in the thousands for national demonstrations in Stoke, Manchester, Dudley, Bradford, and Leicester (Copsey 2010, paras. 27–29).

In recent years the EDL has suffered several setbacks. Most prominently, Robinson quit as leader in 2013 amid much publicity, throwing the group into disarray. In addition several hacking attacks on its website have slowed down its ability to reach an audience, and the emergence of similar groups such as Pegida UK and Britain First have siphoned off a large slice of its membership. These latter groups favour spectacular direct action, marching into mosques while carrying crosses and aggressively questioning worshippers. Notwithstanding the shifting focus of public attention to these more interventionist groups, the EDL remains an important force in the British 'counter-jihad' movement. The group continues to hold regular protests in cities and towns considered particularly endangered by 'Muslim extremism', although they are much less well attended. More important is the continued ideological reach that the group has sustained despite these difficulties. Boasting more than 320,000 Facebook and over 6500 Twitter followers, the EDL is able to maintain a firm hold over the contemporary narrative of Islamophobia in Britain.

The group has no formal system of membership, and invites people of any political persuasion, ethnicity, race and sexuality to demonstrate under the EDL's banner. Group organisation centres on a series of area 'divisions', each directed by a regional organiser. As of 29 February 2012 there were 94 local divisions listed on the group's website. In addition to these there are a number of special interest groups, including a Jewish division, a women's division (EDL Angels), and a lesbian, gay, bisexual and transgender (LGBT) division. The existence of such groups provides the EDL with an important point of differentiation from traditional far-right groups, and sustains the group's claims to be anti-racist, liberal and tolerant.

As the movement grew, expensive security operations to police the protests and violent clashes with local Asian youth and counter-protesters led to increased media coverage which questioned what the EDL hoped to achieve with its increasingly high-profile demonstrations. In response the group set up a website to complement its presence on social networking sites *Twitter* and *Facebook.Englishdefenceleague.org* comprises a mission statement explaining the purpose of the EDL, a forum which allows sympathisers to network, and even an online shop which sells branded clothing, flags, and toys. An important section of the website is *EDL News*, which represents an effort to justify demonstrations, explain the EDL's concern with 'radical Islam', and rally supporters to its cause.

It is crucial to note that although *EDL News* presents the 'acceptable face' of the movement, the nature of EDL protest has often been far removed from the apparently liberal tolerance espoused on this site. The group has repeatedly stressed that it is not opposed to all Muslims, only 'extremists', yet studies of demonstrations indicate supporters have little grasp of any difference between the two. It will be shown that official EDL discourse represents all Muslims as suspiciously dangerous to British people and 'values'. At street level, however, this distinction has entirely disappeared, with protest chants including: 'I hate Pakis more than you'; 'Give me a gun and I will shoot the Muzzie scum'; and

'Allah, Allah, who the fuck is Allah?'(See Booth et al. 2009; Garland and Treadwell 2010, 25; Tweedie 2009). Demonstrations have frequently descended into violence as EDL supporters broke through police lines to assault people they believed to be Muslim, and have attacked Asian businesses and property (Copsey 2010, 26). Jon Garland and James Treadwell, who have undertaken important covert ethnographic work at EDL demonstrations, have highlighted that supporters espouse a much more traditional racism than the group's leadership would be willing to admit, particularly against young Muslim males who are seen as fair targets for violent aggression (Garland and Treadwell 2010, 29–30; Treadwell and Garland 2011, 625).

Because of the amorphous structure and lack of formal membership, studies into the demographic profile and ideological motivations of EDL supporters have proven difficult. The only such study to date estimated that the EDL had approximately 25,000–35,000 active supporters, concentrated around the London area, with a higher proportion of male (81%) to female (19%) members, and an older and more educated profile than perhaps would be expected, with 28% of supporters over the age of thirty and 30% holding a university or college degree. The primary reasons cited for joining and demonstrating with the EDL were opposition to Islam or Islamism and a desire to preserve national and cultural values (Bartlett and Littler 2011, 4–6).

The tactics and discourse of EDL demonstrations, as well supporters' comments on its social networking sites, have led to difficulties in conceptualising the movement. As noted, protests have often involved racist chanting and hate speech, yet the EDL's online articles consistently advocate anti-racism. The liberal tropes that infuse EDL discourse, as well as its efforts to recruit ethnic and sexual minorities, are apparently incongruous with claims that the group is simply racist. This paradox has implications for considering the group a far-right organisation. Several scholars have noted that contemporary extreme right parties have sought to cast off their thuggish image and appeal more to the electorate by careful avoidance of overtly racist language (Atton 2006; Eatwell 2006; Goodwin 2007; Halikiopoulou and Vasilopoulou 2010; Newman 2007). Is the EDL merely a new manifestation of this phenomenon? A brief comparison with Britain's most successful far-right party, the British National Party (BNP) serves to illustrate that although similarities exist, there are important differences which make the identification of the EDL as a far-right movement problematic.

The BNP and the EDL

While BNP and EDL ideology share surface level resemblances, these should not be overstated. Both groups focus on Islam as a central danger threatening Britain, but for the former Muslims are merely a particular symptom of the wider problem of immigration and multiculturalism. Muslims are considered racial 'others' by the BNP, lacking the white Anglo-Saxon 'liberal gene' that genetically predisposes the British to liberal democratic culture (Williams and Law 2011, para. 5.7–5.8). This focus on Muslims as biologically not-British is illustrated by the party's representation of the 2005 London bombings as '...genocidal race attacks by immigrant Islamic Fascists against White Christian British people...' (Wood and Finlay 2008, 713). The BNP's proposed solution to the problem of Islamist terrorism (closure of borders, an end to immigration, a programme of expulsion and abolishment of multiculturalism) exemplify its preoccupation with racial purity. It is true that the increased hardening of public attitudes towards Muslims has provided a platform of populist legitimacy on which the BNP has argued for its racist policies, but it is precisely this focus on race that distances it from the EDL.

In contrast, the EDL disavows crude biological determinism, and uses a more sophisticated discourse of culture to mark out Islam out as a sociological, rather than a biological, impediment to assimilation. The movement rejects the BNP's conflation of Muslims, immigrants and non-whites, and does not concern itself with multiculturalism in general. In EDL discourse Muslims are sharply distinguished from other immigrant communities in the UK, which are looked upon favourably in comparison. In distinction to the BNP's repatriation policies, EDL solutions centre on presenting the 'real facts' about Islam to the public and the demand that Muslims reform their religion. It should also be noted that a strong vein of anti-Semitism runs through the contemporary BNP (Copsey 2008, 162; Richardson 2013, 107–109). Manifested in claims of media control and the attribution of multiculturalism to a Jewish conspiracy, this ideological pillar of the far right is certainly not shared by the EDL. With its firm support of Israel, the existence of a Jewish division within its ranks and its regular denouncement of anti-Semitism, the EDL cannot be said to subscribe to such conspiracy theories, at least regarding Jews.

In addition, ideological differences have been noted by both groups. Until recently BNP members were proscribed from attending EDL demonstrations or making links with the group (Griffin 2012), and when Tommy Robinson announced his defection from the EDL in October 2013, he claimed that the proliferation of far-right activity within the group had led to him spending 'too much time keeping goose stepping white pride morons' away from demonstrations (BBC 2013). Joel Busher (2013, 68) has noted that being anti-racist is an important element of identity construction for EDL activists, and the consistent rejection of BNP advances are a point of pride for the movement (EDL 2011h). Although there are reasons to be cautious about future directions, particularly with regard to the type of supporter it potentially attracts and the malleability of the group's ideology, at this point in its history there are clearly marked and profound differences between the EDL and the established far right. The English Defence League does not biologically racialise the threat from Islam or blame multiculturalism and immigration for the 'Muslim problem' it perceives, and the ends sought are far removed from the repatriation policies advocated by the BNP.

One reason the EDL has been categorised within the far right is that previous studies have concentrated predominantly on the attitudes and ideology of supporters. These have included examinations of the nature and threat of EDL protest (Allen 2010; Burnett 2011), studies highlighting the demographic profile of self-identified members (Bartlett and Littler 2011; Goodwin and Evans 2012), and ethnographic studies which have investigated the discourse and ideology of EDL supporters (Busher 2015; Garland and Treadwell 2010; Treadwell and Garland 2011; Goodwin 2013). This chapter is not concerned with the attitudes of supporters, and focuses instead on what may be termed the official ideology of the English Defence League.

There are significant differences between the EDL's stated ideology and the concerns of those who claim ideological affinity with the group. Previous studies have suggested that anti-Islam prejudice accounts for only one part of supporters' concerns. Matthew Goodwin, for example, found that those who agreed with the ideals and/or methods of the EDL were more likely to be authoritarian and xenophobic, and held more negative attitudes towards immigration and ethnic minority groups (Goodwin 2013, 9–10). In contrast, it is striking the extent to which the issue of immigration is ignored by the EDL in its official material. Only two of 117 *EDL News* articles discussed immigration, and neither politicised the issue, stating only that the government's approach had been seriously flawed, but: 'just because the government has been far too focused on the advantages of immigration (without consideration of the possible problems), is no reason to forget the advantages altogether' (EDL 2011a, h). Indeed, in contrast to the generalised xenophobia and opposition to immigration espoused by supporters, some articles specifically argued against this, stating the benefits that immigration brought to Britain and emphasising positive aspects of cultural diversity (EDL 2011h, m). In the pages of *EDL News*, immigration and multiculturalism are not in themselves problematic: '... it is not multiculturalism, but Islam, that has failed' (EDL 2011c). While supporters may hold generalised anti-immigration prejudice, official EDL discourse either disregards or specifically argues against this.

It is important, therefore, to emphasise ideological variance between the movement and its supporters. The group operates as an umbrella organisation for anyone who wishes to demonstrate against 'Islamic extremism', and those who protest under its banner will surely have additional anxieties. The EDL itself, however, quite consciously shuns wider issues to focus exclusively on Islam. To some extent, these differences afford the group an element of plausible deniability against charges of racism, Islamophobia and extremism. The fact that the EDL has no formal structure of membership and exists as an organisation to which people are affiliated (and can therefore become dis-affiliated) is advantageous, as those using overtly racist language at protests or on its social networking sites can be dismissed as outside agitators; since the EDL is avowedly anti-racist why would racists want to join its protests? This rhetorical question underlines the need to analyse the official discourse of the group. Why, indeed, are those with the attitudes described by Goodwin attracted to the EDL?

Since the EDL claims to have no interest in electoral politics it does not produce pamphlets explaining its purpose and goals. In the absence of such platforms, the only texts which elucidate the group's official ideology are the articles which make up the *EDL News* section of the website *englishdefenceleague.org*. These represent an effort to justify demonstrations, deflect negative media attention, explain the EDL's concern with 'radical Islam', and rally supporters to its cause. Links to these articles are provided on the group's *Facebook* and *Twitter* pages, and consequently every online follower receives regular exposure to this material on their social network newsfeed. As the EDL's internet popularity continues unabated, an analysis of its ideological representation of Muslims is crucial.

The Discourse of EDL News

EDL News contains articles and commentary, as well as information for forthcoming demonstrations and campaigns. As of 29 February 2012 there were a total of 117 publicly available articles, 86 of which discussed Muslims and/or Islam. These articles were used as the corpus for analysis in the present chapter, with each subjected to predicate analysis, which focuses analytical attention on the ideational collocates of the nouns 'Islam' and 'Muslim' in order to determine central narratives, frames and themes of EDL representation (Richardson 2009, 360). Three recurring narratives were identified. First, Muslims were seen as uniquely problematic, posing a distinctive threat to British people and to 'British values'. Second, the problems caused by Muslims were thought to be traceable to Islam itself: through scripture, the example of the Prophet and 'Islamic ideology'. Third, Muslims were held collectively responsible, for both the actions of their co-religionists and the reform of Islam. By failing to speak out against fellow Muslims and root out problematic individuals within their communities, the EDL claimed that Muslims had abandoned their responsibilities and must therefore be coerced into reform. These narratives appeared consistently, regardless of which topic a particular article focused on, suggesting that they form the core of EDL ideological representation of Muslims.

Taking each narrative in turn, the chapter proceeds by identifying how Muslims were problematised by the EDL and critically examining these claims, before moving onto consider the rhetorical strategies employed and demonstrate how EDL discourse functioned ideologically as a form of racial discourse.

NARRATING ISLAMOPHOBIA: THE CENTRAL THEMES OF EDL REPRESENTATION OF MUSLIMS AND ISLAM

Muslims as Uniquely Problematic

One of the EDL's central concerns was to represent Muslims as a unique and exclusive threat to Britain. This was achieved through repetitive lists of negative behaviours attributed exclusively to Muslims and recycled across the articles. Violence, anti-democratic tendencies, intolerance, separatism, homophobia, anti-Semitism, honour killing, child grooming and hatred of the West were the key charges, but the group was careful to ascribe these specifically to Muslims, as a direct result of their culture:

> ...[the] problems associated with the Muslim Community are [not] just down to a few bearded lunatics. If we're to put an end to "home-grown" terrorism so-called "honour-killings", child grooming (which, sadly, is dominated by Muslim men), the preaching of extremism on our streets and in British Mosques, and all of the other problems that stem from the Muslim Community, then we can't be afraid to make serious and considered criticisms. (EDL 2011a)

These repeated lists of negative behaviour were presented as the exclusive preserve of Muslims. The most common activities highlighted were extremism and terrorism however Muslims were also associated with violence more broadly. Two cases in particular serve to highlight how particular local incidents were used by the group to further their agenda: the case of Rhea Page, who was attacked in Leicester by a group of Somali women in June 2010; and the assault of Daniel Stringer-Prince in February 2012 by a group of Asian youths in Hyde, Greater Manchester. In response to these incidents the EDL organised demonstrations against 'Islamic extremism' in both Leicester and Hyde (in the latter case against the family's wishes). *EDL News* justification of the demonstrations, as well as speeches made at the rallies, explicitly connected Islam to the violence. In an article that discussed the Hyde rally, for example, the author claimed that since Islamic extremism and Muslim religious supremacism were barely out of the news, it was reasonable to ask whether Daniel Stringer-Prince had been attacked because he non-Muslim (EDL 2011d).

In neither of the cases that the EDL mobilised against was there a link between the attacks and the religious background of the offenders. In the Stringer-Prince case the religion of the assailants was not clear (Carter 2012). Similarly, although the Rhea Page case was complicated by the possibility that it was racially aggravated (the attackers shouted 'white bitch' as they assaulted her (Telegraph 2011)), the notion that she had been targeted as a non-Muslim was suggested by neither police nor the prosecution. The EDL nevertheless organised a demonstration against the 'two-tier' justice system that had handed suspended sentences to Page's attackers, reportedly because they were Somali Muslims not used to drinking alcohol, and justified the rally in *EDL News* by asserting that given the supremacist beliefs of Muslims, Page *may* have been targeted as a non-believer. The article stated that as members of the religion of peace 'they should be uniquely placed to know that violence is wrong? Or is it not too bad when it's aimed at the non-believers?' (EDL 2011b). The group was careful in its language regarding these incidents, never explicitly stating that Muslim supremacism or extremism was the driving factor behind the attacks, but strongly implying it. Such tenuous associations between the supposed background of the attackers and their violent behaviour were made on the basis of assumptions about who the attackers were and what drove their actions. This cavalier attitude to available evidence was present throughout the articles, and serves to demonstrate the contentious nature of the EDL's claims.

In addition to repeatedly highlighting the violent and threatening behaviour of Muslims, the EDL used the example of other minorities to illustrate their uniquely problematic nature. Other minorities, they claimed, had integrated within the national community without difficulty. Through a narrative that stressed this 'seamless integration' of other minorities, the EDL emphasised the unique challenges posed by Muslims while simultaneously neutralising possible objections that racist attitudes had hampered Muslim integration. The group held up Buddhism, Jainism and Christianity as peaceful in contrast to Islam's supposed problem with suicide bombing (EDL 2011i), and Sikhs in particular were repeatedly referred to as a shining example of unproblematic integration (Greenfield 2011; EDL 2011d). As one article stated, '... there have never been any problems with Sikh integration in this country... Sikhs have shown an impressive willingness to integrate, to accept the laws of the land, and to confront and defeat any form of extremism' (EDL 2011m).

This narrative is both ideological and ahistorical, disregarding the long history of struggle in which minority communities have engaged to have their cultures and customs recognised. The suggestion that Sikhs had been unconditionally accepted by British society overlooked the protracted struggle to be allowed to carry the *kirpan* (ceremonial dagger), as well as the turban disputes at work (and for motorcyclists), both of which resulted in national debates about Sikh's ability to integrate (Nesbitt 2011, 227). The threat to social cohesion and national identity posed by black communities has similarly been a consistently recurring theme of national debate (Christian 2005). Such ideas remain contemporarily relevant, as demonstrated by the intense discussions around the

2011 English riots, which singled out 'black culture' as a major contributory factor (2011). These debates are far from settled in the twenty-first century, regardless of the EDL's deliberate distortion of the history of minority communities and their acceptance into the nation.

Having established that the major problems facing British society stemmed from one particular 'community', the EDL sought to explain why this should be, situating the negative behaviours they perceived in the shared 'ideology' believed to inspire it. Islam was identified by the EDL as the crucial causal factor that provided Muslims with motive and justification for their behaviour.

The Problematic Nature of 'Islamic Ideology'

The EDL explained perceived Muslim over-representation in anti-social behaviour by referring to Islamic teaching. Scripture was believed to sanction such activities, and this was illustrated with selective and de-contextualised passages from the Qur'an, regarded as the rationale for all Muslim action and the source of the problems identified. Considered intrinsically Muslim problems, extremism and terrorism were understood to be embedded within the religion. One article argued that since suicide bombers were always described as devout Muslims, Islam itself must be the issue (EDL 2011i), another was more explicit: 'The primary cause [of terrorism] is right in front of us. It's simple. It's what Islamic terrorists and Islamists have in common. That's right, it begins with an I' (EDL 2011c).

But terrorism was not the only criminal activity that the EDL ascribed to Islam. In 2011 *The Times* reported on child grooming rings in Rochdale and the West Midlands, in which several men of largely Pakistani origin had sexually exploited dozens of underage white girls in 2008 and 2009. What is remarkable about the EDL's treatment of the case is not the racial connotations, which were the focus of national attention, but the group's insistence on marking them out as Muslim crimes, traceable to Islamic scripture. The Prophet was called up again and again to bolster claims that those involved in the exploitation were merely following the example set by 'a murderer and a rapist who had sexual intercourse with a girl of 9 (or younger according to some sources)' (EDL 2011e). Further, the group claimed that since the Qur'an asserted the inferiority of non-Muslims the men involved likely saw their victims as acceptable targets, stating '... many Muslim men see little wrong with applying the example of the prophet (sex with young children) to those who they regard as 'dirty kuffar' (non-Muslims, not worthy of the same rights as Muslims under the Sharia—Islamic Law)' (EDL 2011m).

The group's assertion that these were Muslim crimes was based on the Pakistani heritage of the majority of the perpetrators. The extent to which the men involved were practising Muslims is unknown, and any notion that 'Islamic supremacism' may have fuelled their activities was certainly not reported by any of the authorities involved in the prosecution of the cases. However, as with the cases of Rhea Page and Daniel Stringer-Prince, the EDL were confident enough to demonstrate outside court at both hearings in order to protest the 'Islamic extremism' they claimed had resulted in these crimes. The idea that members of 'Muslim child grooming' gangs were 'Islamic extremists' stretched the term beyond recognition. Men who plied young girls with alcohol and exploited them for sexual gratification were clearly not following any interpretation of the Qur'an, extreme or otherwise, and sexual offences can hardly be deemed a 'Muslim' problem. The authors of the unpublished report that had been cited in the original *Times* article urged against attempts to racialise the crimes, stating that claims that Pakistani grooming gangs represented a national problem could not be sustained from the small sample of the original study. Further, they argued, the notion that white girls were being targeted due to racial or cultural factors did not stand up to scrutiny in the cases analysed. Black and ethnic minority victims were in fact overrepresented in relation to the demographics of the local population (Davies and McVeigh 2011), and those abused were likely selected because of opportunism rather than a specific agenda to target *white* girls (Cockbain and Wortley 2015). The fact that 85% of sex offenders in the UK are white men (Crown Prosecution Service 2011) has not led the EDL to deeply question the ideological foundations upon which masculinity is constructed, yet the assumed Muslim background of the perpetrators in these cases was focused upon as if it had explanatory value.

Muslims' supposed self-segregation was also represented by the EDL as traceable to Islamic teaching, which was deemed to undermine the ties of national identity. These culturally conditioned anti-integration tendencies were believed to not only preclude peaceful co-existence, but were also presented as exemplary of a general, scripturally sanctioned desire to colonise all social spaces. From this perspective the group argued that Muslims had no loyalties but to Islam (EDL 2011j) and were commanded by the Qur'an to wage war: 'Whether it's physical, cultural, economic, social or political warfare, it's incumbent upon all Muslims to follow the example of Mohammad' (EDL 2011e).

For the EDL, Islam itself, devoid of distinction between 'ordinary' and 'radical' practitioners, was the problem. All Muslims were therefore seen as potentially prone to such behaviour. The understanding that scripture provided the rationale for Muslim criminality endorsed the conviction that Islam was inherently dangerous to British society. As a consequence every Muslim, indeed every person with a Muslim background or name, was considered suspicious and (potentially) guilty by association. Accordingly, nothing less than total reform of Islam was demanded.

Muslims as Responsible for Reforming Their Religion

The EDL stressed that all Muslims shared responsibility for the ills they identified, and therefore must make efforts not only to root out those engaged in such behaviours but also to make Islam more acceptable through reform. Because such efforts (if they had been made at all) were considered to have failed, the EDL contended that Muslims had shown themselves unwilling to make the changes demanded of them, and their commitment to 'British values' was questioned (EDL 2011g). Muslims were deemed to have wilfully ignored thriving extremism in their midst, complaining about discrimination and those who insulted Islam, rather than addressing the *Islamic* root of such behaviour and making efforts to prevent radicalisation: 'Islamic extremism is an Islamic problem, and the Muslim community needs to get its house in order' (EDL 2011l).

For the EDL, Muslims had failed to stem the tide of negative behaviour within their communities because they did not see the need, or have the will, to take action. The group claimed that Muslims were shirking their responsibilities and attempting to deflect attention from their failures by remonstrating about discrimination instead of tackling difficult issues: 'You cannot moan about being treated with suspicion when you do nothing to deal with those extremists within your communities' (EDL 2011f). This unwillingness to accept the blame for extremism was taken by the EDL to be indicative of a deep failure within Muslim communities that could only mean that they did not consider it a problem (EDL 2011b).

The notion that Muslims had their priorities wrong was further pressed by the group's contrasting of Muslim willingness to protest when Islam was offended with the 'silence' when 'British liberal values' were contravened (EDL 2011f). Again, the distinction between Muslim and non-Muslim was thought to be the basis for this perceived double standard: 'Cartoonist draws Mohammed—angry Muslims on the street. Muslims kill innocent people in the name of Islam—relative silence' (EDL 2011l). The allegation that Muslim leaders had failed to undermine extremist ideas from an Islamic perspective was set forth as evidence that Muslims were evading their responsibilities and, through their silence, providing implicit support for such ideas.

The contention that Muslims had not addressed these issues deliberately disregarded the myriad voices that have condemned violence and terrorism over the past decade. To mention just a few: Pakistani religious scholar Dr Tahir il-Qadri, who, in March 2010, issued a 600 page *fatwa* against terrorism and extremism, rebutting every Islamic justification used by al-Qaeda (Casciani 2010), the *Minhaj-ul-Quran* International peace conference at Wembley arena, organised to mark the 10th anniversary of the 9/11 attacks, which had an attendance of 12,000 and included a range of Muslim speakers who all unequivocally denounced terrorism (Press Association 2011); the '*jihad* against violence' campaign by British Muslim women's group *Inspire* which aimed to ideologically and practically combat violence (particularly against women) justified in the name of Islam (Siddique 2011); and the Muslim Council of Britain's repeated condemnations of Islam inspired terrorism (Bari 2007; Muslim Council of Britain 2001, 2005). These few examples illustrate that diverse Muslim organisations have recognised the need to tackle extremist ideas, and were willing to take on the challenge. The EDL's insistence that Islam *was* the source of extremism and violence rendered these voices meaningless.

The perception that Muslims had failed to confront extremism led the EDL to suggest that a pool of support for 'extremist' ideas must exist:

> We're always told that this silent majority reject extremism, but if that is the case then why are they so silent? We can think of three possible reasons: either they do not really reject extremism, they are terrified of speaking out against the radicals, or they do not feel any need to press for reform. (EDL 2011d)

The group considered Muslim rejection of extremism disingenuous, and implied this was due to insincerity and lack of will. Pointing to 'Islamic extremist' groups such as *al-Muhajiroun,* the EDL claimed that if Muslims were serious about eradicating extremism such groups would not exist. The actions of *Ahlus Sunnah wal Jammah* at the Royal Anglian Regiment homecoming parade was used to support this contention, and portrayed as exemplary of thriving extremism and evidence that Muslim words were empty. Yet the EDL's analysis of this incident, in its assumption that these actions were entirely religiously motivated, discounted the intrinsically *political* nature of the act. *Ahlus Sunnah wal Jammah* may have protested as an Islamic group, using religious language and symbolism in their demonstration, but the protest was essentially political. The religious discourse of the protesters was incidental to their central message; opposition to the Iraq war and the actions there of British soldiers and the British government.

The conviction that 'extremism' was thriving, along with the belief that Muslim pledges to fight it were insincere, led to the conclusion that there must be widespread support for such ideas within Muslim communities. The EDL chose to accept the rhetoric of 'extremist' groups as representative; concluding that if such groups could religiously justify their claims there must be a large number of less vocal Muslims with the same ideas. By blaming Muslims for the ills identified, the group's assertion that Islam must be reformed, through coercion if necessary, had a semblance of legitimacy.

The themes identified above form the spine of the EDL's official ideological position, which professed to identify problematic elements in British society (Muslims), isolated the root and source of these problems (primarily Islam, but also Muslims' unwillingness to reform), and proposed possible solutions (pressure on Muslims). The adaptability of such an ideology to a wide range of situations is evident, and the EDL has used this to justify its own existence as well as the numerous protests and campaigns it has organised. However, it is equally apparent that the facts upon which these narratives are based are highly contestable. As the above critique has demonstrated, EDL ideology relies heavily upon distortion, reductionism, and the recycling of myths to explain the problems that the group associates with Muslims.

It is important to note that Islamophobia exists as a functional ideology beyond its explanatory purpose: on one hand it attempts to explain who is responsible for any given problem; on the other, this representation of Muslims serves to delineate the contours of British identity. How EDL discourse performs this function has to be taken into account if we are to understand the racialised nature of Islamophobic expression. The following section considers how rhetorical strategies within EDL discourse shaped shared mental representations of Muslims as an existential threat to British identity, while simultaneously bolstering 'British values' and the EDL's claim to them.

THE IDEOLOGICAL EFFECTS OF EDL DISCOURSE

That the English Defence League blamed Muslims and Islam for the problems they perceived in British society is perhaps not surprising. As the vanguard of the UK 'counter-jihad' movement, their representations followed a familiar pattern of Islamophobic discourse and constructed an antagonistic Muslim enemy believed to be undermining the nation in myriad ways. More significant is the way in which these representations served to construct an oppositional identity that dangerous Muslims were thought to threaten. Throughout the articles, a range of rhetorical strategies were employed to construct opposing and irreconcilable 'Muslim' and 'British' identities, representing the former as intrinsically and inescapably not-British, and in doing so presenting the latter as inherently superior. Such discursive constructions are the hallmark of racist discourse, and the following section delineates these strategies in order to demonstrate how, despite its protestations to the contrary, the EDL is a (culturally) racist organisation.

First, the group made liberal use of positive-self and negative-other representations to show that deviant Muslims were breaking well established British norms. This was evident not only from the extensive negative topics across the texts, but also within-text rhetorical strategies which monotonously repeated long lists of socially unacceptable Muslim behaviour. In their positive self-representation the EDL laid claim to British tolerance and convivial values. The integration of other minority groups was represented as an account of British acceptance and hospitality, which simultaneously portrayed Muslims as rejecting integration and testing the boundaries of acceptability with their persistent demands. The EDL's commitment to liberalism functioned in much the same way.

Through its claim to welcome all races, faiths, and political persuasions, including 'moderate' Muslims, the group presented itself as embodying British liberal values. Muslims who rejected the EDL could therefore be dismissed as 'extremist', since rejecting the group was a rejection of the values it claimed to embody.

An important part of this strategy is the denial of prejudice (Berry and Bonilla-Silva 2008, 150–151), and the EDL achieved this by marking a distinction between 'ordinary Muslims' and 'Islamic extremists' and claiming to oppose only the latter. This distinction continually broke down, as the group identified Muslim culture and Islamic scripture as the source of all problems, but it did not reduce the efficacy of the strategy. By claiming to have no problem with ordinary Muslims, the EDL could discursively operate in a territory of apparently legitimate concerns.

The claim that Muslims were making unreasonable demands that exceeded the cultural tolerance of British society further exemplified this positive-self/negative-other representation. This rhetorical strategy is linked to the power relations of racist discourse, where the majority group considers itself at liberty to decide whether demands are reasonable or unreasonable and marks the limits of tolerance in order to determine whether the out-group has transgressed the boundaries of social acceptability (Augoustinos and Every 2007, 126). This found expression particularly in the discourse of the EDL's campaigns against mosques, which implicitly drew upon the notion that the dominant (non-Muslim) group was entitled to decide the number of 'necessary' mosques and the range of views that were allowed to be expressed within them. The EDL's belief that, as part of the majority group, it had the right to police and challenge Muslim behaviour reflected its desire to preserve the traditional ethno-cultural dominance of British society against Muslim demands for religious recognition.

Second, the group used projection strategies, asserting that Muslims had a superiority complex. 'Islamic supremacism' was a key concern of almost a fifth of the articles and relied on the notion that Muslim behaviour could be explained by their supposed insistence on the superiority of their religion and culture. This projection of cultural racism onto Muslims served to represent them as violating established egalitarian norms, while simultaneously casting non-Muslims as victims. The discourse of white victimhood has been highlighted as a central feature of contemporary racial ideology (Bonilla-Silva et al. 2004, 567–568; Feagin et al. 2001, 189–194), where those espousing this discourse share an ideological world in which equality legislation has erased discrimination. Claims by minorities that they are victims of discrimination are thus met with scepticism and viewed as attempts to use their race to gain unfair advantages ('playing the race card').

EDL insistence on the inherently supremacist nature of Islam meant that all Muslim actions were considered expressions of this supremacism. Mosques were thus deemed symbolic of Muslim desires to dominate, increasingly available *halal* meat was seen as evidence of the 'creeping Islamification' of Britain, and Muslim political participation was viewed with deep suspicion as entrism and an attempt to expand the reach of Islam within the British political system. Muslims were believed to be culturally colonising the UK, and the EDL claimed that non-Muslims were, and would increasingly be, disadvantaged and victimised as a result. This projection of supremacist motivation thus formed the basis for EDL counter-mobilisation against Muslim demands, ideologically formulated as a fight for equal treatment (Doane 2006, 269).

A third strategy was the presentation of views as reflecting external reality rather than internal psychology. Racist discourse entails an outlook in which negative perceptions of minorities are articulated not as irrational fears, but as factually grounded in the out-group's transgression of norms (Augoustinos and Every 2007, 127). Islamophobia works in much the same way. The EDL's preoccupation with Muslims was explained as a natural reaction to their negative behaviour, a consequence of living in proximity that politicians and the 'liberal elite', whose lives were far removed from the 'Islamic ghettoes', could not possibly understand. The English Defence League constantly referred to itself as a *symptom* of 'Islamic extremism', and stated that if the government could be trusted to tackle it there would be no need for the group. The contention that a group like the EDL is merely the consequence of unacceptable Muslim behaviour is an ideological claim which naturalises Islamophobia as a reasonable reaction, rather than a prejudicial ideology, and effectively blames Muslims for anti-Muslim sentiment.

A fourth strategy employed by the group was the use of denials ('I'm not racist but...'), which function in racist discourse to present a positive self-image of tolerance and reasonableness (van Dijk 1992, 91–92). The EDL utilised this strategy in its refutation of the existence of Islamophobia. Ridiculed and dismissed as the paranoid fantasies of Muslims, who should be directing their energies towards rooting out extremists, Islamophobia, conceptualised as an irrational fear, was believed to be nonsensical and the group insisted that no one in the EDL had a 'mental illness' that would prejudice them against Muslims (EDL 2011k). This reduction of Islamophobia to individual prejudice served to deflect accusations of bigotry, however, as the discourse and narratives discussed in this chapter demonstrate, Islamophobia is much more than this. Far from being merely a negative assessment of Islam and a fear of individual Muslims, it is cultural racism: an ideological discourse that demarcates an in-group and an out-group and presents the former as superior and its privilege endangered.

Etienne Balibar has argued that culture may have replaced biology in new racism but, predicated on a fear of the 'other' and giving rise to an identical denial of rights, the ideological underpinnings remain the same (Balibar 2007, 83–84). The EDL constantly represented culture as a bounded and naturalised sociological signifier, and characterised Muslims as the bearers of an innate and opposing Islamic culture which could not be absorbed into Britain until Islam was entirely reformed. The assumption that integration must be one-way and on the terms of the dominant group was implicitly an expression of the superiority of 'British culture', and the constant refrain that Muslims held unacceptable and inassimilable values contained within it a denial of the right to challenge 'traditional values' as British citizens. While the EDL instrumentalised 'British values' for decidedly illiberal ends in order to vehemently criticise Islam, the reverse would be unthinkable. Muslims were constrained by the discourse to such an extent that any conception of the social good expressed in religious terms would be considered exemplary of latent extremism.

The deeply ideological nature of EDL discursive representation of Muslims supports the conceptualisation of Islamophobia as cultural racism, working on one hand to preserve traditional ethno-cultural dominance and privilege, and on the other to contain challenges to this dominance, believed to stem primarily from Muslim communities. The representation of Muslims by the EDL reproduced and sustained the cultural dominance of non-Muslims over Muslims based on a set of 'British values' that the latter were thought to violate, and the right of the bearers of these values to decide the boundaries of tolerance and police the behaviour of others.

Available scholarship on the EDL has highlighted the pessimism of its supporters, their view that England is entering a period of decline, and the belief that white working-class men (of which the EDL is predominately composed) are being disadvantaged in comparison to other groups (Bartlett and Littler 2011, 30–32). The attraction of a discourse that identifies Muslims as responsible for perceived social decay is not surprising if supporters feel that the traditional power and sense of superiority of white communities is dissipating in the face of the demands of other groups. EDL street protest may accomplish psychological benefits for those who attend, alleviating these feelings of inferiority and marginalisation through a performative masculinity that involves a show of strength and solidarity and the possibility of violent confrontation as a way to work out problems (Treadwell and Garland 2011, 625). In this sense the group performs an important function as a means of expressing discontent, erasing its supporters' feelings of despair and transforming them from passive into active subjects. The EDL thus affirms a certain kind of white working-class identity, and demands that it be recognised and acknowledged as an heir to the historical privileges of the dominant (white) group.

The analysis of Islamophobia as an affective prejudice (a *fear* of Islam or Muslims) has led to difficulties of conceptualisation that the EDL have gleefully exploited in their dismissal of the term as nonsense. Yet, if we retreat from the notion that Islamophobia is an individual negative attitude, and instead consider it a shared social narrative, its ideological usefulness becomes more apparent. Islamophobia has currency enough to motivate thousands to take to the streets, and hundreds of thousands to claim some affinity to the EDL because, like all racial discourse, it has ideological value. In its explanation of social problems as resulting from cultural deviance, Islamophobia not only identifies Muslims as problematic, but also relieves the rest of society of responsibility. The EDL's constant chastisement of Muslims, whether for their lack of will or success in tackling extremism, or their failure to see that it is *their* problem, reflects the group's belief that the rest of British society bears no responsibility. Islamophobia has ideological appeal precisely because it finds non-Muslim Britons blameless.

CONCLUSION

In April 2011, Adrian Tudway, the Metropolitan Police's National Co-ordinator for Domestic Extremism, sent an email to the National Association of Muslim Police, stating:

...[the EDL] are not extreme right wing as a group. Indeed if you look at their published material on their web-site, they are actively moving away from the right and violence with their mission statement etc.... I really think you need to open a direct line of dialogue with them, that might be the best way to engage them... (Quoted in Dodd and Taylor 2011)

Tudway's comments suggest either that he has taken the EDL's claims at face value, or that he subscribes to some extent to the 'problematic Muslims' discourse. It is difficult to imagine these comments addressed to any other group in society; they are only acceptable because there is some social currency to understanding Muslims as problematic and the 'Muslim community' as responsible for changing anti-Islam views. To underscore this point, it is worth considering whether an Islamist web-site, which drew constant attention to the criminal deviance of non-Muslim Britons, explained this behaviour through inferior British values, and organised thousand-strong demonstrations throughout the country which regularly resulted in non-Muslims being targeted with violence and intimidation, would be considered 'extremist'. It is equally absurd to imagine that Jews would be advised by the National Co-ordinator to engage with an openly anti-Semitic group that was, nonetheless, 'moving away' from violence.

This chapter has argued that the English Defence League's Islamophobia is a culturally racist discourse. Racist discourse construction involves the demarcation of an in-group and an out-group, where the former considers itself superior and claims the right to decide who can belong, while the latter is represented as threatening its privileges and position. EDL discourse performed this function by racialising Muslim culture as the source of Muslim behaviour and conferring the role of arbiters of acceptability to culturally superior non-Muslims. The group utilised rhetorical strategies such as denial of prejudice, projection of culturally racist motivations onto Muslims, positive-self and negative-other representation, and denials such as 'we are not against all Muslims, but...' These strategies worked to construct Islam as oppositional to British values and identity and contained an implicit assumption of the latter's superiority. The EDL's claim that it only opposed 'radical Islam' dissolved into a discourse that laid the blame for the problems of society at Islam's door and made aggressive demands that the religion be reformed to be more acceptable. Whether the EDL's leadership sincerely believed itself not to be Islamophobic is a moot point. But knowingly or otherwise the group employed a discourse which stratified British society hierarchically, constructed opposing subject positions for Muslims and non-Muslims, and endeavoured to protect the privileges of (traditionally white) non-Muslim British people against real and imagined demands for Muslim recognition.

Adrian Tudway's assessment that Muslims should consider engaging with the EDL indicates a broader problem. The group's analysis of Muslims and Islam is not considered extremist precisely because it is not particularly 'extreme' to hold such views—they are articulated every day in newspapers, by government ministers and by think-tank intellectuals who all converge around the same theme: that Muslims in Britain are dangerous. In such a climate the soaring popularity of the group and the dramatic spike in Islamophobic hate crimes following high-profile instances of terrorism should come as no surprise.

The English Defence League are indeed a symptom; not, as they claim, of 'Islamic extremism', but of the increasingly socially acceptable discourse of 'problematic Muslims'. The challenge posed by the group, and others like it, is therefore not simply to quell its violence or confront the more caustic elements of its protests. Rather, it requires deep reflection and confrontation of the entrenched societal Islamophobia that makes such a movement possible.

REFERENCES

Allen, Chris. 2010. Fear and Loathing: The Political Discourse in Relation to Muslims and Islam in the British Contemporary Setting. *Contemporary British Religion and Politics IV* 2: 221–236.

Atton, Chris. 2006. Far-Right Media on the Internet: Culture, Discourse and Power. *New Media & Society* 8 (4): 573–587.

Augoustinos, M., and D. Every. 2007. The Language of 'Race' and Prejudice: A Discourse of Denial, Reason, and Liberal-Practical Politics. *Journal of Language and Social Psychology* 26 (2): 123–141.

Balibar, Etienne. 2007. Is There a 'Neo-Racism'? In *Race and Racialization: Essential Readings*, ed. Tanya Das Gupta, 83–88. Toronto: Canadian Scholars' Press Inc.

Bari, Muhammad Abdul. 2007. Statement from the Muslim Council of Britain on Recent Terrorism. *Muslim Council of Britain*, 3 July. http://www.mcb.org.uk/features/features.php?ann_id=1617. Retrieved 31 May 2012.

Barrett, David. 2011. Historian Starkey in 'Racism' Row over Riot Comments. *Telegraph*, 15 August. http://www.telegraph.co.uk/news/uknews/crime/8700109/Historian-Starkey-in-racism-row-over-riot-comments.htm. Retrieved 3 June 2012.

Bartlett, Jamie, and Mark Littler. 2011. Inside the EDL: Populist Politics in a Digital Age. *Demos*. London. http://www.demos.co.uk/publications/insidetheedl. Retrieved 27 March 2012.

BBC. 2013. EDL Leader Tommy Robinson Quits Group. *BBC News*, 8 October. http://www.bbc.co.uk/news/uk-politics-24442953. Retrieved 17 Feb 2015.

Berry, Brent, and Eduardo Bonilla-Silva. 2008. 'They Should Hire the One with the Best Score': White Sensitivity to Qualification Differences in Affirmative Action Hiring Decisions. *Ethnic and Racial Studies* 31 (2): 215–242.

Bonilla-Silva, Eduardo, Amanda Lewis, and David G. Embrick. 2004. 'I Did Not Get That Job Because of a Black Man...': The Story Lines and Testimonies of Color-Blind Racism. *Sociological Forum* 19 (4): 555–581.

Booth, Robert, Matthew Taylor, and Paul Lewis. 2009. English Defence League: Chaotic Alliance Stirs up Trouble on Streets. *Guardian*, 12 September. http://www.guardian.co.uk/world/2009/sep/11/english-defence-league-chaotic-alliance. Retrieved 1 Jan 2012.

Burnett, Jon. 2011. The New Geographies of Racism: Stoke-on-Trent. *Institute of Race Relations*. London. http://www.irr.org.uk/pdf2/New_geographies_racism_Stoke.pdf. Retrieved 28 Nov 2011.

Busher, Joel. 2013. Grassroots Activism in the English Defence League: Discourse and Public (Dis)order. In *Extreme Right-Wing Political Violence and Terrorism*, ed. Max Taylor, P.M. Currie, and Donald Holbrooke, 65–83. London: Bloomsbury.

Busher, Joel. 2015. *The making of anti-Muslim protest: Grassroots activism in the English Defence League*. London: Routledge.

Carter, Helen. 2012. Man Held over Alleged Race Hate Attack. *Guardian*, 7 February. http://www.guardian.co.uk/uk/2012/feb/07/alleged-race-hate-attack-hyde. Retrieved 3 June 2012.

Casciani, Dominic. 2010. Islamic Scholar Tahir Ul-Qadri Issues Terrorism Fatwa. *BBC*, 2 March. http://news.bbc.co.uk/1/hi/8544531.stm. Retrieved 31 May 2012.

Christian, M. 2005. The Politics of Black Presence in Britain and Black Male Exclusion in the British Education System. *Journal of Black Studies* 35 (3): 327–346.

Cockbain, Ella, and Richard Wortley. 2015. Everyday Atrocities: Does Internal (Domestic) Sex Trafficking of British Children Satisfy the Expectations of Opportunity Theories of Crime? *Crime Science* 4 (1).

Copsey, Nigel. 2008. *Contemporary British Fascism: The British National Party and the Quest for Legitimacy. Labour*, 2nd ed. Hampshire: Palgrave Macmillan.

———. 2010. *The English Defence League: Challenging Our Country and Our Values of Social Inclusion, Fairness and Equality*. London: Faith Matters. http://faith-matters.org/images/stories/fm-reports/english-defense-league-report.pdf. Retrieved 28 Nov 2011.

Crown Prosecution Service. 2011. Violence against Women and Girls: Crime Report 2010-2011. *Area*. http://www.cps.gov.uk/publications/docs/CPS_VAW_report_2011.pdf. Retrieved 28 May 2012.

Davies, Caroline, and Karen McVeigh. 2011. Child Sex Trafficking Study Sparks Exaggerated Racial Stereotyping, 6 January. *Guardian*. https://www.theguardian.com/law/2011/jan/06/child-sex-trafficking-racial-stereotyping. Retrieved 23 Aug 2013.

Doane, Ashley. 2006. What Is Racism? Racial Discourse and Racial Politics. *Critical Sociology* 32 (2): 255–274.

Dodd, Vikram, and Matthew Taylor. 2011. Muslims Criticise Scotland Yard for Telling Them to Engage with EDL. *Guardian*, 2 September. http://www.guardian.co.uk/uk/2011/sep/02/english-defence-league-muslims-police. Retrieved 18 May 2012.

Eatwell, Roger. 2006. Community Cohesion and Cumulative Extremism in Contemporary Britain. *The Political Quarterly* 77 (2): 204–216.

EDL. 2011a. "99% of Daily Star Respondents Support the EDL." *EDL News*, 1 December. http://englishdefenceleague.org/edl-news-2/178-99-of-daily-star-respondents-support-the-edl. Retrieved 1 March 2013.

———. 2011b. A Two-Tier System. *EDL News*, 11 December. http://englishdefenceleague.org/edl-news-2/181-a-two-tier-system. Retrieved 28 Feb 2012.

———. 2011c. Birmingham Demonstration: October 29th. *EDL News*. http://englishdefenceleague.org/birmingham-demonstration-october-29th/. Retrieved 1 March 2012.

———. 2011d. British Muslims Support the Poppy Appeal. *EDL News*, 14 November. http://englishdefenceleague.org/edl-news-2/163-british-muslims-support-the-poppy-appea. Retrieved 1 March 2012.

———. 2011e. Islam: The Religion of Peace? *EDL News*. http://englishdefenceleague.org/islam-the-religion-of-peace/. Retrieved 28 Feb 2012.

———. 2011f. Life in the UK Is Generally Pretty Good. *EDL News*, 10 November. http://englishdefenceleague.org/edl-news-2/167-life-in-the-uk-is-generally-pretty-good. Retrieved 1 March 2012.

———. 2011g. Speeches from the Birmingham Demonstration. *EDL News*, 1 November. http://englishdefenceleague.org/edl-news-2/160-speeches-from-the-birmingham-demonstration. Retrieved 1 March 2012.

————. 2011h. Suspicions Raised about Nationalist Demonstration on 8th October... And Neo-Nazi Named and Shamed. *EDL News*, 19 September. http://englishdefenceleague.org/edl-news-2/138-suspicions-raised-about-nationalist-demonstration-on-8th-october-and-neo-nazi-named-and-shamed. Retrieved 1 March 2012.

————. 2011i. The Cultic and Beastly Nature of Islam. *EDL News*, 10 July. http://englishdefenceleague.org/edl-news-2/70-the-cultic-beastly-nature-of-islam. Retrieved 1 March 2012.

————. 2011j. The Rise of the British Taliban. *EDL News*. http://englishdefenceleague.org/the-rise-of-the-british-taliban/. Retrieved 1 March 2012.

————. 2011k. Tommy Robinson Challenges David Cameron to a Live Debate. *EDL News*, 30 August. http://englishdefenceleague.org/edl-news-2/122-tommy-robinson-challenges-david-cameron-to-a-live-debate. Retrieved 1 March 2012.

————. 2011l. Tommy Robinson Vs. Weyman Bennett. *EDL News*, 26 October. http://englishdefenceleague.org/edl-news-2/158-tommy-robinson-vs-weyman-bennett. Retrieved 1 March 2012.

————. 2011m. What Does It Mean to Be Asian? *EDL News*, 22 August. http://englishdefenceleague.org/edl-news-2/116-what-does-it-mean-to-be-asian. Retrieved 28 Feb 2012.

————. 2012a. EDL Featured in BBC Documentary. *EDL News*, 20 February. http://englishdefenceleague.org/edl-news-2/239-edl-featured-in-bbc-documentary. Retrieved 1 March 2012.

————. 2012b. National Demonstration: 25th February 2012, Hyde, Greater Manchester. *EDL News*, 15 February. http://englishdefenceleague.org/edl-news-2/230-national-demonstration-25th-february-2012-hyde-greater-mancheste. Retrieved 28 Feb 2012.

————. 2012c. Open Letter to Leicester Businesses. *EDL News*, 25 January. http://englishdefenceleague.org/edl-news-2/194-open-letter-to-leicester-businesses. Retrieved 1 March 2012.

————. 2012d. Successful Demo in Hyde (and No, We're Not Paying for It). *EDL News*, 29 February. http://englishdefenceleague.org/edl-news-2/255-successful-demo-in-hyde-and-no-we're-not-paying-for-it. Retrieved 1 March 2012.

Feagin, Joe R., Hernan Vera, and Pinar Batur. 2001. *White Racism*. New York: Routledge.

Garland, Jon, and James Treadwell. 2010. 'No Surrender to the Taliban!': Football Hooliganism, Islamophobia and the Rise of the English Defence League. *Papers from the British Criminology Conference 10*. British Society of Criminology: 19–35. http://www.britsoccrim.org/volume10/2010_PBCC_full.pdf#page=23 Retrieved 28 Nov 2011.

Goodwin, Matthew. 2007. The Extreme Right in Britain: Still an 'Ugly Duckling' but for How Long? *The Political Quarterly* 78 (2): 241–250.

———. 2013. The Roots of Extremism: The English Defence League and the Counter-Jihad Challenge. *Chatham House Briefing Paper*. http://www.open-briefing.org/docs/rootsofextremism.pdf. Retrieved 13 May 2013.

Goodwin, Matthew, and Jocelyn Evans. 2012. From Voting to Violence? Far Right Extremism in Britain. *Hope Not Hate*. http://www.channel4.com/media/c4-news/images/voting-to-violence(7).pdf. Retrieved 20 May 2012.

Greenfield, Daniel. 2011. Anglophobia or Islamophobia—What's the Real Problem? *EDL News*. http://englishdefenceleague.org/anglophobia-or-islamophobia-whats-the-real-problem/. Retrieved 1 March 2012.

Griffin, Nick. 2012. An Opportunity to Be Seized—Why We Have Lifted the Proscription on the English Defence League. *BNP News*, 25 February. http://www.bnp.org.uk/news/national/opportunity-be-seized-why-we-have-lifted-proscription-english-defence-league. Retrieved 24 Feb 2015.

Halikiopoulou, Daphne, and Sofia Vasilopoulou. 2010. Towards a 'Civic' Narrative: British National Identity and the Transformation of the British National Party. *The Political Quarterly* 81 (4): 583–592.

Jackson, Paul, Mark Pitchford, and Trevor Preston. 2011. The EDL: Britain's 'New Far-Right' Social Movement. *Radicalism and New Media Research Group*. http://www.radicalism-new-media.org/images/pdf/The_EDL_Britains_New_Far_Right_Social_Movement.pdf. Retrieved 28 May 2015.

Muslim Council of Britain. 2001. MCB Expresses Total Condemnation of Terrorist Attacks. *Muslim Council of Britain*, 11 September. http://www.mcb.org.uk/media/pr/110901.htm. Retrieved 31 May 2012.

Muslim Council of Britain. 2005. British Muslims Utterly Condemn Acts of Terror. *Muslim Council of Britain*, 12 July. http://www.mcb.org.uk/features/features.php?ann_id=1046. Retrieved 31 May 2012.

Nesbitt, Eleanor. 2011. Sikh Diversity in the UK: Context and Evolution. In *Sikhs in Europe: Migration, Identities and Representations*, ed. Knut A. Jacobsen, and Kristina Myrvold, 225–252. Surrey: Ashgate.

Newman, Naomi. 2007. The New Frontier of Racism. *Public Policy Research* 80–89.

Press Association. 2011. UK Muslims Cheer for Global Peace. *Guardian*, 24 September. http://www.guardian.co.uk/uk/feedarticle/9863616. Retrieved 31 May 2012.

Richardson, John E. 2009. 'Get Shot of the Lot of Them': Election Reporting of Muslims in British Newspapers. *Patterns of Prejudice* 43 (3–4): 355–377.

———. 2013. Ploughing the Same Furrow? Continuity and Change on Britain's Extreme-Right Fringe. In *Right Wing Populism in Europe: Politics and Discourse*, ed. Ruth Wodak, Majid KhosraviNik, and Briggitte Mral, 105–119. London: Bloomsbury Academic.

Siddique, Haroon. 2011. Muslim Women's Group Launches 'Jihad against Violence'. *Guardian*, 6 June. http://www.guardian.co.uk/uk/2011/jun/06/muslim-womens-group-jihad-violence. Retrieved 31 May 2012.

Telegraph. 2011. Muslim Women Not Used to Drinking Walk Free after Attack on Woman. *Telegraph*, 6 December. http://www.telegraph.co.uk/news/uknews/crime/8937856/Muslim-women-not-used-to-drinking-walk-free-after-attack-on-woman.htm. Retrieved 3 June 2012.

Treadwell, James, and Jon Garland. 2011. Masculinity, Marginalization and Violence: A Case Study of the English Defence League. *British Journal of Criminology* 51 (4): 621–633.

Tweedie, Neil. 2009. The English Defence League: Will the Flames of Hatred Spread? *Telegraph*, 10 October. http://www.telegraph.co.uk/news/6284184/The-English-Defence-League-will-the-flames-of-hatred-spread.html. Retrieved 23 April 2012.

van Dijk, T.A. 1992. Discourse and the Denial of Racism. *Discourse & Society* 3 (1): 87–118.

Williams, Sasha, and Ian Law. 2011. Legitimising Racism: An Exploration of the Challenges Posed by the Use of Indigeneity Discourses by the Far Right. *Sociological Research Online* 17 (2). http://www.socresonline.org.uk/17/2/2.html. Retrieved 19 May 2013.

Wood, C., and W.M.L. Finlay. 2008. British National Party Representations of Muslims in the Month after the London Bombings: Homogeneity, Threat, and the Conspiracy Tradition. *The British Journal of Social Psychology* 47 (4): 707–726.

CHAPTER 5

Islamophobia and National Identity in Europe

INTRODUCTION

On 22 July 2011 a car bomb was detonated outside government buildings in the Norwegian capital of Oslo, resulting in eight deaths. Within an hour the *Observer's* foreign affairs editor, Peter Beaumont, had declared that the explosion was most likely the work of a 'Jihadist' group, and speculated that Norway had likely been targeted because of its involvement in the war on Afghanistan, its reprinting of controversial Danish cartoons, and the filing of terror charges against an Iraqi-born cleric who had threatened politicians with death if he was deported from the country. A few hours later, reports about further developments began to emerge. A man dressed in police uniform had opened fire on young people attending a Labour Party youth camp on the island of Utøya. Sixty-nine youths were killed on the island before police apprehended Anders Behring Breivik, a 32-year-old ethnic Norwegian.

In his 1500 page manifesto, entitled *2083: A European Declaration of Independence,* Breivik explained that his motivation had been the desire to spark a revolution against the 'Islamification' of the continent. Political correctness, 'cultural Marxism', radical feminism, and the EU's deliberate attempt to Islamise Europe, were all implicated in what he perceived as the cultural treason against Europe's essence. For Breivik, Islam was quietly colonising Europe with the support of multiculturalist politicians and he considered himself a warrior whose duty was to defend Western Europe against this onslaught. Breivik's actions were universally

© The Author(s) 2018
L.B. Jackson, *Islamophobia in Britain*,
DOI 10.1007/978-3-319-58350-1_5

condemned by European governments, yet the ideology that spurred him to action finds support across the continent, in both national debates about the integration of Muslim minorities and the civilisational discourses that seek to define European belonging.

The construction of both European and national identity has been predicated historically on the construction of 'others', and in the post-2001 period Muslims have increasingly taken this role, identified as possessing values and identities antithetical to the societies in which they reside. In this sense, Breivik's ideology is not an aberration but a radical continuation of mainstream discourses that view multiculturalism as a dangerous to European identity and solidarity, and Muslims as the most profound threat. Across Europe the assertion of stable national identities defined in cultural terms has been deemed essential to ensuring social cohesion, and within this discourse Muslims have been singled out as most threatening and most in need of coercive assimilation by the state.

This chapter considers how Muslim identity has increasingly been constructed within European states as an 'other' against which to articulate national identity. The chapter explores culturalist conceptions of national identity in four European countries: Switzerland, Denmark, the Netherlands, and France. These countries diverge in their political culture, their immigration history, the state's official position towards immigrants, and state management of claims for religious recognition. Yet despite these variations, there has been a remarkable convergence across all four countries in debates that centred on questions of Muslim belonging. Through a critical consideration of the identities articulated, this chapter explores both contradictions within the discourses and the political effects of these narratives of exclusion.

THE DISCURSIVE CONSTRUCTION OF NATIONAL IDENTITY

National identity is only understandable in the realm of discourse, through the language and other semiotic practices that build belonging to the imagined national community (De Cillia et al. 1999). The discursive work of national identity lies in its capacity to mark an inside and an outside, a native and a foreign, and expresses a relative feeling of belonging that only makes sense when compared with the feelings members of a nation have towards foreigners (Triandafyllidou 1998). National identity therefore requires difference in order to demarcate those who belong and those who do not, and this difference is often interpreted as danger.

By telling us what to fear these discourses are able to fix who we are. In this way alternative identities are often represented as the negative 'other' against which national identity is contrasted: what the nation is not is used to affirm what the nation is.

This chapter is concerned with how national identity has been constructed in contrast to Muslim identity. In Switzerland, Denmark, the Netherlands, and France, Islamophobic discourses which identified Muslims as dangerous and threatening to the nation led to high-profile public debates about national identity and values. These states demarcated their boundaries through the invocation of 'Muslim culture', conceived as diametrically opposed to national values inherited from the Enlightenment. Those values deemed 'European' or 'Western' were represented as natural and essential *national* characteristics, and were used to police the boundaries of who did or did not belong to the nation. The concepts considered particularly demonstrative of the character of the nation differed among the four countries studied, but all used the idea of the inherent and eternal 'otherness' of Muslims as a way to shore up both national identity and enlightened European belonging. The Islamophobic dimension of these discourses lies in the way that Muslim culture was considered *the* impediment to national belonging, in such a way that even descendants of immigrants from Muslim majority countries, born and educated in Europe, were marked out as dangerous to the existence and continuance of the nation.

The chapter focuses on 'construction moments' in order to delineate Islamophobic discourses of national identity. These are events which have led to Muslims being represented in particular ways. They are the catalysts for the emergence, recycling and reframing of discourses, which occur when a given event leads to public debate and an attempt to represent subjects in a particular way. The construction moments detailed in this chapter represent changes in, or reaffirmations of, national discourses. They may be triggered by a specific event and occur over a relatively short period of time, as in the anti-minaret initiative in Switzerland and the Danish cartoon controversy, or they may be much more well-entrenched positions that are nonetheless reawakened by particular incidents, as with Dutch homoemancipation policy or French gender equality arguments in relation to Islamic dress. The key is that a debate is initiated in which identities are questioned and discourses of national identity come to be articulated. This chapter demonstrates how those discourses of national identity were articulated in opposition to 'Muslim identity' and 'Islamic values'.

In each of the countries discussed, Muslim identity, values and culture were articulated in opposition to national culture. In the case of Switzerland, the minaret referendum was more than a question of whether the architectural expression of religious diversity should be permitted. By tying the vote to questions of national identity the initiative became an opportunity to symbolically reject Islam and the values it was supposed to promote. In Denmark, escalating anger at Muslim outrage towards the Jyllands-Posten Muhammad cartoons created a dichotomy of identities which demanded not only that Muslims in Denmark choose sides in an increasingly international conflict, but also that Danes choose between sensitivity to the feelings of others and a commitment to absolute free expression, newly defined as a central premise of Danish national identity. In both the Netherlands and France, Islam was constructed as the exclusive domain of particular illiberal positions, which were represented as absolutely antithetical to national culture and Enlightenment values. Culturally determined 'Muslim homophobia' in the Netherlands was constructed as existentially threatening to the tolerant 'homo-friendly' Dutch nation. Correspondingly, the conflicts over Islamic dress in France focused (among other things) on the danger that veiling was thought to pose to gender equality.

In each country Islam became central to representations of the nation, marking the boundaries of belonging according to certain values deemed 'European'. In this sense the construction moments gave rise to nationally specific discourses that not only sought to define the identity of the nation in opposition to this 'other', but also reaffirmed national belonging to the *idea* of Europe, considered superior, rational and liberal.

The Swiss Minaret Referendum and the Symbolic Rejection of Islam

The Swiss minaret referendum represents the first, and to date only, time that a specifically anti-Islam popular vote has been undertaken in Western Europe. Initiated by the right-wing populist Sweizerische Volkspartei (SVP), with the backing of a minor Christian evangelical party (Eidenossische Demokratische Union, EDU), the referendum proposed a constitutional ban on the construction of minarets, and was passed in November 2009 with a majority of 57.5% in favour.

Most striking about the anti-minaret initiative was its symbolic nature. The central issue of the referendum was whether minarets, a symbol of Islam, should be tolerated in Switzerland. The vote itself was also largely symbolic, entailing no economic or political consequences that may otherwise have impacted on individuals' decision to vote in favour or against the initiative. In addition, the discourse promoted by the SVP to support its anti-minaret position consisted largely of emotive symbols which helped to escalate the matter from a local building permission issue into a nationwide referendum that sought to define the place of Islam in Switzerland.

The referendum was sparked by an application for the country's fifth minaret in the town of Langenthal, Berner Mitteland. The 2006 application for the fourth (and final) minaret, in Wangen bei Olten, had caused controversy when local resistance against construction led to a long spell of legal wrangling in local and national courts before the application was finally approved in 2009 by the Supreme Court. Conceptualising the issue as an intolerable aesthetic attack on the nation's skyline, the SVP launched a 2007 initiative calling for the prohibition of minarets in the country and this was submitted in July 2008 with 114,895 supporting signatures (Matyassy and Flury 2011).

Apart from the EDU, all other political parties in Switzerland were opposed to the initiative, and the Federal Government issued four arguments recommending rejection, claiming that it: violated religious freedom and was discriminatory since it was directed exclusively at Muslims; was contrary to the Swiss constitution and breached fundamental human rights conventions; was ineffective in fighting extremism and would not stop the influence of Islam; and would hinder the integration of Muslims in Switzerland, as well as potentially damaging the country's standing in the world and negatively impact national security and the economy (Mason et al. 2010). Despite pre-referendum polls which predicted that the ban would be rejected, the vote passed with a 57.5% majority, as well as a cantonal majority, with only four of Switzerland's 26 cantons opposed to the initiative. As a result, Article 72 of the Federal constitution was amended to read: 'the construction of minarets is prohibited' (Orlanskaya and Gunther 2010).

A remarkably similar debate over public space as a site of identity contestation emerged during discussions of the Park 51 Islamic centre near the 'ground zero' site of the former World Trade Center. As Jeanne Kilde (2011, 306) has noted, the debates about the site's reconstruction focused on the need to use the space sensitively, implying that the close proximity of Muslims would be insensitive. Proponents of the discourse sought to exclude Muslims from this particular public space in deference to the grieving families of victims, suggesting that the connection between Islam and the September 11, 2001 attacks meant Muslims were less entitled to the space than other Americans. The symbolic incompatibility of an Islamic centre near the 'ground zero' site thus provided the rationale for the exclusion of Muslims as not fully American and entitled to fewer rights than other members of the national community. The Park-Zero controversy illustrates how discursive representations have material political effects, making some actions inevitable and others unthinkable. The exclusion that begins through a discursive questioning of Muslims can lead to concrete exclusionary practices when Muslims are prevented from accessing public space on the same terms as non-Muslims. The Swiss minaret referendum followed a similar logic.

The increased visibility of Muslims in Switzerland over the last decade has been shaped both by public criticism of court decisions which affirmed Muslim religious claims (such as the High Court decision to allow the construction of the fourth minaret, as well as struggles within municipalities over Islamic burial sites) and an increased resentment of Islam after the September 11, 2001 attacks and especially the 2004 attacks in Madrid. While the New York attacks led to increased media stereotyping of Islam, the Madrid attacks unleashed a more profound change in reporting, and threat became a central motif. Muslims were no longer presented as victims of inadequate integration, but perpetrators who shunned mixing, and 'Muslim culture' was presented as threatening to Swiss norms and values (Ettinger 2008). The 2006 World Values Survey revealed that negative opinions of Muslims in Switzerland had increased relative to general xenophobic sentiments, with 19.8% reporting that they would not want a Muslim for a neighbour as opposed to 7.1% who would not want a foreigner for a neighbour (Dolezal et al. 2010).

The SVP's anti-minaret campaign escalated a planning issue into a matter of national identity through a dual process of politicisation-and culturalisation. Minarets were politicised through an argument that stressed they were unnecessary. Since Islam could be practised freely without the feature, the desire to construct a minaret was cast as inherently suspicious; an aggressive symbol of non-conformity and a mark of the ascent of Islam on the Swiss landscape which, if not countered, would lead to the spread of Sharia. Architectural features themselves, of course, pose no objective threat, but minarets were made contentious through an association with Islamic fundamentalism, which served to re-ascribe them as symbols not of religion, but of power. The SVP's Ulrich Schlüer, co-president of the Stop the Minarets Movement, stated that as a symbol of political power the minaret had nothing to do with religion, and was rather a prelude to the introduction of Sharia law (Traynor 2009). By linking minarets to the inevitable growth of Sharia in Switzerland, the anti-minaret campaign invoked an intolerant Islam diametrically opposed to European values. Should voters reject the initiative, they would be responsible for the encouragement of a plethora of negative consequences to the nation:

> We do not want to limit freedom of religion, we want to outlaw the political symbol.... The fear is great that the minarets will be followed by the calls to prayer of the muezzin... Sharia is gaining in importance in Switzerland and in Europe. That means honour killings, forced marriages, circumcision, wearing the burqa, ignoring school rules, and even stoning. (Ulrich Schlüer, quoted in Institute of Race Relations 2010, 2)

As a symbol of the power of Islam, the minaret was represented as an intolerable challenge to Swiss constitutional values and a claim to sole representation that undermined democracy. When prominent radical feminist Julia Onken called on women to support the initiative she further entrenched this discursive construction. Stating that 'mosques are male houses, minarets are male power symbols', (Traynor 2009), she maintained that the minaret must be opposed because it represented the visible sign of the state's acceptance of the oppression of women. Through the symbolic representation of minarets as emblematic of Muslim power designs on Swiss public space, the cultural threat posed by Islam became the central theme of the anti-minaret campaign.

One of the most contentious symbols of the campaign was the poster produced by Goal advertising agency, which depicted an ominous burqa-clad figure alongside a Swiss flag pierced with looming missile-like minarets and the words: 'Stop. Yes to the minaret ban'. The poster accessibly gathered together the central tropes of the anti-minaret position, representing a threatening and dangerous Islam that would not only blot the Swiss landscape but would also implicitly challenge Swiss values by sanctioning Islamist social models that allegedly professed inequality between the sexes. Proponents of the ban thus explicitly demonstrated a causal relationship between Islam, violence, and social models incompatible with Swiss gender equality norms. This semiotic display emotively linked minaret construction to the dissolution of Swiss culture and society, and the ability of the minaret initiative's backers to bring these larger issues into the debate illustrates how the process of culturalisation worked. By enfolding discourses of culture into a debate about the suitability of architecture, minarets formed a proxy for a larger rejection of Islam, defined negatively and in opposition to Swiss culture.

This discourse appears to have been successful in politicising and culturalising the minaret issue. Post-referendum polls revealed that the majority of those who voted in favour of the ban had done so to set a sign against both the spread of Islam and Islamic social models and to emphasise that the limits of Swiss tolerance had been stretched too far by Muslim demands. That no evidence existed to suggest mosques with minarets were any more likely to propagate these values than those without was irrelevant. The referendum became a symbolic rejection of a constructed threat through the representation of the minaret as a political symbol that encouraged both the spread of Sharia and the relegation of women to second-class status. This discourse transformed the referendum from a planning into a civilisational issue, and constructed the vote as a simple choice between incompatible and oppositional cultures. The fact that only 15% of those who voted in favour of the ban cited specific criticisms of Muslims living in Switzerland suggests that it cannot be understood as a general rejection of Swiss Muslims (Mason et al. 2010). Rather, the referendum should be understood as a symbolic vote against the perceived Islamisation of Switzerland. It is unlikely that a mere planning issue would have gathered such popular support in a national referendum had proponents of the ban not discursively constructed the initiative as symbolic of a wider issue. Through the employment of a civilisational discourse, which explicitly pitted Swiss values against 'Muslim values', the anti-minaret campaign was able to unite a disparate nation without linguistic, cultural or ethnic homogeneity against an 'other' that was not just outside the nation, but outside of Europe itself.

The Danish Cartoon Controversy and the Politics of Outrage

On 30 September 2005, as a result of Culture Editor Flemming Rose's request that cartoonists stop self-censoring, the Danish newspaper Jyllands-Posten published twelve cartoons in an article entitled *The Face of Muhammad*. The discourse which emerged in the din of controversy that followed worked to emphasise the centrality of free expression as a Danish and European value, against the intolerance of Muslims and their demand for special treatment. The article accompanying the cartoons articulated what was to become the central premise of the discourse: that Muslims demanded a respect not accorded to other groups and which undermined the principle of freedom of speech. The construction moments that occurred during the cartoon controversy worked to underscore this representation. Prime Minister Anders Fogh Rasmussen's unwillingness to meet with Muslim ambassadors to diffuse the conflict was articulated as a decisive refusal to engage with those who wished to see him censor the press. At the same time, violent protests across the world were represented as archetypal Muslim reactions to perceived provocation, and this understanding encouraged Danish Muslim protest to be viewed as demonstrations against freedom of expression rather than a (freely expressed) call for their voices to be heard.

The immediate background of the cartoons was a heated discussion in Denmark about growing Islamic extremism in Europe and perceived increase in media self-censorship with regard to Muslim issues. The difficulty experienced by Danish writer Kåre Bluitgen in finding an illustrator for his children's book on the life of Muhammad was much publicised, as was the attack on a lecturer at the University of Copenhagen, who was set upon by a gang apparently because he read aloud Arabic passages from the Qur'an during lectures. Flemming Rose claimed that the idea for the article had emerged from a frustration with this increased climate of timidity and self-censorship, along with a stifling European culture of political correctness which made it impossible to criticise minorities.

Each of the illustrations took up a different theme; one portrayed Muhammad with a stick walking through the desert; another poked fun at the newspaper, depicting a school child named Muhammad pointing at a chalkboard on which was written in Arabic: 'the editors of Jyllands-Posten are a bunch of reactionary provocateurs'. The most inflammatory cartoon, however, and certainly the most discussed, was Kurt

Westergaard's depiction of Muhammad with a lit fuse in his turban. Alongside the twelve drawings, the article's text stated:

> Modern secular society is rejected by some Muslims. They demand an exceptional position, insisting on special consideration for their own religious feelings. This is incompatible with secular democracy and freedom of speech, where one has to put up with insults, mockery, and ridicule. It is certainly not always attractive and nice to look at, and it does not mean that religious feelings should be made fun of at any price, but that is of minor importance in the present context (Kublitz 2010).

Placing Muslims in opposition to modernity, secularism, democracy and freedom of speech, this justification for publication set the tone of the representations that were to follow and was eagerly employed by a variety of Danish actors.

As the conflict was escalated on to the world stage the reaction to the cartoons' publication took different forms. In October 2005, Prime Minister Rasmussen refused to meet with 11 ambassadors from Muslim countries to discuss the article, and in response a delegation of Danish imams travelled to the Middle East to actively gain support outside Denmark, claiming that Rasmussen's refusal illustrated that the government failed to take Muslim concerns seriously. This decision dramatically expanded the stage upon which discontent was voiced. Pakistani Islamist group Jamaat-i-Islami offered a $10,000 bounty on the head of the cartoonists, the Organisation of the Islamic Conference put the issue on their agenda, and protests in Muslim majority countries saw Danish flags burned in demonstrations in Gaza and elsewhere. In response to this German and French newspapers printed part of the cartoons on 1 February 2006, and this led to further escalation of the conflict and an apparent drawing of stark ideological opposition between 'the West' and the 'Muslim world'. In Lebanon and Tehran, Danish embassies were attacked, the Norwegian embassy was burned down in Syria, and protests in Afghanistan, Pakistan, Libya, and Nigeria led to several deaths. These international protests were represented as emblematic of Muslim anger and intolerance, and undeniable evidence that freedom of expression must be defended in the face of violent demands for Muslim recognition. The cartoons and the reactions that followed had the effect of constructing an oppositional relationship between Danes and Muslims, with the former represented as championing the enlightenment value of freedom of speech and the latter constructed as mired in violent intolerance of any criticism of Islam. This binary encouraged Muslims in Denmark to be seen as internal carriers of a culture which rejected Danish values and posed an existential threat to the ongoing life of the national community.

The Prime Minister's reaction to the eleven ambassadors who wrote in October 2005 to request an interview illustrates how these positions became entrenched. The ambassadors' letter highlighted their concerns with what they perceived as a growing Islamophobia in Denmark, and the cartoons were mentioned as just one example of an ongoing 'smear campaign' against Muslims. Rasmussen refused to meet with the ambassadors and responded instead with a letter which explained that 'freedom of expression has a wide scope and the Danish Government has no means of influencing the press' (Mason et al. 2010). According to the Egyptian ambassador, the purpose of the letter had been to ask for nothing more than a moral condemnation of the cartoons from the Prime Minister, however Rasmussen interpreted and subsequently represented it to the media as a call for the government to constrain press freedom, claiming that there was no reason to meet with the ambassadors since he had neither the power nor the desire to limit the press (Belien 2005). Despite the diplomats' protestations that they merely wanted to diffuse the situation through dialogue, Rasmussen continued to claim that their appeal for a meeting was a demand for censorship and beyond the pale of acceptability in a democratic society, stating: 'In my opinion, this reveals an abysmal ignorance of the principles of a true democracy as well as a complete failure to understand that in a free democracy, the government neither can, must or should interfere with the press' (Engelbreth Larson 2006). The continued representation of the diplomats' request in such stark terms indicated Rasmussen's adherence to the discursive construction originally laid out by the cartoons, and this lent some official respectability to the notion that Muslim opposition to the images was based on anti-secular and anti-free speech leanings.

A further illustration of this may be gleaned from reactions to the 14 October 2005 protest organised by Muslims in Denmark. The demonstration was called in order to provide a focal point for Muslim opposition, to counter the possibility that someone may take up violence, and to show that Muslims were peaceful and could operate dissent democratically. Holding banners in both Danish and Arabic which read: 'No to the clash of civilisations, yes to the dialogue of civilisations' and 'No to racism and fanaticism, yes to peace and co-existence', the 3000 strong demonstration moved from Nørrebro Station, near the largest mosque in Copenhagen, to the town hall square, where a request was made by organisers to participate in a common prayer. A few hundred joined in the prayer, claiming that this was the most peaceful act that one can undertake. However, as Anja Kublitz has highlighted, this protest dramatically revealed the different interpretative spaces of the Muslims who participated and the general public who witnessed it. The sight of thousands of Muslims protesting seemed to confirm prevailing views on how Muslims demonstrate and what they demonstrate for. In this sense the protest was perceived not as a demonstration for dialogue, peace and co-existence, rather, it was interpreted within a worldview that considered all Muslim political action as essentially Islamic: *for* Islam and therefore *against* the West. Some onlookers, confronted by the sight of Muslims praying, interpreted the demonstration as a protest against secular freedom of expression. This visual understanding of what was occurring was supported by a misinterpretation of the sounds of the demonstration. The slogan '*Islam er fred*'(Islam is peace) was misheard as '*Islam er vred*' (Islam is angry), leading pedestrians to ask the demonstrators if they were going to war (Kublitz 2010).

The demonstration confirmed for some the bipolar positions entrenched by the discourse of Muslims vs. secular freedom. What was seen by onlookers seems to have been fitted to a mental representation of what they expected to see, based on perceptions of how Muslims usually behave when protesting or expressing dissent. As the form of the demonstration appeared religious, the mishearing of slogans, which transformed an assertion of peace into a declaration of war, combined with the prone submission of prayer fit a mental model congruent with media representations of Muslim protest. It is little wonder that for spectators the belief that the demonstrators were protesting Danish freedom of expression seemed to be confirmed by the form the protest took.

The increasingly opposing subject identities constructed by the discourse surrounding the cartoons meant that the ostensibly positive, progressive value of free speech was used to mark the boundaries of Danish national identity. This was tied to larger civilisational narratives by underscoring difference, formulated as the binary opposition between modernity and tradition. The publication of the cartoons developed an already existing narrative that centred on the incompatibility between Western values and Islam and promoted it to national and international attention. The West, aligned with democracy, individualism, secularism and liberalism, was increasingly represented in contrast with Islam's backward primitivism, oppression of the individual and failure to accept the separation of religion and state, and this interpretative frame marked the discourse to such a degree that to be both European and Muslim was considered a contradiction in terms. Muslims were perceived to have allegiance to their religion over Danish values and to be signalling their difference in a way that undermined the fundamental underpinnings of Danish national identity: the separation of religion and state and the freedom to express critical opinions of religion. Freedom of expression became an absolute value in the discourse surrounding the cartoons.

Flemming Rose claimed that the decision to publish the cartoons sent a positive message, signalling that Muslims were accepted as an integral part of Danish daily life, and as such were subject to the same treatment as anyone else. The cartoons, he claimed, were an act of inclusion:

> It's humiliating and discriminating to treat any minority as a kind of odd, special group. It's very important to treat everyone equally. The cartoonists were just doing what they are doing every day with all kinds of figures, issues, institutions. It's an act of love and inclusion to satirize people. There is some kind of recognition in that, to know you can laugh and make fun of one another (Rose, quoted in Malek 2007, 18).

The notion that the cartoons were an expression of inclusion, however, was strongly undermined by their instrumentalisation as objects of revenge. In the early hours of 12 February 2008 police arrested three Muslim men (two Tunisian nationals with permanent residency in Denmark and one Moroccan man with Danish citizenship) on suspicion of plotting to assassinate Kurt Westergaard, illustrator of the most contentious cartoon. The arrests provided a pretext for reprinting the cartoons across the media, starting with Jyllands-Posten. This mass reprinting of the cartoons illustrates how the entrenched positions generated by the original controversy had created a binary opposition of Islam vs. freedom of speech that could now be wheeled out in response to any perceived Muslim provocation. The centre-left Danish newspaper *Information* justified its printing of the cartoons in an editorial, claiming: '*Information* chose not to print the cartoons first time around. Back then we felt that they were a clear provocation against the Muslim community. Not this time though. People have been plotting to kill an innocent seventy-three-year-old man. This is completely unacceptable' (Brun and Hersh 2008). This statement illustrates how the controversy's escalation allowed the cartoons to be transformed from offensive to defensive symbols. What began as a 'clear provocation' against Muslims had now been re-ascribed as an emblem of solidarity with the champions of freedom. Muslims, linked with the alleged plotters by virtue of their religion, were considered legitimate targets for collective punishment and no longer entitled to feel provoked.

The (Homo)Sexualisation of Dutch National Identity

In the Netherlands, the discourses that constructed national identity in opposition to a supposed Muslim culture have taken many forms, but one of the most interesting and prominent was the representation of homosexual tolerance as a Dutch cultural value. As Mepschen, Duyvendak and Tonkens (2010, 963) have observed, sexual liberation has been used to frame Europe as the avatar of modernity and freedom, while depicting Muslims as the cultural bearers of backward homophobia. Nowhere in Europe is this discourse more prevalent than in the Netherlands, where homosexual freedom has been instrumentalised to mark the borders of belonging in discursive, symbolic and concrete ways.

Several construction moments have brought this discourse to the foreground, including the anti-gay comments of imam El-Moumni in 2001, which were characterised as typical and representative of all Muslims; the rise of openly gay and Islamophobic populist politician Pim Fortuyn; and government policies such as the 2008–2011 'homoemancipation' strategy, which particularly targeted young people of Muslim background, and the 'integration abroad act' which utilised tolerance of homosexuals (among other 'national values') as a means of testing potential immigrants' suitability for family reunification in the Netherlands.

Sexual freedom, and the particular sexual freedom of gay people, has been used in the Netherlands as an indicator of modernity, creating a dichotomy of identities, with those who are modern represented as accepting and embracing homosexuality and those who are premodern represented as opposing it. Through a process of what Jasbir Puar (2007) has termed 'homonationalism,' the liberatory struggle of gay people has been defined as a central tenet of Dutch national identity, and not only juxtaposed against a perceived Muslim cultural homophobia, but instrumentalised as a means of coercion and exclusion to mark the boundaries of the Netherlands and regulate access to the national community.

The Dutch positioning of homosexual tolerance as a national value has become central to identity construction over the last decade. In 2001, the Netherlands became the first country to confer equal marriage rights to homosexuals, effectively removing all legal discrimination against same-sex couples and paving the way for the development of a national myth that viewed Dutch society as entirely 'homo-friendly'. In this climate of national self-congratulation, Muslim homophobia came to be seen as the only obstacle remaining to gay equality, and focus began to shift to immigrants and their descendants as the carriers of culturally sanctioned anti-gay attitudes that threatened the unity of Dutch society. This debate gained prominence in May 2001 when a relatively unknown Rotterdam imam, Khalil El-Moumni, was interviewed on national television about the legalisation of gay marriage. El-Moumni stated that homosexuality was an illness that threatened the reproduction and future of society, and his comments were taken to be an endorsement of increasing homophobic attacks in the area perpetrated by young men of Moroccan and Turkish descent. In fact, the imam unequivocally condemned the violence in a portion of the interview that was not aired (Mepschen 2009). Nevertheless, his religiously conservative views were framed by Dutch media as representative of the entire Muslim community of the Netherlands and taken to be symbolic of the lack of cultural integration of Muslims. Responding to the crisis, Prime Minister Wim Kok spent the full 10 minutes of his weekly television address explaining that Muslims must tolerate homosexuals and all imams were invited to a 'tolerance conference' by the Liberal Democratic Minister of Large Cities Affairs. The intervention of the government escalated and politicised the issue, allowing a discourse to crystallise which placed Muslim homophobia in direct opposition to Dutch tolerance.

The rise of openly gay and Islamophobic politician Pim Fortuyn and his List Pim Fortuyn Party, which found political success after his 2002 assassination, further reinforced the antithetical identities constructed by this discourse. Fortuyn's populist politics focused on the perceived cultural gulf between Islam and the West, and his public gay identity positioned him perfectly to take up the defence of Dutch progressive sexual values against the threat believed to be posed by Islamic tradition. He claimed that Islam was a backward culture, and linked the increasing presence of Muslims to the retreat of women's and gay rights, stating that he did not want 'to do women's and gay liberation all over again' (Bracke 2012). By representing Muslim homophobia as essential and culturally sanctioned, Fortuyn strengthened the discourse of homonationalism in which Islam in the Netherlands symbolised a regressive cultural assault that threatened not only the hard-won freedoms of homosexuals, but the very project of European modernity itself.

The need to protect the gains of modernity from Muslims who wished to restrict such freedom became so deeply rooted in the discourse around homosexuality that it became impossible to talk about LGBT politics in the Netherlands without discussing Islam and Muslims. The policy document 'Simply Gay', launched in 2007, addressed this issue, albeit without explicitly discussing Islam. The document laid out the 2008–2011 'homoemancipation' strategy for the country and identified Turkish and Moroccan communities as the primary targets of a policy that would create a 'third emancipatory wave' and greater social acceptance in those parts of Dutch society where homosexuality was still a sensitive issue (Ministry of Education Culture and Science 2007). As with Britain's community cohesion policy, it was not necessary to specifically state in the document that Islam was the problem, since it was implicit from the communities targeted that *Muslim* homophobia was considered the prime danger to gay freedom. Since the problem was culturalised as emanating from specific (Muslim) communities, the solution lay in targeting them with coercive measures that demanded these problematic communities tolerate homosexuality.

The Integration Abroad Act 2005 (*Wet inburgering in het buitenland*) instrumentalised homosexual tolerance as a tool of coercion in a similar way. One of the provisions of the Act was the overseas integration test, introduced in 2006, where all non-Western foreign nationals who wished to join family members or spouses in the Netherlands were required to sit a pre-entry integration exam in their home country before being issued a visa. Part of the test required applicants for immigration to look at a photograph of two men kissing and report whether the picture offended them and whether they understood it to represent an expression of personal liberty. But not every applicant had to take the test. Citizens of presumably modern countries (EU and US nationals, Canadians, Australians, Swiss, and other 'Western' nations), as well as those whose income exceeded €45,000, were exempt, underscoring the assumption that acceptance of homosexuality is a temporally located modern and culturally advanced position (Butler 2008). The sexual freedom of gay people was in this way used to exclude those considered pre-modern and culturally regressive from access to the Netherlands (including their Dutch families), as well as being used as an instrument of coercion to force the adoption of cultural norms.

The examples above illustrate how the Netherlands has made its 'homo-friendly' identity a tool of coercive nationalism, considering homosexual tolerance a key measure of integration and a precondition of citizenship. As in other European countries, an ostensibly progressive value—in this case homosexual acceptance—was used as a means of excluding and disciplining Muslims in a national project that identified Islam as the prime danger to social cohesion. Muslim homophobia was constructed along a binary axis of civilisation/barbarism, in which the comments of imams were thought to be representative of the views of all Muslims, homophobia within Muslim communities was considered indicative of a cultural and religiously sanctioned backwardness, and homophobic attacks by Turkish and Moroccan youths were deemed emblematic of the failure of Muslim integration and the multicultural project.

The effects of this discourse were to shore up Dutch identity as Western, modern, tolerant and enlightened, in contrast to a pre-modern Muslim culture figured as incompatible and dangerous to the precarious freedoms won by gay people in the Netherlands. As a result, homophobia came to be seen as the exclusive domain of Muslims, and ethnic Dutch homophobia was rendered invisible. The state was then free to utilise a certain conception of freedom in order to discipline Muslims and compel them to shed their unacceptable cultural preconditioning. Judith Butler wryly hinted at this discursive change when she asked, referring to the integration abroad test, whether gay and lesbian people were being tested by the Dutch government to make sure they were not offended by the visible practices of Muslims Ibid., 4. This is an important point, and highlights what Halleh Ghorashi has identified as a dual discourse of citizenship, where the 'real Dutch' are considered responsible citizens, while the 'unwanted Dutch' must be coerced by the state into behaving acceptably (Ghorashi 2003). In the present period, Muslims represent the unwanted Dutch: passive, immature subjects who must simply do as society dictates without being allowed to enter the debate or raise their voices. This discourse underwrites a national project that is based on the incompatibility of cultures and the need to assimilate all into a culturally fundamentalist notion of Dutchness, exemplified by the populist right's declarations of European cultural supremacism:

> Why are we not allowed to say that Muslims should adapt to our way of life, because our standards and values are of a higher, better, more pleasant and more humane level? It is not about integration, it's about assimilation! At home they can wear their headscarves and slaughter their sheep; outside they have to behave like every Dutchman does. (Geert Wilders, quoted in Hylarides 2005, 76)

While the acceptance of diverse sexualities is a value that most progressives would applaud, its use to discipline and demonise Muslims in an Orientalist constellation of modern civility vs. barbaric traditionalism represents a perverse misuse of freedom for purposes of exclusion.

Coercive Undressing and Gender Equality in France

In France, cultural anxiety over Islam has concentrated primarily on the symbolic threat represented by Islamic dress. Construction moments such as: the 2004 ban on religious symbols in schools, which focused primarily on Muslim girls' right to wear the hijab; the reaction to the New Anti-capitalist Party's fielding in the 2010 elections of 'veiled' candidate Ilham Moussaid; and the burqa ban in 2010, which criminalised the full body covering, illustrate what Vincent Geisser (2010) has described as French 'hijabophobia', where Islamic dress is represented as a danger to basic secular republican values.

The debates emerging from this aversion to the various veiling practices of Muslim women have been underpinned by the French legal principle of laïcité, the strict separation of (private) religion and the public sphere. Yet despite this central principle of the French Republic, it is striking the extent to which issues of gender equality and feminism have taken an integral role. This section focuses on the centrality and instrumentalisation of such arguments, which were employed to oppose Islamic veiling specifically to protect women's rights in France (particularly, though not exclusively, Muslim women's rights), and worked to shore up a particular version of French identity as enlightened and modern in contradistinction to backward and patriarchal Islam.

France has the largest Muslim population in Europe, but has historically been hostile to recognition of ethnic and religious identities, viewing individuals as French only and requiring social conformity as the price of political equality. Anxieties about the extent to which Muslim women threatened the idea of an indivisible republic became evident in the 1980s as post-war migration, until then perceived as temporary and solely masculine, began to be viewed as permanent with the arrival of women and children through family reunification. As Muslim women became more visible in France, they became a political issue through a dual representation which identified them as both threatening to the Republic, because of their embodied attachment to, and transference of, Islamic practices, and as victims of the patriarchal dominance of Muslim men. This ambiguous representation was apparent in then Minister of Interior Nicolas Sarkozy's 2006 New Year's Day address to the nation, in which he spoke of the 'immigrant woman, trapped at home, who doesn't speak the language because her husband doesn't let her leave and doesn't put her in contact with literacy groups or French lessons' (Quoted in L. Fekete 2006, 6). As a victim the Muslim woman was prevented from being part of French society by her husband, but her isolation also endangered the integration of her children and thus threatened the future of France.

It is in this context that the debates surrounding the veil, which in France means any covering of the head or face, including the headscarf (hijab), face covering (niqab), and full body cover (burqa), have not only centred on the sacrosanct principle of laïcité, but are also increasingly about patriarchal Islam and the need to rescue Muslim women from men's power. Feminist arguments have been appropriated for the purpose of targeting Muslim women, and emancipating them from their patriarchal culture, and the veil, from this perspective, is pre-eminently a symbol of sexist Islam, and thus not only symbolic of Muslim women's oppression but also a visible challenge to gender equality in France.

It is in this sense that the veil in France is viewed as symbolically announcing the wearer's attachment to values that are incongruous with French commitment to gender equality and the values of autonomy and freedom. There is, of course, no objective violation of gender equality inherent in any type of veil. As Susanna Mancini has pointed out, it is merely a piece of fabric and there are no laws in Europe banning the right to wear any other type clothing, even when, as with high heels and tight trousers, it may actually harm health (Mancini 2012). It is the subjective perception of the veil that causes difficulties in France (and elsewhere in Europe), based on its symbolic connotations. Covering the hair or face implies an unwillingness to engage in established protocols of interaction with the opposite sex, and carries with it a stark visual reminder of a different value system that, in the context of the 'war on terror', is understood as confrontational and opposed to the values of the West.

The understanding that veiling is predominantly symbolic of diametrically opposed gender relations, and specifically of the submissive role of women in Islam, has led to the discursive construction of any veil as dangerous to equality in France. This position, exemplified by the statements of feminists, asserts that no woman wears the veil autonomously, even if she believes she does. Thus the philosopher Elisabeth Badinter could stress that since the veil represented oppression, choosing to wear it was equal to renouncing personal autonomy (Fekete 2006). As symbolic of the patriarchal values of Islam, a woman who embodied these values by covering a part of herself was thought to be publicly renouncing her rights, and in doing so signalling to society that equal rights with men were not important to her. This interpretation of the purpose of veiling has been used over and over in France to sustain limitations on women's rights to wear it, and was employed by President Sarkozy in June 2009, when he proposed banning the burqa, stating: 'That is not the idea that the French republic has of women's dignity. The burqa is not a sign of religion, it is a sign of subservience' (Quoted in Carland 2011, 470). Sarkozy's statement foregrounds the centrality of a particular form of feminism to this debate, where the burqa is perceived as being fundamentally about gender relations and the submissive position of women in Islam. Autonomy can only be restored to these women by forcing them to uncover.

Wearing a burqa in public, or compelling someone else to do so, was banned in France in 2010, and the penalties imposed illustrate the centrality of the gender equality argument. Those breaking this law are required to pay a fine and attend a mandatory citizenship course. The penalties imposed indicate that the law addresses gender equality rather than secularism. Those who force others to cover are considered more problematic to the French government and have to pay one hundred times the fine (€15,000) of those who choose to cover (€150). The disparity in penalties signals that it is women's rights that are being addressed, since if secularism were the principle being defended, one would expect the fine to be equal for both offenders Ibid., 469–470. The difference in financial penalty suggests that the government has made provisions within the law for the presumed patriarchy of Islam by punishing more harshly those who force others to cover. Yet the assumed passivity of Muslim women, which lies at the heart of this two-tier penalty system, contains a paradox: Would not the presumed power of these Muslim fathers, husbands and brothers be so great over these women that they could be coerced into claiming they had chosen to cover in order that dominant men escape the higher penalty? And with the implicit assumption at the heart of French debate that wearing a veil is a renunciation of one's autonomy, how can the covered woman's views be trusted as her own? Could the testimony of a veiled woman ever be accepted?

The Stasi Comission, convened in 2003 by Jacques Chirac to debate the proposed ban on the hijab in schools, illustrates that this lack of trust in the autonomy of veiled women's opinions persists at the highest levels. Of 150 people invited to give testimony only one (Saida Kada, founder of Activist French Muslim Women) was a veiled French Muslim woman, invited on the very last day of discussion and subjected to interrogatory and hostile questioning (Laborde 2008).

The distrust of veiled Muslim women and the threat they represented to French gender relations was further exemplified by the reaction to the New Anti-capitalist Party (NPA) fielding of Ilham Moussaid in the 2010 elections. Moussaid, who covers her hair, has described herself as 'feminist, secular, and veiled' (Guha 2010), yet her candidacy drew widespread criticism and led to an official complaint by right-wing feminist group *Ni Putes Ni Soumises* (Nether Whores Nor Submissives), who stressed that her candidacy was evidence that: 'the NPA is perverting the values of the Republic and suggesting we reread them in a manner which conforms with regressive visions of women' (Davies 2010). This statement signals how the very presence of a veiled woman in the political sphere was thought to endanger France, despite the fact that Moussaid stated continuously her commitment to feminists principles, including contraception and abortion rights, and her autonomous decision to cover her hair: 'Try as I might to explain that I am not oppressed and it shows, there is still a lack of understanding' (quoted in Davies 2010).

The dominant monolithic construction of the veil in France as a symbol of gender oppression silenced the voices of those women, like Moussaid, who claimed agency in their choice to cover some part of their body. While there is no doubt that in some societies Muslim women are subject to enforced dress codes, there is an increasingly assertive

Muslim feminist perspective in the West which claims that covering, far from being oppressive, is actually an emancipatory practice that liberates women. Veiling, for some, represents freedom. Pnina Werbner's work with veiled British Muslim women has demonstrated that through their religious observance these women have opened up a space for autonomous decision making that includes the right to work, be educated, move around un-chaperoned in public and choose their own marriage partners (Werbner 2007). Interviews with French Muslim women have similarly shown that their reasons for wearing the headscarf differed significantly from mainstream French discourse that represented it as an oppressive religio-political symbol. Young French women of Moroccan descent opposed traditional patriarchal interpretations and argued that Islam advocates equality, authorises women to work and legitimises love marriages. The veil in this context may signal both attachment to traditional Moroccan culture and an assertive Islam which granted these women greater freedom, where their Muslim identity reassured their parents (who were often worried by their daughters' French affiliation) and their practice of Islam allowed them to negotiate a greater freedom and transgress other rules (Skandrani et al. 2012).

The trajectory of Western feminism has been so entwined with the freedom to uncover that the use of a discourse of women's emancipation to underpin authoritarian practices which control (Muslim) women's bodies is considered by many to be unproblematic. The liberatory discourses of the veil put forward by Muslim women are incongruent with mainstream discursive constructions which represent it as monolithically oppressive. Based on an assumption that the only way to be liberated is to be uncovered, Muslim women who claim that sexual freedom is not the only or most important freedom a woman can have are silenced by a discourse that assures them they are deluding themselves and playing into the hands of patriarchal men. The effect of these discourses for French Muslim women who veil is, paradoxically, a restriction of their freedom. Renee Le Mignot, co-president of French NGO Against Racism and For Friendship Between Peoples, has emphasised the increased discrimination against women who wear the headscarf, including their being refused access to voting booths and driving lessons, barred from their own wedding ceremonies in town halls, ejected from university classes, and in one case prevented from withdrawing cash from her own account at a bank counter (Carland 2011). The visual symbol of the veil, believed to indicate a lack of belonging to French society, thus invited discrimination and encouraged the treatment of covered women as lesser citizens.

THE CONSTRUCTION OF EUROPEAN IDENTITY IN OPPOSITION TO ISLAM

The examples above illustrate the extent to which national identities in the post-2001 period have been constructed in opposition to an imagined Muslim identity. In each case, certain 'Western' values that were thought to encapsulate the identity of the nation were seized upon as timeless and essential characteristics and contrasted with 'Muslim values' that were oppositional and threatening. The debate about the suitability of Islamic architecture in Switzerland quickly mutated into a value-laden dispute about the place of Islam in Swiss society. Based on the notion that minarets were representative of unacceptable Islamic social models, the national virtue of tolerance was represented as being in direct competition with Muslim politico-religious power desires, and Swiss neutrality was deemed threatened by Islam's inability to relegate religion to the private sphere. Danish debates about 'The Face of Muhammad' cartoons similarly positioned a national commitment to freedom of expression in opposition to a perceived Muslim demand that their religion be respected above all else. Muslims were represented as intolerant and authoritarian, incapable of understanding the liberal concept of press freedom, and prone to violent rage when provoked. Dutch sexual diversity was also portrayed as deeply threatened by Muslims who could not shed their cultural predisposition to homophobia. The Netherlands was represented as possessing an excessive national tolerance that was endangered by Islamic intolerance and repression of sexual freedom. Finally, French debates over the right of Muslim women to cover coalesced around the threat that veiling practices were believed to pose to gender equality. The veil was constructed as symbolic of Muslim patriarchy and female oppression and thus a direct challenge to feminism and women's freedom in France. In every case, national values were represented as rational, enlightened and superior, and this hierarchical construction highlights the Eurocentric self-understanding that guided these discourses of national identity.

The internalisation of the civilised/barbaric dichotomy was central to the discursive creation of national identity for each state. This binary construction was used to designate the nation as modern, enlightened, rational and progressive, in opposition to an imagined Islam within its midst and outside its borders which was considered pre-modern, obscurantist, irrational and regressive. This bipolarity is a central construction of Eurocentrism, giving rise to identities which are deemed entirely oppositional and irreconcilable and containing a logic that demands the 'barbaric' is subsumed entirely into the 'civilised' as a condition of residence in Europe. This closing down of symbolic borders is evident in the discourses of those states which consider themselves immigration countries (France and the Netherlands), as well as traditional isolationists for whom immigration is a relatively new reality (Denmark and Switzerland).

The dominant discourses adopted worked to represent Muslims as monolithically opposed to whichever value was being nationally championed, and the superior values of the enlightened Europeans were instrumentalised as disciplinary tools in an authoritarian discourse that demanded Muslims shed their cultural impediments to modernity. The threat to Switzerland that Muslim social models were believed to pose was countered by prohibiting the construction of minarets. Danish discourse sought to protect free expression by condemning and silencing the freely expressed outrage of some Muslims. The Netherlands utilised a culturally racist discourse which considered anti-gay feeling inescapably inscribed in the mindset of anyone with a Muslim background in order to discipline actual and potential Muslim citizens. And France sought to practice gender equality by silencing and excluding from French civic culture those women who claimed that their freedom and equality could best be served by their own autonomous choice to cover whatever they saw fit.

Yet, it should be clear that these discourses did not serve only as a means of excluding Muslims to forge national cultural homogeneity. Despite the varied starting points; tolerance (Switzerland), free expression (Denmark), (homo)sexual freedom (the Netherlands), and gender equality (France) are all ostensibly progressive values that were intrinsically linked and explicitly articulated as European and Western. The national discourses did not only exclude, they also provided pivotal ideals around which European belonging could be reaffirmed. This highlights the central place of the civilised/barbaric binary. Anti-Muslim feeling in Europe has a long history, but the Islamophobia that we are now witnessing is a product of and nourishes the post-September 11, 2001 international order and the discursive constructions of the 'war on terror'. In a world that was deliberately, discursively, and self-consciously structured by the appealing Manichean logic of 'with us or against us', to be 'with' is to be civilised, enlightened, and Western. The fluid boundaries of this identity are policed and fortified by values recognised as products of the European historical trajectory. In affirming these Eurocentric values, states affirm their belonging to the 'right' side in the 'war on terror'.

The understanding of such values as inherently Western requires that they be constantly reaffirmed as such, and this was achieved through a politicisation of culture and a culturalisation of politics (Gudrun Jensen 2008; Wright 1998). Culture is politicised when social and political issues are linked to the essentialised culture of groups. This may be achieved in a negative sense, for instance by linking social problems such as 'ethnic ghettoes', low socio-economic status or crime to the culture of Muslims. It may also be positively politicised, through discourses which assert that political systems and values such as secularism, democracy and liberalism are the preserve of a particular culture. The culturalisation of politics is a process whereby this essentialised notion of cultural difference is instrumentalised in a political project which seeks to discipline those cultures perceived as antithetical. Those national projects that viewed Islam as internally problematic to the practice of Western liberal democracy employed culture as a means of exclusion. Integration tests, the coercive assimilation of Muslims through civic training and the prohibition of Muslim practices all serve as examples.

By considering political systems to be cultural artefacts, and by using culture as a political disciplinary tool to mark the boundaries of the nation, these discourses advanced a Eurocentric notion of national identity. The ideological representation of these national values as the universal and progressive standards to which all the West aspires allowed states to cultivate a civilisational sense of belonging in their affirmation of European/Western values. These Eurocentric values were also used to mark the borders of identity, policing who could and could not belong to the community by interrogating their commitment to such values, based on culturalist notions of essential difference. In this sense, they were instrumentalised to exclude individuals and groups from belonging both to the (European) value community and to the national community that predicated its identity on these values.

There is, however, a central paradox at work in projects which seek to protect the freedom of some by sacrificing the liberty of others, and this underscores the superiority intrinsic to Eurocentric ideology. The impulse to authoritarianism was revealed in each nation's attempt to work through the problems perceived to be posed by Muslims and their inassimilable and oppositional cultural identities. Despite the fact that Muslims make up a significant percentage of Europe and its nations, the integration of Islam into European and individual national identity has been disregarded in favour of projects of national cultural chauvinism. Muslim voices and opinions, it seems, are not required by those who seek to define national identity. This underscores what Haleh Ghorashi (2003, 7–9) has highlighted as the dual discourse of citizenship. Muslims are increasingly considered the passive 'unwanted Europeans', who must be coerced into acting as society dictates without being permitted input into the debate. Such practices contribute to the isolation of Muslims in Europe by refusing equal access to the shaping of national identities, and increase the perception of a cultural gulf by asserting a Eurocentrism which identifies Muslim values as oppositional, barbaric, and inferior, and therefore not worthy of discussion or integration into new European and national identities.

CONCLUSION

Matti Bunzl (2005, 502) has emphasised that the question of civilisation lies at the heart of Islamophobia, which considers Islam to have a worldview fundamentally incompatible with Western civilisation. Unlike biological racism and anti-Semitism, it functions less in the interests of national purification than as a means of fortifying Europe, by questioning whether Muslims, with their alternative civilisation and mindset, can be European at all. Each of the discourses studied in this chapter has posed the same question through the identification and reification of a particular 'European' value as sacrosanct and endangered by Muslims and their practices. These values were represented as modern, rational and superior, in contrast to traditional, irrational, and inferior Muslim values. The civilised/barbaric binary central to Eurocentric discourse thus created the conditions for discriminatory and exclusionary practices, allowing for ostensibly positive values to be instrumentalised in order to quash alternative identity conceptions that were represented as dangerous and threatening to the solidarity and cohesion of the nation.

This chapter has analysed the discursive construction of Islam as antithetical to national identity in Switzerland, Denmark, the Netherlands and France by focusing on construction moments in which Muslim identity was politicised as irreconcilably 'other' to the nation's conception of itself. In emphasising the Eurocentric assumptions that have upheld narratives of national identity, the aim has been to illustrate the discursive mechanisms through which these identities have been ideologically constructed. By demonstrating alternative positions that challenge the dominant narratives, I have attempted to de-naturalise the logic of these discourses and highlight the subjectivities that are silenced. My intention has not been to suggest that each nation considers Islam as a threat in the same way or to the same extent. Islamophobia is in each case subject to national particularities, and the varying construction moments and their accompanying discourses illustrate the extent to which different conceptions of Islam's otherness were instrumentalised. Yet noting that Islamophobia is not homogenous across Europe should not blind us to the Eurocentric suppositions that sustain these narratives of identity. As David Theo Goldberg has pointed out, Islam is viewed in the dominant European imaginary to represent a collection of lacks: of freedom, civility, and equal respect for women and gays (Goldberg 2006). In contrast, the West is considered to hold these values in abundance. The binary of Western values/Islamic values thus provides an abundance of oppositions from which to cherry pick in times of identity crisis and a bounty of discourses which may be instrumentalised to discipline and exclude those who are considered to occupy the inferior side of this civilisational border.

When Anders Behring Breivik attempted in July 2011 to 'start a revolution' in Europe, he was drawing upon the very same conceptions of identity that have been discussed in this chapter. Viewing his actions as the precursor to a long war which would wrest the very soul of European civilisation from the clutches of Muslims, his justifications employed an identical civilised/barbaric binary that viewed Western society as existentially endangered by the presence of Islam. Breivik's actions should caution us to the dangers of stark binaries that essentialise culture and employ it as a coercive tool in projects of national hegemony. His violent solution to the problem perceived to be posed by Muslims in Europe is only the extreme end of a spectrum of exclusionary and discriminatory practices made possible by Eurocentric discourse.

REFERENCES

Belien, Paul. 2005. Europe Criticises Copenhagen Over Cartoons. *The Brussels Journal.* http://www.brusselsjournal.com/node/589 Retrieved 25 Oct 2012.

Bracke, S. 2012. From 'Saving Women' to 'Saving Gays': Rescue Narratives and Their Dis/continuities. *European Journal of Women's Studies* 19 (2): 237–252.

Brun, Ellen, and Jacques Hersh. 2008. The Danish Disease: A Political Culture of Islamophobia. *Monthly Review.*

Bunzl, Matti. 2005. Between Anti-Semitism and Islamophobia: Some Thoughts on the New Europe. *American Ethnologist* 32 (4): 499–508.

Butler, Judith. 2008. Sexual Politics, Torture, and Secular Time. *The British Journal of Sociology* 59 (1): 1–23.

Carland, Susan. 2011. Islamophobia, Fear of Loss of Freedom, and the Muslim Woman. *Islam and Christian-Muslim Relations* 22 (4): 469–473.

Davies, Lizzy. 2010. Election Candidate in Headscarf Causes Uproar in France. *The Guardian.* http://www.guardian.co.uk/world/2010/feb/10/french-election-headscarf-candidate. Retrieved 5 Oct 2012.

De Cillia, R., M. Reisigl, and R. Wodak. 1999. The Discursive Construction of National Identities. *Discourse & Society* 10 (2): 149–173.

Dolezal, Martin, Marc Helbling, and Swen Hutter. 2010. Debating Islam in Austria, Germany and Switzerland: Ethnic Citizenship, Church-State Relations and Right-Wing Populism. *West European Politics* 33 (2): 171–190.

Engelbreth Larson, Rune. 2006. The Cartoon Crisis and Danish Islamophobia. *Panhumanism.* http://www.panhumanism.com/articles/2006-02.php. Retrieved 25 Oct 2012.

Ettinger, Patrik. 2008. Problematisation of Muslims in Public Communication in Switzerland. In *Conference: Representing Islam, Comparative Perspectives.* University of Zurich. Zurich. www.foeg.uzh.ch/analyse/publikationen/Problematisierung_Muslime.pdf. Retrieved 2 Sep 2012.

Fekete, L. 2006. Enlightened Fundamentalism? Immigration, Feminism and the Right. *Race & Class* 48 (2): 1–22.

Geisser, Vincent. 2010. Islamophobia: A 'French Specificity' in Europe? *Human Architecture* VIII (2): 39–46.

Ghorashi, Halleh. 2003. Ayaan Hirsi Ali: Daring or Dogmatic? Debates on Multiculturalism and Emancipation in the Netherlands. In *Multiple Identifications and the Self,* ed. Toon an Meijl and Henk Driessen, 163–172. Utrecht: Stinchting Focasl.

Goldberg, David Theo. 2006. Racial Europeanization. *Ethnic and Racial Studies* 29 (2): 331–364.

Gudrun Jensen, Tina. 2008. To Be 'Danish', Becoming 'Muslim': Contestations of National Identity? *Journal of Ethnic and Migration Studies* 34 (3): 389–409.

Guha, Keshava. 2010. Gauche Politics: Radical Leftism Resurges in France. *Harvard International Review.* Spring: 9–10.

Hylarides, Peter C. 2005. Multiculturalism in the Netherlands and the Murder of Theo van Gogh. *Contemporary Review* 286 (1669): 73–78.

Institute of Race Relations. 2010. The Swiss Referendum on Minarets: Background and Aftermath. Briefing Paper No. 1 February 2010. http://www.irr.org.uk/pdf2/ERA_BriefingPaper1.pdf Retrieved 29 March 2013.

Kilde, Jeanne Halgren. 2011. The Park 51/Ground Zero Controversy and Sacred Sites as Contested Space. *Religions* 2 (3): 297–311.

Kublitz, Anja. 2010. The Cartoon Controversy: Creating Muslims in a Danish Setting. *Social Analysis* 54 (3): 107–125.

Laborde, Cécile. 2008. *Critical Republicanism: The Hijab Controversy and Political Philosophy.* Oxford: Oxford University Press.

Malek, Alia. 2007. Beyond the Cartoon Controversy. *Columbia Journalism Review* 45 (6): 18–19.

Mancini, Susanna. 2012. Patriarchy as the Exclusive Domain of the Other: The Veil Controversy, False Projection and Cultural Racism. *International Journal of Constitutional Law* 10 (2): 411–428.

Mason, Simon J A, Abbas Aroua, and Annika Åberg. 2010. Mediating Tensions over Islam in Denmark, Holland, and Switzerland. *Center for Security Studies, ETH Zurich and Cordoba Foundation, Geneva Center for Security Studies (CSS) Swiss Federal Institute of Technology.* http://129.132.199.42/var/ssn/storage/original/application/f4900bb611904ea6ef86caf1a507da38.pdf Retrieved 2 Sept 2012.

Matyassy, Johannes, and Seraina Flury. 2011. *Challenges for Switzerland's Public Diplomacy: Referendum on Banning Minarets.* Los Angeles: Figueroa Press. http://uscpublicdiplomacy.org/sites/uscpublicdiplomacy.org/files/legacy/publications/perspectives/CPDPerspectives_P4_2011.pdf. Retrieved 2 Sep 2012.

Mepschen, P., J.W. Duyvendak, and E.H. Tonkens. 2010. Sexual Politics, Orientalism and Multicultural Citizenship in the Netherlands. *Sociology* 44 (5): 962–979.

Mepschen, Paul. 2009. Against Tolerance: Islam, Sexuality, and the Politics of Belonging in the Netherlands. *Monthly Review.* http://mrzine.monthlyreview.org/2009/mepschen130709.htm. Retrieved 9 Jan 2012.

Ministry of Education Culture and Science. 2007. Simply Gay: Dutch Government's LGBT Policy Document 2008–2011. *The Council for Global Equality.* http://www.globalequality.org/storage/documents/pdf/simply-gay_dutchlgbtpolicy.pdf. Retrieved 16 Oct 2012.

Orlanskaya, Olga, and Gunther G Schulze. 2010. The Determinants of Islamophobia—An Empirical Analysis of the Swiss Minaret Referndum, 1–31.

http://crem.univ-rennes1.fr/EPCS11/submissions/epcs2011_submission_256. pdf. Retrieved 18 June 2011.

Puar, Jasbir K., and Terrorist Assemblages. 2007. *Homonationalism in Queer Times*. Durham, N.C.: Duke University Press.

Skandrani, S.M., O. Taieb, and Marie Rose Moro. 2012. Transnational Practices, Intergenerational Relations and Identity Construction in a Migratory Context: The Case of Young Women of Maghrebine Origin in France. *Culture & Psychology* 18 (1): 76–98.

Traynor, Ian. 2009. Swiss to Vote on Mosque Minarets Ban. *The Guardian*. http://www.guardian.co.uk/world/2009/nov/26/swiss-mosques-minarets-ban-vote. Retrieved 24 Oct 2012.

Triandafyllidou, Anna. 1998. National Identity and the 'Other'. *Ethnic and Racial Studies* 21 (4): 593–612.

Werbner, Pnina. 2007. Veiled Interventions in Pure Space: Honour, Shame and Embodied Struggles among Muslims in Britain and France. *Theory, Culture & Society* 24 (2): 161–186.

Wright, Susan. 1998. The Politicization of 'Culture'. *Anthropology Today* 14 (1): 7–15.

CHAPTER 6

Eurocentric Islamophobia

INTRODUCTION

All of the discourses explored in this book have in common the cultural problematisation of Muslims. This can be understood as the central organising principle that holds together the diverse enunciations and practices that fall under the rubric of Islamophobic discourse. The previous chapters have sought to demonstrate how Islamophobia functions as a culturally racist discourse, by problematising Muslim culture and with ideological effects that disadvantage Muslims and advantage non-Muslims. The present chapter aims to understand why this discourse has such salience at the present historical moment and how it serves those who employ it.

Understanding Islamophobia as cultural racism implies that there is more going on than merely a prejudicial stance against Muslims. As an ideology, racism (in whatever form it may take at any given historical moment) performs particular functions for those employing its discourse and practices. Islamophobia is no exception, and the functions it performs are related to an understanding of (culturally) racialised space. Whether it appears at the local, national or international level, Islamophobia emerges from a cultural anxiety generated by the notion that previously Western spaces are being undermined by the presence of Muslims. Those who employ this discourse consider that their previously special relationship with a particular territory is now under strain because of Muslim presence, and they use Islamophobia as a means of regaining

© The Author(s) 2018
L.B. Jackson, *Islamophobia in Britain*,
DOI 10.1007/978-3-319-58350-1_6

control over the objects (Muslims) which block their identity as Western subjects.

In his 2000 book *White nation: Fantasies of white supremacy in a multicultural society*, Ghassan Hage explored this territory in relation to nationalism, arguing that both those considered 'racist' and those considered 'multiculturalist' share in common the conviction that they are masters of the national space and it is up to them to decide who stays and who ought to be kept out of that space. Hage argued that this is a fantasy of white supremacy, the belief in white mastery over the nation and the conception that ethnic minorities are merely national objects to be moved or removed according to white national will. This understanding of race relations as an expression of nationalism centres the notion of territorial power as a motivating ideology.

Although he discussed Muslims as 'ethnic others' within the nation, Hage's specific focus was on racist practices and how they are better conceptualised as nationalist practices. I wish to extend this theoretical position specifically in relation to Islamophobia and in doing so I argue that something greater than national identity is at stake. While nationalist practices do inform many Islamophobic discourses, a larger understanding is at work that situates local and national expressions of Islamophobia in a more global context. Islamophobia entails not only the understanding that Muslims block the special relationship between locals and their localities, nationals and their nation, but also the idea that Muslims' existence within the West problematises the privileged relationship between Westerners and the imagined *civilisational* space of the West.

This global dimension of Islamophobia can be understood as an expression of resurgent Eurocentrism, which aims to reconstitute threatened spaces through a subject/object dichotomy in which Western subjects are positioned as the legitimate cultural managers of local, national and global territories, while Muslims are constructed as objects whose presence changes or contaminates the fantasised ideal spaces appealed to.

The present chapter first considers the spatial dimension of Islamophobia, before going on to analyse how the Muslim undesirable is constructed within this discourse as spatially threatening to particular territories. Islamophobia operates as a discourse of control that works to put Muslims in their place as local, national and civilisational objects to be directed by subjects whose claims on the territories in question are considered greater. Both exclusionary and ostensibly inclusive discourses draw upon the articulation of spatial dominance, and it is in this sense that Islamophobia can be best understood as Eurocentrism. Through the assertion that Western values are superior and the demand that Muslims integrate into them, Islamophobia provides its adherents with a means of reconstituting their privileged relationship with the territories that Muslims are believed to threaten.

THE SPATIAL DIMENSION OF ISLAMOPHOBIA

They talk of integration, but they are the ones not wanting to integrate, they alone wish to take over! They believe their religion is the best and refuse to accept other religions, so why should we allow the Muslim community to trample all over our historic market town of Dudley? (Letter to the Editor, Dudley News, 2 February 2007)

Islam is not just a religious system, but a political and social ideology that seeks to dominate all non-believers and impose a harsh legal system that rejects democratic accountability and human rights. It runs counter to all that we hold dear within our British liberal democracy... (EDL 2011d)

For the first time in a generation there is an unease, an anxiety, even at points a resentment that our very openness, our willingness to welcome difference, our pride in being home to many cultures, is being used against us; abused, indeed, in order to harm us. (Blair 2006)

The quotes above are taken from radically different sites, enunciate very different perspectives, and have different purposes. The first is a letter to the Editor in the local newspaper *Dudley News*, the second is from the English Defence League's Mission Statement, and the third is from Prime Minister Tony Blair's speech, *A duty to integrate*, which discussed integration in the context of the 7 July 2005 London bombings. What the three have in common is an understanding of a space of values and heritage that is threatened by the presence of Muslims, and a shared conviction among these diverse speakers that they have the right to decide the values of the spaces they seek to protect. It is this spatial dimension of Islamophobia that I wish to explore.

In each of the above statements the word 'our' was used to denote a relationship that the speaker felt he or she had with a given territory. Whether local, for the *Dudley News* correspondent, or national, for the EDL and Blair, this territory was considered in some way endangered by Muslims. In each case Muslims were presented as destructive (trampling over our history, dominating non-believers, harming us) and antagonistic (refusing to accept other religions, rejecting British liberal democracy, exploiting our openness to other cultures). For each of these speakers, Muslims occupy the position of 'the undesirable'.

Constructed as undesirables, Islamophobic discourse represents Muslims as blocking the relationship between speakers and the territories imagined as theirs. Each appealed to a fantasy space rife with positive attributes (a historic market town, a dearly held British liberal democracy, a nation that is an open and welcoming haven for all cultures)—spaces which had, in the past, been infused with positive ideals, but whose goodness was now endangered by a Muslim presence that threatened the continued achievement of these ideals. The above examples also underscore the proprietal relationship that speakers believe they have with the space to which they refer. By employing a discourse which fantasised a space once infused with positivity, now threatened by Muslim presence, each speaker claimed some sort of special relationship with that space, which justified his or her perceived right to decide what it should be like.

Islamophobic discourse implicitly understands some relationships with a particular territory to be more legitimate than others—specifically it understands that Muslims have fewer rights over local and national spaces in Britain than non-Muslims. This can be understood as a form of spatial dominance, in which those non-Muslims who employ Islamophobic discourse believe that they have managerial rights over a territory; a feeling of entitlement to decide what this territory should be like, who belongs there and who should be removed.

The Muslim Undesirable

This conceptualisation of Islamophobia as a response to perceived spatial threat foregrounds its function, allowing us to understand its usefulness to those employing it. But why are Muslims considered to pose such a problem to the spaces in question?

Part of the answer to this question lies in the fact that it is not individual Muslims who are considered to be so threatening. Rather, anxiety is caused by the perception of a large Muslim minority with an identical Muslim cultural will. Appreciating the culturally racist aspects of Islamophobia is essential to understanding why Muslims are considered to be the group that frustrates the realisation of the ideal territory imagined by those employing this ideological frame.

There is widespread agreement that there has been a transformation in racist discourse since the end of the Second World War, from overtly biological understandings of race to a focus on culture (Balibar 2007; Durrheim and Dixon 2000). Cultural racism employs many of the tropes of biological racism but averts its attention from race, blood and biology, to focus instead on the cultural heritage of groups and individuals. Although race is rarely mentioned, the essentialisation of culture in such discourse performs the same function. The focus on the deterministic and inescapable culture of a group in terms of beliefs, habits, behaviours and values institutes a hierarchical understanding, within which individuals are naturalised as subjects of superior or inferior cultures which regulate their abilities, attributes and psychology. Islamophobic discourse asserts that a Western subject, socialised within a cultural form that cherishes freedom, equality and liberalism, has imbibed Western values into his or her very being. Conversely, Muslim subjects, socialised within a culture of inferior Islamic values (submission to Allah above all else, clinging to pre-modern traditions and values) are unable to move beyond the strictures of Islamic thought. From the perspective of cultural racism, Muslims will always revert to Islam as the guide for their thought processes and behaviour.

As the previous chapters have demonstrated, the essentialisation of Muslim culture as a driver of behaviour is what makes up the fundamental nature of Islamophobia. Yet, as Hage points out, one can believe that certain groups are essentially different, even inferior, and not act upon this belief (Hage 2000, 32). The imperative for action within the ideological world of Islamophobia comes not from an understanding that Muslims are radically different, but from an understanding that their presence is undesirable and harmful to the wellbeing of non-Muslims. If one understands Muslim culture as being determining, then it does not necessarily follow that individual Muslims are particularly problematic. The problematisation of Muslims comes about when their group presence is seen to threaten the way that things are, based on the perception that Muslim will is widespread, unified, and antagonistic. If Muslims are understood to exercise an Islamic will, then the greater the number of Muslims in a particular territory, the more anxiety will be generated by the possibility that there exists a potential bloc of culturally determined Muslims that may alter the territory to their advantage and to the disadvantage of non-Muslims.

The construction of Muslims as undesirables within Islamophobic discourse always involves a cultural anxiety. This anxiety is not necessarily caused by the belief that Muslims are radically different or inferior, which can exist independently of the need to vocalise or act upon such a belief. Rather, it is the fear that Muslims might change who we are, or the space in which we live, that forms an imperative for Islamophobic acts of discursive or physical exclusion.

The Dudley mosque debates serve to illustrate this point. The mosque caused such anxiety in Dudley not because it represented any real threat to Dudley itself, but because of how it symbolically represented the changing face of the locality. The anxiety of those locals who petitioned *Dudley News* with their views about the undesirability of the mosque was saturated with symbolism, and the idea that the mosque represented was more worrying than its actual existence. This is why a central debate at the time concerned the size of the minaret and fears that it would be higher than the spire of the Church of St Thomas. Local people saw in the mosque Muslim will and ability to transform the landscape, and considered the preservation of Dudley as it is was preferable to the economic investment that the mosque complex would have generated. The maintenance of a privileged cultural relationship with Dudley led those opposed to the mosque to act against their own local economic interests, preferring to stem Muslim cultural will in order to preserve these privileged relationships at the expense of a better economic future for the area. When not exercising a specifically Islamic cultural will, Muslims are not considered dangerous or threatening. It was the possibility that Muslims would change the locality, and by consequence, the locals, that drove the anxiety witnessed during the Dudley mosque controversy.

This fear that the local or national landscape may be changed also helps to explain why Muslims are so relentlessly focused upon. If, as I have argued, Islamophobia is cultural racism, and therefore has the potential to be applied to any culture considered drastically different, then why does Islamophobia have such appeal at the present historical moment? If the terrain of exclusion centres on values, why are Muslims singled out as such a threat, as opposed to other cultural or religious minorities such as Hindus or Sikhs?

The typical answer offered to this question is that Muslims are more culturally antagonistic than other minority groups. In order to unpack this claim, it is useful to consider the example of British Sikhs. Many of the claims made of Muslim culture could be extended to Sikh culture.

British Sikhs are clustered in certain residential areas in much the same way that British Muslims are, due to the racialised housing policies which segregated immigrant groups during the mid-twentieth century. There is a strong symbolic difference between Sikhs and non-Sikhs, manifested in styles of dress, such as covering the hair, the bangle, and the carrying of the *kirpan*, as well as observation of festivals and religiously forbidden activities such as eating meat and eggs. In addition, cultural issues that affect the South Asian population more generally, such as forced and arranged marriages, 'honour' killings, and the status of women, are potentially equally applicable to Sikhs. Many of the issues that are believed to signal Muslim difference and supposed Muslim inassimilability are directly analogous to the Sikh population of Britain. Why then are Sikhs not considered dangerous in the same way? Why is Sikh difference containable?

I venture that the answer to this question lies in the relative power of Sikhs, both within the UK and in the world. Sikhs are considered a containable minority precisely because they are a small minority, while in contrast Islam is experiencing both national and global resurgence. Muslims are considered dangerous not because of something inherently antagonistic about Muslim culture, but because they are considered actually or potentially powerful, and since Muslims are consistently the group which is worse off in almost all national indicators of multiple deprivation (Peach 2006, 648), their perceived power must lie in their numbers. The anxiety that drives Islamophobia is caused by the perception of a demographically increasing Muslim population and a unified Muslim cultural will, and it is this sense that 'we' have lost, or are about to lose, control that feeds the apocalyptic fantasies of individuals like Anders Breivik and groups such as the EDL and Stop the Islamization of Europe (SIOE) (Buuren 2013). The standard counter argument to these claims is that the Sikh community, in Britain and the world, do not pose a terrorist threat. Contrary to this position, there is ample evidence that Sikh militant movements operate from Western states in a transnational capacity (see, for example Razavy 2006). However, the fact that Sikh terrorism exists does not adequately answer this criticism. When individuals explain their discomfort with Muslims because of terrorism they are essentialising Muslim culture as predisposed to violent extremism, and rationalising the general distrust of Muslims because of the actions of some. This argument is only structurally sound within the context of essentialised cultural racism, where Muslim culture is believed to justify, or in some way incline individuals to, acts of terrorism.

The Discursive Reconstitution of Privileged Spaces

My argument so far has emphasised the spatial dimension of Islamophobia, illustrating how the discourse articulates privileged spaces which are considered under threat from Muslim undesirables who do not or will not recognise the specifically non-Muslim character of these spaces. Islamophobia operates as a discourse of control to rearticulate these spaces as closed to cultural change by Muslims, through both exclusionary and inclusive discourses that reemphasise the incontrovertible (non-Muslim) values of a particular territory. The following section aims to explain why speakers who employ this discourse attempt to control Muslims. If Islamophobia is understood as a discourse of control, then to what end is it used?

Islamophobic discourse works to reconstitute the imagined privileged relationship that those employing this discourse believe they have with a particular territory. Islamophobia is thus not just a means of controlling Muslims, but a means of reinstating spatial dominance. It is a discourse that works to restore the fantasised authority of non-Muslims over Muslims in spaces imagined as theirs.

Ghassan Hage conceptualises this operation within nationalist practice as the white nation fantasy, in which immigrants or 'third world looking people' are relegated to the position of national object through a problematisation of their presence. Hage argues that the integration debate performs a socio-anthropological function for those who subscribe to this fantasy, giving them the illusion of power to decide the make-up of the nation and positioning them in a supervisory role with the capability to decide how much and what type of integration is desirable. At a time when widespread cynicism with electoral politics leaves individuals feeling powerless to change national policy through the political process, the immigration and multiculturalism debates become a ritualised alternative. The impotence of conventional political engagement is alleviated through the institutionalised form of the integration debates, and provides ordinary white people with a means of reproducing their sense of control over the nation and its destiny (Hage 2000, 240–241).

Islamophobia accomplishes a similar function by giving non-Muslims the illusion of control over local, national and civilisational spaces. By problematising Muslims as endangering privileged relationships with particular territories, Islamophobia provides its adherents with a discursive means of reconstituting that fractured relationship. The following section explores in greater detail the means by which speakers employ both exclusionary and inclusive Islamophobic discourse for the purpose of reconstructing privileged relationships, and how the local, national and civilisational levels interplay in this ideological operation.

RECONSTITUTING PRIVILEGED SPACES: EXCLUSIONARY ISLAMOPHOBIA

Exclusionary Islamophobia at the Local Level

The ideology of Islamophobia problematises its targets culturally, and for that reason it may be equally articulated to local, national and international/civilisational contexts. Through the identification of Muslims as the problematic objects that prevent an idealised space being the way it should be, Islamophobic discourse attempts to restore the (fantasised) authority of non-Muslims to remake that space discursively and decide its values and culture. For this reason, the local, national and civilisational levels within Islamophobic discourse are heavily intertwined. Privileged relationships with local spaces often include articulations of the ideal nation, as well as a civilisational understanding of where that nation, and the locality in question, belongs. In letters to the Editor of *Dudley News*, correspondents tied the construction of the mosque to the destruction not just of Dudley's culture and heritage, but of English culture more generally, reminding readers of the industrial past of the town and the sacrifices made by working-class ancestors who built the town through their back-breaking labour. Through the appeal to homely imagery, heritage, tradition and an idealised past, speakers connected local landscapes to treasured national ideals. Muslims were constructed within this fantasy as the significant other whose presence and demands effectively dismantled dearly held traditions and blocked the achievement of the imagined and idealised local and national space.

Such utterances illustrate more than merely a fear of change. In their appeals to almost apocalyptic fantasies, speakers expressed a profound dread of Muslim presence and symbols, based on an overinflated and exaggerated understanding of Muslim power. The fear was not change itself, but reflected a deep anxiety that Muslim power had the potential to reverse traditional dominance, to the detriment of the traditionally dominant. The consistent reiteration that Muslim power must not be left unchecked underscores the notion that there are natural managers of particular spaces who are *able* to check this power, and must do so before roles are reversed. It is the naturalness of this managerial cultural position that is perceived as threatened by Muslim demands.

Appeals to Dudley culture and tradition must be seen through this lens if we are to understand why Islamophobia has such sway at this moment in time. When speakers appealed to the heritage of Dudley, therein lay an understanding that this history was implicitly not Muslim. As 'natural Dudleians', correspondents exercised local cultural capital, a construction that pivoted on their attempts to situate themselves as the bearers of Dudley's past and the legitimate owners of its future. Islamophobic discourse was a means by which to make a claim of ownership on the local landscape, and served to legitimise the speaker's claims to represent Dudley. The discussions of Dudley's past were more than an idealised history of monolithic Dudley culture. They were a claim to the right to have an opinion on the cultural landscape of Dudley that only those who believed themselves to be the legitimate bearers of its culture felt able to make.

This certainty that the future is bleak and Muslim-dominated ties into the fear that time is running out, present in Islamophobic discourse in an almost hysterical manner. At its core this anxiety is related to a belief in the ability to stem the tide of Muslim power, believed to be increasing as Muslims make more and more culturally specific demands. As one correspondent to Dudley News stated, 'I seriously think if this mosque goes ahead it's the beginning of the end of our identity as a Christian country... *Like-minded people should get together before it's too late*' (Letter to the Editor, *Dudley News*, 2 October 2006) (Emphasis added). The narrative that time is running out rests on the notion that control is being lost by the natural managers of a privileged local space, and also acts as a call to action before the positions of dominance are unalterably reversed. In the demand to do something 'before it's too late' lies the fantasy of cultural power to stem the tide of role reversal. It is a fantasy because it bestows an illusory power on to the imagined, culturally coherent, 'real' Dudleians. The Islamophobic discourse of the Dudley mosque debate attempted to resolve the identity crisis of those who employed it by restoring imagined power over the cultural landscape of the locality.

The above demonstrates how correspondents to Dudley News understood the town as part of a larger conglomerate, and the fate of the mosque as tied to larger, and more important, questions of identity. Dudley was understood not just as part of the Black Country or Britain, but also as a European town, and thus rightfully heir to the cultural heritage of the West. This helps to explain why correspondents drew upon civilisational discourse, which constructed Dudley's Muslims as part of a threatening and dangerous global Islamic community and represented mosques as inexorably linked with terrorism and disorder. This discourse functioned not only to present an apparently rational opposition to the mosque's construction, but also provided a broader psychological resolution to the identity crisis brought about by the perception that power relations were being redrawn. Dudley's natural Western belonging enabled correspondents to invoke all the positive attributes (of freedom, civilisation, modernity, progress, and superiority) attached to Western identity and claim it for the locality.

This exercise in civilisational capital accumulation is particularly important for individuals who are not perceived to 'naturally' belong to the spaces in question. For those whose skin colour or background marks them out as having been born or descended from the non-West, belonging is not natural and unquestioned but something that must be accrued and articulated (Riley 2009, 60). One way of doing this is to draw a line between oneself and the undesirable, exemplified in the letter from Mrs Kaur, who stated her Sikh heritage before exclaiming the beauty of England and the aesthetic challenge posed by 'these hideous buildings'. Staking her place in the local community by repeating the dominant discourses that had come to form the ideological representation of the proposed mosque, she asserted that Muslims only wanted power over Dudley, England and indeed the world, ending her letter on a plea to her fellow locals to do something before it was too late: 'We want to keep Dudley, not change its name and culture to Islamabad. Wake up Dudley, don't let this happen' (Letter to the Editor, *Dudley News*, 22 February 2007). This rhetorical strategy demonstrates how local, national and civilisational capital was accumulated by individuals whose belonging may have been in question. The correspondent distinguished herself from Muslims by invoking their problematic presence in Dudley, England and the world. Since her Sikh heritage meant that belonging was not auto-matic, she employed Islamophobic discourse to entrench her own posi-tion on the right side of the West/Islam divide and stake her own claim to Western belonging.

Islamophobic discourse always appeals to larger narratives in order to reconstitute a privileged civilisational place for its adherents. The Dudley mosque debate amply demonstrated that the construction of Muslims as possessing a unified cultural will has consequences beyond an abstract understanding of the dangerous 'Islamic world'. Dudley's Muslims were punished for the crimes of their fellow religious adherents, held to account as subjects of a backward religion and viewed as furthering the most apocalyptic of agendas.

The fear of being dominated by Muslims, consistently articulated during the Dudley mosque debate, is a central trope of exclusionary Islamophobia. Why were correspondents so afraid that the construc-tion of a mosque would result in the Muslim domination of Dudley? It is easy to dismiss these anxieties as exaggerated paranoia and fear of change, but this fails to grasp the underlying crisis of dominance that Islamophobia expresses. The anxiety communicated by this trope is that existing patterns of 'natural' dominance in particular spaces will be imminently reversed, and non-Muslims will soon be dominated by an alien faith. This worry expresses both an understanding that relations of domination and subordination are the natural order of things, and the profound dread that if Muslims are emerging from the position of subordination, non-Muslims will soon occupy that position.

The various expressions of Islamophobia during the Dudley mosque debate may be viewed as an hegemonic articulation of Eurocentrism, an attempt to close the gap being opened up by Muslims who were per-ceived as not merely demanding cultural recognition from the tradition-ally dominant, but also claiming an *equal* right to a stake in the cultural values of Dudley. The identity crisis brought about by the expression of Muslim subjectivity was resolved through Islamophobia, a discursive means to reconquer the territory in question and restore to dominance the cultural will of Dudley's 'natural' managers at the same time as pro-viding a means by which the latter could bolster their claim to authority by accumulating local, national and civilisational capital.

Exclusionary Islamophobia at the National Level

Just as the discourse of the Dudley mosque debate employed Eurocentric understandings to rebuff Muslim requests for cultural recognition and reposition subjects in their 'natural' positions, so the English Defence League articulated its Islamophobia according to the same mental model. Although the EDL's stark reductionism meant that almost every Muslim-related issue was considered illustrative of widespread 'Islamic extremism', the group merged local, national and international spaces in the same way as the correspondents to *Dudley News*, and claimed these spaces as rightfully belonging to non-Muslim cultural custodians.

The English Defence League took a special interest in the case of the proposed mosque in Dudley, holding three protests in the town and publishing several articles in *EDL News*. Discussing Dudley council's rejection of the full plans for the mosque in September 2011, *EDL News* stated that the decision sent a clear message to Islam in Britain, that 'we will not be dictated to by a minority with an agenda to destroy us culturally and we will not allow you to destroy the architectural style and heritage of this country with Arabic monstrosities' (EDL 2011c). In this way the group was able to position Muslims as agents of destruction; of British culture, national heritage and even the architectural style of the country. Through such representations, the EDL appealed to homely imagery and deeply held national traditions, understood as threatened by Muslim demands.

Yet, again, a deeper anxiety runs through this extract. The EDL feared being 'dictated to' by Muslims in their own country. Muslims were identified as an antagonistic out-group within a mental model that understood Muslim power to be generally increasing. The council's decision was seen as so important by the EDL because it represented the claiming back of this power from Muslims, and a restoration of the natural dominance of non-Muslims. The refusal of planning permission by the council for a second time had a symbolic meaning for the group, sending a clear message to Islam in Britain and having importance beyond the confines of the locality in which the mosque would have been built. Rejection of the mosque was understood in an ideological universe in which any and every obstruction of Muslim demands was considered a victory for non-Muslims.

This construction of Muslims and non-Muslims as inevitably locked in a battle for power and control of local, national and international space explains the EDL's constant reductionism of all Muslim action to the ideology of 'Islamic extremism'. From this perspective the EDL constantly reiterate that Islam was engaged in a global battle for supremacy. The same article asserted that Dudley's Muslims were merely continuing a long tradition of Muslim domination, invoking historical examples to claim that Islam had sought to replace and eradicate every culture it came into contact with. The fear of being dominated could hardly be articulated more bluntly. Tying up local, national and international space, EDL Islamophobia understood all Muslim action as reducible to 'Islamic extremist' ideology that sought nothing but power. The invocation of historical examples to illustrate the contention that Muslims seek only the eradication of other cultures served to represent Muslims as irreducibly backward, the living enactors of a historical tradition that the West had turned away from. By representing Islam as unchanged over centuries, modern Muslims were presented as similarly intent on domination. Every appeal for recognition or Islamic facilities was viewed through this prism as an attempt by Muslims to stake cultural power and wrest control of a territory that was not rightfully theirs.

For the EDL, as for the correspondents to *Dudley News*, local, national and international spaces were represented as culturally endangered because of Muslim presence. At the same time, these discourses betrayed a conviction that these spaces belonged to someone. They were all considered naturally and rightfully 'ours', and thus any effort by 'them' to alter these spaces endangered the natural order. Discussing the reasons for a planned demonstration in Birmingham in October 2011, the EDL stated that Birmingham's future should be of concern to the whole nation since the growth of 'radical Islam' in the country's second city would be felt nationwide. The article went on to explain that, although Western foreign policy in the Middle East may have had some impact on the growth of radicalism, 'that is not to say that we are responsible for the emergence of Islamic terrorists or Islamists. The primary cause is right in front of us. It's simple. It's what Islamic terrorists and Islamists have in common. That's right, it begins with an I' (EDL 2011b).

As the EDL amply demonstrate, Islamophobic discourse relies on an understanding that the rightful managers of particular spaces are losing control, or have perhaps already lost it. When the group reminded their readers that they should care about the future of Birmingham, they meshed local, national and international space by explicitly positioning Muslims as the main challengers and contenders to these spaces. Since Islam, rather than politics ('Western' foreign policy), lay at the root of violence, the EDL contended that Islam had to be challenged locally, nationally and internationally. But the implication underlying this ideological position, and the central strand running through all Islamophobic articulations, is that these spaces must be defended because they belong to 'us'.

One final example serves to illustrate how the EDL linked local, national and global levels through an Islamophobic understanding of Muslims as essentially one-dimensional and dangerous to all of these spaces. In response to Birmingham City Council's petitions to the Home Secretary to ban the planned EDL protest, *EDL News* likened the attempt to Islamist crackdown on 'Arab Spring' protests in Egypt, claiming that the council was attempting to limit the natural rights of English people:

> Birmingham council, which appears to be run by Muslims and its dhimmi supporters in the Labour Party, have laid down a challenge to the rule of law, the rights of free Englishmen and the people of Great Britain. It's a challenge the EDL are happy to embrace. The EDL will pick up the torch of Freedom and Free speech (EDL 2011a).

By focusing on the deterioration of democratic hopes in Egypt following the revolution, the EDL were able to imply that there was something inherently Islamic in the limiting of free speech and the right to protest. Birmingham council's attempts to have the EDL demonstration banned were then held up as an example of the same *Islamic* drive to silence criticism and undermine rights, presented as a challenge to the nation and the 'rights of free Englishmen'. Islam's global anti-democratic impulse was thus presented as prevailing within Birmingham council. Through this merging of local, national and international space, the EDL presented Birmingham as cracking down on democratic rights *in the same way* as Muslims in Egypt, and since elected representatives ('dhimmi supporters in the Labour party') could not be trusted to defend these rights, the task fell to the EDL.

Because the EDL believes that Islam is an ideological phenomenon, the group sees 'Islamic extremists' wherever it sees Muslims. It follows from this that Muslims are thought to be centrally driven by the desire for cultural domination in each and every space they inhabit. The EDL thus understands itself through this ideological lens as the group which can and must take back control, and, by taking up the torch of freedom, restore dominance to the rightfully dominant. But though its focus and agenda is undoubtedly nationalistic, it relies on the blending of local, national and international levels as spaces which are all being culturally colonised by Muslims.

What drives this discourse and the ideology behind it is the assertion that this is not the way it *should* be. For the EDL, as with other proponents of Islamophobic discourse, these spaces justly belong to non-Muslim cultural managers. The implicit understanding running through such discourse is that rightful cultural managers are 'Westernised', if not explicitly 'Western', and that being 'Westernised' means holding to a particularly Eurocentric cultural superiority. As the EDL, along with other signatories to the 'European Defence Leagues Memorandum of Understanding', stated: 'we must not be afraid to say what should be obvious to all: Our way is better. Not different, better'(EDL 2011e).

RECONSTITUTING PRIVILEGED SPACES: INCLUSIVE ISLAMOPHOBIA

The exclusionary discourses outlined above operate as a means of regaining control over spaces believed to be threatened by the presence of Muslims. This space may be interpreted as physically threatened by Muslims who represent a violent extremist threat, or it may be culturally threatened by Muslims who are believed to be culturally colonising and changing it beyond recognition. However, as I have argued, it is not change itself that is feared. Rather, it is the formerly privileged and now endangered relationship with that space that drives Islamophobic discourse and practice. Islamophobia's imperative for action is based on the attempt to reconstitute this privileged relationship—it is a means of reaffirming the right to be a spatial manager and have a legitimate opinion on that territory's future.

Exclusionary discourses operate to inhibit Muslims in the public sphere, for example by preventing the construction of Dudley mosque, or through EDL intimidation. By impeding Muslim action in this way, proponents of exclusionary Islamophobia reclaimed local, national and civilisational territories as their own, and psychologically reconstituted an imagined privileged relationship with these territories. Yet, if

Islamophobia were made up only of exclusionary discourse and practice, it would not be so effective an ideology. Part of the reason Islamophobia is such a widespread contemporary phenomenon is that it exists not only as bigotry and intolerance, but also takes an apparently rational and reasonable form that may be termed inclusive Islamophobia.

The good/bad Muslim dualism is central to inclusive Islamophobia. Inclusive discourses insist that 'good' Muslims outnumber the 'bad', they demand that the 'moderates' stand up to their 'extremist' co-religionists and take leadership positions within British Islam, and they maintain that integration is achievable and desirable. Yet, while these discourses appear to be conciliatory and inclusive, they still operate to discipline and control based on the same understanding of privileged spaces. 'Good' Muslims, within inclusive discourses, are ideologically structured as objects to be moved around according to the will of the rightful managers of a territorial space, and they are allowed to be Islamic insofar as the particular Islam they practice is considered acceptable by these managers. Should they display an Islamic will which is outside the boundaries of acceptability, their status will change from 'good' to 'bad' and they will be subjected to exclusionary discourse and practice.

While exclusionary discourses of Islamophobia verge on the hysterical in their insistence that the situation is already out of control, inclusive discourses tend to be more measured. Muslim cultural diversity is viewed as excessive and dangerous to privileged spaces and relationships, but the situation is considered remediable through management strategies. The integration and tolerance discourses have important roles within inclusive Islamophobia. They are directed towards different subjects (the former is directed at Muslims, while the latter is entreated to non-Muslim cultural spatial managers), but they both function as discourses which condition behavioural expectations. What marks these discourses out as Islamophobic is not only their central concern with retaining and/or reinstating the relative power of non-Muslims over Muslims, but also the centrality of those British/Western/universal values that Muslims are expected to integrate into.

The Function of Integration Discourse in Inclusive Islamophobia

Tony Blair's speech on multiculturalism and integration, in the context of the 2005 London bombings, provides a very good example of this form of inclusive Islamophobia. At the start of his speech Blair discussed the racial tolerance of Britain in glowing terms and went on to concede that the perpetrators of the attacks had been integrated at the level of lifestyle, but stated that this was not real integration, which was not about culture or lifestyle but happened at the level of (British) values (Blair 2006). He went on to define these values as a belief in democracy, the rule of law, tolerance, equal treatment for all, and respect for Britain and its shared heritage. By defining the boundaries of Britishness through an explicit outlining of the values British people were expected to share, a line of cultural tolerance was drawn which could not be crossed. He went on to state that no distinctive culture or religion superseded this duty to be part of an integrated UK, clearly implying that members of some cultures or religions had focused their loyalties elsewhere. Going on to name that community, he stated that most Muslims were decent, law-abiding and proud to be British, but that a minority, particularly from certain (unnamed) countries, were problematic. However, for Blair the history of British management of problematic communities gave grounds for optimism. The nation had successfully negotiated the Irish 'Troubles', and had created a thriving multicultural society that recognised and respected the various lifestyles and values of a diverse society. Britain's past successes proved, for Blair, that 'integrating people while preserving their distinctive cultures, is not impossible. It is the norm. The failure of one part of one community to do so is not a function of a flawed theory of a multicultural society. It is a function of a particular ideology that arises within one religion at this one time' (Blair 2006).

By relating them to extremism, terrorism and lack of integration, Blair problematised Muslims. But his inclusive discourse made clear that he was referring only to a minority of that community. British values had been contravened, and though not *all* Muslims were the problem, it was within the Muslim community that this problem arose and it was therefore this community that must be targeted with measures to integrate it properly. Blair's assertion that integrating people while preserving their distinctive cultures was the norm betrays an understanding, however, that integration is a one-way process. 'We' integrate 'them', and have had success in doing so, hence his assertion that multiculturalism was not a flawed theory. It was not 'our' way of doing things that was wrong, but problematic Muslims who had failed to grasp what being British meant.

This paternalistic understanding of the relationship between British Muslims and non-Muslims and the domestic, familial imagery of the nation that this implies, was further underlined through the language of disappointment. Blair suggested that Muslims had failed to appreciate what being British meant, misunderstood multiculturalism and neglected their duty to integrate. Multicultural Britain was never supposed to be a celebration of division or an encouragement to discord, he admonished, but a way for people to live harmoniously together (Blair 2006). His discourse of benevolent paternalism was nevertheless essentially optimistic. Since Muslims had *misunderstood* their duties as Britons, they could be drawn back into the nation through education. Although they had failed to live up to their duties, he suggested that it perhaps had not been made clear what was expected, partly because in 'our' desire to be hospitable 'we' had naively showered public funds on communities to entrench 'their' cultural presence . In other words, non-Muslim Britons did bear some of the responsibility for the parallel communities that had developed, because 'we' had simply been too welcoming, too convivial, and too *good*.

Although Blair was making a very contentious point in his linking of the London bombings to issues of integration and multiculturalism, he was able to do so by problematising Muslims at several levels (linked to extremism and terrorism, refusing to integrate, misunderstanding multiculturalism) and representing 'values' as the solution to the numerous problems associated with them. His assertion that most Muslims were not at fault was undermined by his constant referral to this community as the target of state intervention. The ideological structure of inclusive Islamophobia thus mirrors its exclusionary twin. Through a process of objectification, Muslims were not addressed as equal citizens with whom one can have a discussion about values. Rather, they were represented as a community to be *targeted* with these values, deployed as weapons of control.

Although the discourse of integration implies something positive, it is saturated with a conception of Muslims as objects to be directed and controlled. The call to integrate contains within it an understanding that something exists into which individuals *can* integrate, something larger that will contain them and within which they can be included. As Blair's narrative of paternal disappointment demonstrated, social divisions were caused by 'their' misunderstanding of the meaning of 'our' benevolent encouragement of diversity. By reaffirming what the spirit of multiculturalism truly meant, the then Prime Minister not only relieved it of any blame for contemporary social division and terrorism (blame lay firmly with 'them'), but also reassured the nation that its values were good. The integration debates always contain an implicit understanding of what the nation is and what it is not. But further, they address nationals as equals, enjoined to aid in the project of remaking the nation through espousing the ideals and values it holds dear. Problematic communities, on the other hand, are addressed as subordinates, patronisingly instructed that their efforts to be part of the nation have failed and it is not 'us' who are responsible, but 'them'.

The demand for integration is a mode of power within Islamophobic discourse that works to discursively construct Muslims as national objects. The implicit understanding that 'our' values are what Muslims need to integrate into reinforces this power relationship, and integration becomes a disciplinary process which restores contested relationships of power by positioning non-Muslims as national spatial managers with the right to decide, supervise and direct the level of acceptable integration. Such a discourse rearticulates and reproduces the differentiation between the national subject, who exercises will, and the national object, who submits to it. The uncontested centrality of the non-Muslim subject as someone whose opinion is legitimate and who is entitled to feel concerned about the level of integration is reaffirmed each time these debates resurface.

The Function of Tolerance Discourse in Inclusive Islamophobia

Integration discourse functions in tandem with tolerance; both assert rights and duties, yet they address different subjects. While integration is pitched towards Muslims, and confers the right to be British on the condition that Muslims integrate into British values, tolerance affirms the acceptance of difference as a duty which goes hand in hand with the right to be British. The latter is an address to non-Muslims to relinquish their power to be intolerant, and the former conditions this by stipulating its boundaries. When taken together the dual power of these discourses lies not only in the central uncontested power of non-Muslims to set thresholds of tolerance and levels of expected integration, but also the implication that if integration is not achieved, then intolerance is natural. In other words, if Muslims fail to integrate as directed, then the intolerance of non-Muslims is to some extent predictable, justifiable and legitimate.

Former Home and Foreign Secretary Jack Straw's intervention into the 'veil debate' is a good example of how integration and tolerance operate within Islamophobia as an expression of hegemonic power. Writing in his weekly column in the *Lancashire Evening Telegraph*, Straw discussed an encounter with one of his veiled Muslim constituents, in which he had been struck by the incongruity between her apparent Englishness and the niqab she wore to cover her face. Straw set out a dichotomy between the veil and Englishness based on his perception that the former signalled separation from common national bonds. The woman's accent indicated that English was her first language and her education, he stressed, was entirely in the UK. These facts served to indicate to the reader that the woman was British born and bred, yet the veil weakened the common bonds Straw felt with her. He went on to explain the effect that this incident had upon him:

> Above all, it was because *I felt uncomfortable about talking to someone "face-to-face" who I could not see. So I decided that I wouldn't just sit there* the next time a lady turned up to see me in a full veil, and I haven't... I can't recall a single occasion when a lady has refused to lift the veil; most seem relieved. (Straw 2006) (Emphasis added).

Straw's discomfort led him to decide that in future he would be proactive in assuaging his unease by requesting that veiled women show their faces. His recounting of this incident can be understood within the rubric of inclusive Islamophobia because of the interplay between tolerance and integration. Straw asserted that on most levels this woman was integrated. She spoke English with an English accent and had a British education, yet the fact of the veil represented to him a weakening of these bonds of commonality and above all, it made him uncomfortable. His decision to no longer 'just sit there' with a veiled woman indicates that the incident led him to abandon his diffidence and assert his desire to conduct interviews with constituents in a way that would not make him feel uncomfortable.

There are two things to note about this incident and Jack Straw's interpretation of it. First, in framing the veil as a signal of separation he marked it as a difference that exceeded his level of tolerance, and resolved to no longer accept this state of affairs by henceforth requesting that veils be removed. Second, he formulated this decision, and acted out its consequences, from a position of power. This is not just the power delegated to him by society as an elected representative, but a position of cultural power from which his entitlement to feel 'comfortable' was judged as normatively more important than Muslim women's right to veil. His acknowledgement of this power is revealed in his statement that most 'seem relieved' when he asked them to remove their veil, suggesting to his audience that by conferring permission to unveil he was in some sense liberating these women, portrayed as eagerly awaiting powerful men to authorise their undressing.

Muslims are expected to integrate and non-Muslims are expected to tolerate. Yet both of these discourses, apparently inclusive as they are, maintain the cultural power of non-Muslims, who are free to set both the boundaries of tolerance and the expected levels of integration, Muslims have only the power to endure or resist. Later in the article he relayed a story of his request in action, where the woman in question removed her veil immediately and she and Straw went on to debate the merits of veil wearing, which 'contained some surprises. It became clear that the husband played no part in her decision. She had read books about the issue. *She felt more comfortable wearing the veil when out. People bothered her less*' (Straw 2006, emphasis added).

More important than Straw's 'surprise' that the decision to veil may be autonomous and educated, is the fact that the central signifier upon which his own decision to request unveiling turned was itself an object of struggle. Both Straw and the veiled woman were seeking to go about their daily lives in a way that made them feel 'comfortable', and both, in exercising this right were causing discomfort to others. Placed in a wider context of good community relations, if the veil is constructed as a mark of separation and difference, then its removal becomes a nod towards integration and similarity, but the symbolism of the veil—its meaning in society—is decided a priori. Muslim women could thus grant or refuse Straw's request to unveil but they were denied any power to challenge his reading of the meaning of the cloth itself.

Veiled women were presented as contravening a particular value, in this case Jack Straw's right to feel 'comfortable', which was placed in a wider context of good community relations in order to generalise and naturalise it as something normatively desirable. In requesting the removal of veils, Straw prioritised his own comfort, restored his cultural will to dominance and put Muslims back in their place as objects to be directed.

The purpose of this discussion is not to mark individuals out and censure them as Islamophobic. Rather, what I have tried to show is that Islamophobia is an ideological entity that may take exclusionary and inclusive forms, but is basically dependent on an understanding that Muslim difference is excessive and dangerous and that the cultural power of non-Muslims must remain dominant in the face of increasing Islamic demands.

The integration and tolerance discourses within inclusive Islamophobia function to situate culturally defined individuals in positions of power and subordination. This discourse is usually conducted at the national level and appeals to national belonging and the rights and duties of British citizens. Yet its power goes beyond nationalism. The integration and tolerance discourses are heavily reliant on the internalisation of a subject/object construction, which determines who is a subject, with the right to set expected levels of integration and boundaries of tolerance, and who is an object, duty bound to fulfil the roles decided in advance by national subjects. Once objectified as articles of national will, to be directed and managed according to the whims of culturally dominant and value-superior non-Muslims, Muslim difference must be contained through Islamophobic discourse which reaffirms the right of national subjects to tolerate them only insofar as they have integrated.

CONCLUSION

The preceding chapters have argued that it is most useful to understand Islamophobia as a form of cultural racism. Analysing Islamophobic discourse as such brings to the fore the essentialisation of Muslim culture as something that structures the attitudes and behaviours of Muslims, is 'biologised' in some way as innate and inescapable, and is antithetical to British cultural norms. It is this understanding of Muslim culture as 'other' that drives Islamophobic expression and structures Islamophobic discourse.

Yet, the belief that Muslims are different, and even the conviction that they are culturally inferior, does not necessarily provide an imperative for acting upon these beliefs through Islamophobic discourse and practices of exclusion. Individuals may hold such beliefs without feeling any need to express them. An analysis of contemporary British Islamophobia is thus incomplete without an attempt to understand why this ideology has such salience at the present historical moment, and why Islamophobic discourse and practices occur at such varied sites and are employed by such diverse actors. What is the attraction of Islamophobic discourse?

What benefits does it provide to its adherents? And what does it achieve ideologically for those employing it?

The present chapter has aimed to answer these questions by conceptualising Islamophobia as a discourse of spatial dominance, where non-Muslims are considered to have managerial rights over a particular territory, a more legitimate claim on its values and an entitlement to decide what that territory should be like, who belongs there and who should be removed. The diversely situated expressions of Islamophobia analysed throughout this book share in common the perception that a particular space has been, or is being, culturally comprised by Muslims and a desire to reclaim that space as belonging to the dominant cultural group, whether local (Dudleians), national (English/British, French, Dutch, etc.) or civilisational (Western/European). In every articulation of Islamophobia, whether explicitly exclusionary or apparently inclusive, the illusion of the power of the dominant group to decide the cultural component of the spaces believed to be endangered is implicit, even if only expressed as the right to have a legitimate opinion. Islamophobia provides those who subscribe to its ideological tenets with a sense of control over the destiny of those spaces they consider their own.

In each of the cases discussed, because the values at stake were presented first as threatened by Muslims, and second as incontrovertible, Muslims were represented as endangering the very essence of the space held dear. In order that the space remain authentic, Muslims had to be put back in their place as an unobtrusive and inconspicuous minority who did not make specific demands that could potentially change the territory in question. Islamophobia, as a discourse of control, exists ideologically to restore to dominance the will of non-Muslims, and action, in the form of Islamophobic discourse and practice, occurs when the privileged position of non-Muslims is challenged by Muslim presence and will. It is not the fact that Muslims exist as Muslims, being different in a particular space, which is the issue. Rather, it is that they are perceived to be seeking to change this space, exercising their own Muslim will and refusing to recognise the supremacy of non-Muslims.

Within this ideological universe, Muslims occupy the position of the undesirable. As a discourse of control, Islamophobia provides its adherents with a means of reconstituting threatened identities and privileged relationships to spaces through an objectification of Muslims as the problematic significant other which prevents an idealised space being what it ought to be. The presence of Muslims is understood through this prism as deeply threatening to settled identities because of their perceived unwillingness to accept the cultural dominance of the legitimate spatial managers. Islamophobia provides a discursive means of reconstituting these fractured privileged relationships and reinstating fantasised authority. While exclusionary discourses assume that control has already been lost, inclusive discourses work on the assumption that control may still yet be retained.

Although inclusive Islamophobia appears to be conciliatory, it works on the same assumptions. When Muslims were asked to set an example by integrating into the nation, requested to remove their veils, told to declare themselves against extremism and terrorism, and exhorted not to complain about discriminatory counterterrorism practices such as stop and search, house raids and increased airport security, they were being told to put the nation above their cultural and religious difference, at the same time as the nation itself was focusing unrelentingly upon this difference. In the case of inclusive discourse, the impulse to control took the form of demands for more integration. Muslims were problematised as radically different from other Britons and within this understanding was an imperative for action. Inclusive Islamophobia aimed to integrate by only offering recognition to those Muslims who acknowledged national values as their primary identification. In doing so, it privileged non-Muslim nationals as the bearers of the right to decide who should be integrated and according to which values they should be accepted as British. The dominance of non-Muslims as legitimate deciders of, and actors upon, the national will remained in place. Even as Muslims were apparently invited into the nation, they were invited conditionally—the nation welcomed them only in so far as they accepted their pre-decided place within it.

Such a discourse need not be exclusively applied to Muslims. Other minorities have historically been, and are contemporarily, excluded (and 'included') through the same process. However, Islamophobia gains its specificity through the rather obvious fact of being directed at Muslims. There is no reason to believe that similar structural discourses could not and would not be directed at other racially or culturally defined minorities at other historical periods. By the same token, Islamophobia may lose its grip on the current British situation. At the present time, however, Islamophobia—the cultural problematisation of Muslims as Britain's significant 'others' and the drive to manage them through disciplinary discourses of control—is a principal discourse at a number of social and political sites.

It is clear from the examples discussed that Islamophobia, instrumentalised to safeguard privileged spatial relationships, does not end at the particular spaces that proponents seek to protect. Even when Islamophobic discourse is employed at a local level for very specific aims, such as in the Dudley mosque debate, proponents draw upon larger civilisational discourses in order to rationalise and prop up their claims. Every assertion of the values of a local territory, and every investigation as to whether these values had been contravened, contained within it an understanding of who was a subject with agency and the right to direct change and who was an object to be moved around according to the former's will. This subject/object construction is a central feature of Eurocentric ideology.

Eurocentrism is usually understood as a special case of ethnocentrism, the tendency of human beings to view their own social group as the basis of evaluative judgments concerning the practices of others, with the attendant implication that their values and practices are superior. What makes Eurocentrism worthy of its special status is the historical trajectory of this particular ethnocentrism. Carried by the conquistadors to the New World in the fifteenth and sixteenth centuries, spread globally by imperialist and colonialist practices of the European powers in the eighteenth and nineteenth centuries, and accompanied by Enlightenment rationality and the scientific method, the sense of Western superiority that constituted the societies of Europe (and synonymously the West) was imbibed with a claim to universality (Hobson 2006, 2–3; Heit 2005, 727–728; Dussel 1993, 74). Eurocentrism, as it historically developed, contained within it not simply an assertion that West is best, but also a claim that the rational philosophy at its core transcended cultural baggage and was thus available to all societies, who could (and should) imitate the West in order to join the march to progress that was humanity's historical mission.

Eurocentrism developed along with conquest and colonial exploitation as the ideology that justified and sustained them intellectually. Eurocentric thought held, (and holds) that Europeans had a natural advantage of culture or nature, and in each moment of history some natural essence of superiority that was bred into their very being was working itself out (Amin 2004, 2; Grosfoguel and Mielants 2006, 8). From this perspective, the conquest of the 'New World' was the natural working out of an essentially adventuresome nature, the French and American revolutions represented the natural yearning for freedom within European DNA, the industrial and scientific revolutions were explained as the result of essential European rationality, and the period of high imperialism and colonialism during the late nineteenth and early twentieth centuries was considered the historical working out of natural European civilisational superiority. Eurocentric ideology explained the West's position at the centre of the world system and world market as the natural result of centuries of supremacy at every level, a place in the world carved out by European innovation and superiority.

It is useful to consider Islamophobia under Eurocentrism as analogous to racism in a system of white supremacy, understood here as a *system* of privilege in which ordinary white people receive a variety of benefits by virtue of belonging to the racial majority and seek to defend their racial privilege through racist practices (Bonilla-silva 2000; Foster 2009). Under white supremacy, non-white races are subordinated and inferiorised, while those considered white receive social, material and psychological benefits. Eurocentrism similarly operates as a racialised social system with a civilisational thrust, in which (usually white) European 'Westerners' are considered superior in culture and values to non-Europeans. The exclusionary and inclusive forms of Islamophobia serve to maintain this system of Eurocentric dominance; a hegemonic form of control, that interpellates subjects as Western or non-Western and provides economic, social, political and psychological benefits to the former, while seeking to manage, contain and assimilate the latter. Those considered to be Western receive benefits by virtue of being the bearers of a progressive, liberal and egalitarian civilisation. Western values are considered the norm, and the standard by which other cultural subjects are judged, and Westerners have the honour of being considered subjects, capable of having an effect by directing and changing, or retaining and restricting the values of a territory. Muslims within this system are positioned as the bearers of a particularistic culture constructed as the West's antagonistic other. While Eurocentric, Western subjects accumulate all positive signifiers, Muslims are perceived as culturally deficient and required to assimilate into Eurocentric culture, imbibing its norms and values and shedding their cultural difference.

As part of a wide and deep global racial structure which provides benefits to those racialised as white, Western and European, the particular cultural racism that is Islamophobia benefits those whose values are understood as Western. This is why the concept of Eurocentrism is so important. In Britain the allocation of material and psychological benefits still depends to a large extent on white skin, but not only white skin—in a multiracial society, contemporary national belonging has a value dimension. Those whose values are considered to be in line with the dominant Eurocentric values of society receive greater benefits than those whose values are considered antithetical, opposed or inferior. Islamophobia is a (cultural) racism of values, a racism that posits the values of Eurocentric culture as superior and claims Muslim culture to be inferior, dangerous, and threatening to the maintenance of Eurocentric privilege.

If there were no benefit to employing Islamophobia, proponents would not do so. What Islamophobia offers to those who utilise its narratives and mental models is the prize of subjectivity, the positive attributes drawn into the West as an imagined civilisational territory and the consequent positive identity that is associated with it. Westerners within Eurocentrism are subjects, all others are objects. Understanding the great investment of identity that Eurocentrism represents helps explain its appeal. Eurocentrism tells a story of adventure, the conquering of the globe, the riches of the 'New World', the subjugation of the rest, and the political and technological revolutions of the early modern period. It is a history of glory and success populated by brave conquistadors and great innovators. It is an intellectual history of discovery and science, great ideas and noble principles. And it is the story of freedom; revolution from the tyranny of priests and kings and the centring of man as the creator of his destiny. By accumulating Western civilisational capital, individuals are able to claim a share of this history, and one of the most effective ways to do this is to draw a line between oneself and the cultural other whose values are believed to be absolutely antithetical.

Conceptualising Islamophobia as a shared social narrative of the West, rather than an expression of prejudicial affectation, suggests that attempts to eradicate anti-Muslim sentiment through myth-busting and contact theory are approaching the problem from the wrong angle. Similarly, integration debates are unlikely to yield positive results as long as they are structured within a Eurocentric understanding of values to be integrated into. If we understand Islamophobia as an expression of resurgent Eurocentrism then rising to its challenge implies a radically more inclusive agenda. Not only does it require that integration be reformulated away from assimilative policies that prioritise the values of one group over another, but it also demands that space be made for an open debate about the relevance and normative commitments of the values to which society subscribes.

REFERENCES

Amin, Ash. 2004. Multi-ethnicity and the Idea of Europe. *Theory, Culture & Society* 21 (2): 1–24.

Balibar, Etienne. 2007. "Is There a 'Neo-Racism'?" In *Race and Racialization: Essential Readings*, ed. Tanya Das Gupta, 83–88. Toronto: Canadian Scholars' Press Inc.

Blair, Tony. 2006. A Duty to Integrate. Speech on Multiculturalism and Integration. No. 10: The Official Site of the British Prime Minister's Office. http://www.number10.gov.uk/Page10563. Accessed 14 Feb 2011.

Bonilla-silva, Eduardo. 2000. 'This Is a White Country': The Racial Ideology of the Western Nations of the World-System. *Sociological Inquiry* 70 (2): 188–214.

Van Buuren, Jelle. 2013. Spur To Violence? *Nordic Journal of Migration Research* 3 (4): 205–215.

Durrheim, Kevin, and John Dixon. 2000. Theories of Culture in Racist Discourse. *Race and Society* 3 (2): 93–109.

Dussel, Enrique D. 1993. Eurocentrism and Modernity (Introduction to the Frankfurt Lectures). *Boundary 2* 20 (3): 65–76.

EDL. 2011a. Betrayed by Birmingham Dhimmi Council. EDL News. http://englishdefenceleague.org/birmingham_betrayed/. Accessed 1 Mar 2012.

EDL. 2011b. Birmingham Demonstration: October 29th. EDL News. http://englishdefenceleague.org/birmingham-demonstration-october-29th/. Accessed 1 Mar 2012.

EDL. 2011c. Dudley Mosque Defeat. EDL News. http://englishdefenceleague.org/dudley-mosque-defeat/. Accessed 1 Mar 2012.

EDL. 2011d. EDL Mission Statement. EDL: About Us. http://englishdefence-league.org/mission-statement. Accessed 14 Jan 2011.

EDL. 2011e. European Defence Leagues: Memorandum of Understanding. EDL News. http://englishdefenceleague.org/european-defence-leagues/. Accessed 2 Feb 2012.

Foster, J.D. 2009. Defending Whiteness Indirectly: A Synthetic Approach to Race Discourse Analysis. *Discourse & Society* 20 (6): 685–703.

Grosfoguel, Ramón, and Eric Mielants. 2006. The Long-Durée Entanglement Between Islamophobia and Racism in the Modern/Colonial Capitalist/Patriarchal World-System: An Introduction. *Human Architecture* V (1): 1–12.

Hage, Ghassan. 2000. *White Nation: Fantasies of White Supremacy in a Multicultural Society*. New York: Routledge.

Heit, Helmut. 2005. Western Identity, Barbarians and the Inheritance of Greek Universalism. *The European Legacy* 10 (7): 725–739.

Hobson, J. 2006. East and West in Global History. *Theory, Culture & Society* 23 (2–3): 408–410.

Peach, Ceri. 2006. Muslims in the 2001 Census of England and Wales: Gender and Economic Disadvantage. *Ethnic and Racial Studies* 29 (4): 629–655.

Razavy, Maryam. 2006. Sikh Militant Movements in Canada. *Terrorism and Political Violence* 18 (1): 79–93.

Riley, Krista Melanie. 2009. How to Accumulate National Capital: The Case of the 'Good' Muslim. *Global Media Journal–Canadian Edition* 2 (2): 57–71.

Straw, Jack. 2006. I Want to Unveil My Views on an Important Issue. Telegraph. http://www.telegraph.co.uk/news/1530718/I-want-to-unveil-my-views-on-an-important-issue.htm. Accessed 4 Aug 2013.

CHAPTER 7

Conclusions: The Waste of Islamophobia

INTRODUCTION

This book has had two major goals: one analytical and one theoretical. My analytical goal was to examine the nature of post-2001 Islamophobic discourse in the UK. My theoretical goal was to understand the purpose of Islamophobic discourse, the advantages that it holds for those employing it and the reason this discourse is so widespread.

Employing critical race theory as a theoretical and analytical framework, I have developed an interpretation of Islamophobia that reformulates the racialised system of white supremacy as one of Eurocentric supremacy, where Western subjects are awarded a better social, economic and political 'racial contract' and seek to defend these privileges against real and imagined Muslim demands. Under a system of Eurocentric supremacy, Islamophobia is not an 'unfounded hostility', as the Runnymede report describes it, but exists rather as a rational defence of collective Eurocentric advantages.

I have argued that as a cultural racism, Islamophobia can be conceptualised within a critical race theory framework as the racist discourse and practice that upholds a system of Eurocentric supremacy. This has been understood by other scholars as white supremacy, a historical development emerging from the colonialist and imperialist expansions of the fifteenth and sixteenth centuries that led to the development of a racialised social system which provided whites with greater benefits (Bonilla-Silva 2001, 193). I agree with this conceptualisation of white supremacy;

© The Author(s) 2018
L.B. Jackson, *Islamophobia in Britain*,
DOI 10.1007/978-3-319-58350-1_7

however, I think it is better formulated as Eurocentric supremacy in the present historical moment. Although the structures and privileges remain the same, this reformulation focuses on the universalising aspects of Western culture and the conditional invitation extended to non-Western subjects to join the march to progress that is humanity's historical mission and which is only possible through Western cultural forms.

Eurocentric Islamophobia has developed a number of narratives that enable those employing it to argue rationally that they are not against all Muslims, only extremists. In Chap. 2, I delineated the dominant state-sponsored discourses that have focused on Muslims in the post-2001 period. Community cohesion and counterterrorism were identified as the central organising discourses which aimed to represent Muslim identity and control and contain their cultural diversity. Analysis of these high-lighted the centrality of the good/bad Muslim binary and the related understanding that (bad) Muslims represented a threat to Britain's internal cohesion and external security. This binary can be understood as a representation that constructs Muslims as Britain's 'significant others', both internally and externally threatening and thus requiring careful management and surveillance.

From the critical perspective, which argues that all discourse has concrete social effects, it follows that Islamophobic discourse will be used by individuals to argue against change that is perceived to advantage Muslims and disadvantage non-Muslims. Chapter 3 considered how the dominant discourses outlined in Chap. 2 were rearticulated and reformulated for particular local purposes during the Dudley mosque debate. By isolating representations of Muslims articulated by ordinary local people for the purpose of preventing the mosque's construction, a deeper understanding of Islamophobic discourse may be obtained. This chapter demonstrated that discourses which presented Muslims as dangerous, threatening and antithetical were readily applied to a local context for the purpose of preventing change in the area.

The theoretical position outlined rests on the understanding of Islamophobia as cultural racism, yet this is a controversial conceptualisation. Chapter 4 dealt directly with this controversy, analysing the discourse of an overtly Islamophobic group, the English Defence League, and attending to their central conviction that they are 'not racist.' This chapter detailed how Islamophobia operates as culturally racist discourse by essentializing Muslim culture and employing a number of strategies typical of racist discourse construction in order to present speakers as within the boundaries of liberal tolerance. This chapter also demonstrated how the EDL laid claim to both the nation and European civilisation by presenting itself as the defender of these values and positioning Muslims as consistently and inveterately antagonistic.

If Islamophobia is an expression of Eurocentrism then its appeal will not be limited to Britain. Rather, we would expect to see any nation that has a claim to European/Western values invoking them in order to discipline and control Muslims. This was the focus of Chap. 5, which considered the way Islamophobic narratives had been used to mark national boundaries in Switzerland, Denmark, the Netherlands and France. By considering key construction moments, this chapter attempted to understand how Muslims were represented as national 'others' through a problematisation of their culture as antithetical to dearly held national values. This chapter argued that the national values appealed to were always positioned as cherished and timeless European values whose national expression was challenged and prevented full realisation by the presence of Muslims.

The four empirical chapters revealed a remarkable convergence in discourse structure, narratives used to represent Muslims and larger discourses appealed to. Yet this convergence does not provide sufficient answer to the question of why individuals and groups employ these narratives. Chapter 6 attempted to explain this phenomenon by extending Ghassan Hage's theoretical formulation of racism as nationalist practices to Islamophobic discourse. Whether employed for specific local purposes, as in the Dudley mosque debates, or for national purposes as Chaps. 4 and 5 demonstrated, Islamophobia relies on the notion that space has been culturally compromised by Muslims and must be restored to authenticity by legitimate non-Muslim cultural managers. As such it represents a discourse of control whose purpose is to put Muslims back in their place as an invisible and silent minority who do not make faith-based demands of the society in which they live. As a discourse of control, Islamophobia relies on Eurocentrism to give it rationality and legitimacy. Eurocentric binaries play a central role in this, the most important of which is the subject/objectbinary around which all other attributes of non-Muslims and Muslims are scattered in the Eurocentric imaginary.

By demonstrating the form and structure of Islamophobic discourse I have drawn attention to the culturally racist frames, styles, and ideological understandings that it recycles and relies upon, and in doing so have sought to illuminate the nature of Islamophobia. I have also addressed a significant gap in the literature; the purpose that Islamophobic discourse serves for those employing it. To this end I have conceptualised Islamophobia as a culturally racist discourse of Eurocentric supremacism, which operates to restore fantasised dominance to the supposedly legitimate cultural managers of particular spaces. Understanding Islamophobia as such allows a greater appreciation of why it has such prevalence at the present time. From the perspective of those employing the discourse, Muslims are culturally changing a space they consider their own in an unacceptable way.

THE NATURE, CHARACTER AND PURPOSE OF ISLAMOPHOBIC DISCOURSE

At the beginning of this book I posed three questions regarding the nature, the character and the purpose of Islamophobic discourse. In order to conclude, I now turn to each of these questions and offer answers.

What Is the Nature of Islamophobic Discourse?

Much of the discussion about Islamophobia has been concerned with how to conceptualise the phenomenon. The present book has analysed empirical examples of discourses that represent Muslims and Islam for their structure and form in order to contribute to this debate. From the focus within community cohesion and counterterrorism on the good/bad dichotomy, to the discourses of threat and blame which made up the discourse of opposition to Dudley mosque, the strategies of cultural racist discourse construction employed by the EDL, and the dichotomy of Western/Muslim values employed in Switzerland, Denmark, the Netherlands and France, Islamophobia relies upon binary oppositions that allow its proponents to lay claim to a host of positive values, while denigrating, disciplining and excluding Muslims.

Across these diverse sites, representations invoked an essentialized and determinative 'Muslim culture' as threatening. It is this essentialisation of culture that can be understood as the central organising principle of Islamophobia; the belief that Muslims are intrinsically different.

What Is the Character of Islamophobic and How Does It Work to Mark Boundaries of Identity?

Understanding Islamophobia as a culturally racist discourse foregrounds the way Muslims are constructed as other through particular discursive strategies. As discussed in detail in Chap. 4, racist discourse employs a number of strategies to mark its 'others' out as, while at the same time allowing those articulating the discourse to make claims to rationality and reasonableness. In Islamophobic discourse these take the form of denial of Islamophobic prejudice, projection of culturally racist motivation on to Muslims, positive-self and negative-other representations, and diminutives such as 'I'm not against all Muslims, but...' In exclusionary discourses, such as those witnessed during the Dudley mosque debate and in EDL news articles, these are often explicit and obvious. Yet inclusive discourses, such as community cohesion and integration, which constructed a good/bad Muslim binary and conditionally embraced the former while targeting and disciplining the latter, operated the very same discursive strategies.

Any discourse that essentialises culture as determining in such a way must be considered culturally racist. The discourses of threat and blame that centrally inform Islamophobia further support this conceptualisation, but it is the essential function of binaries within the discourse that help to explain how boundaries of identity are marked through Islamophobic articulation. Islamophobia turns on the central construction of us and them. Every other construction is scattered around these two identities, and each has a number of attributes attached to them that are so embedded in the discourse that to invoke one always invokes its oppositional pair. The good/bad Muslim binary that is repeatedly invoked always represents a positive identity (good Muslims who are like us and can be integrated) and (bad) Muslims with excessive and problematic cultural diversity who are present as antagonistic and must be contained.

What Is the Purpose of Islamophobic Discourse and Why Do Diversely Situated Speakers Appeal to It?

The belief that Muslims are intrinsically 'other' is not an imperative for action, and understanding that Muslims are represented as good or bad in order to draw them in or exclude them from particular sites does not explain the purpose of Islamophobic discourse. Why do diverse speakers across differing social sites appeal to the same narratives each and every time in order to mark Muslims out as different?

Even when instrumentalised for a very particular purpose, Islamophobia draws upon wider narratives that serve to link local struggles with a broad civilisational understanding of their importance. Articulated in diverse sites, Islamophobia nonetheless relies upon a restricted number of tropes that serve to represent Muslims as deeply threatening to the values and identities of the spaces they occupy. Throughout this book I have tried to show that Islamophobia, whether employed for specifically exclusionary ends or to ostensibly promote inclusion and integration, shares the same structure. This structure is ultimately a discourse of control which fantasises the authority of non-Muslims over Muslims, and it works at local and national sites in Britain and other European countries to shore up boundaries and restore control to those who feel that Muslims are changing the spaces to which they relate.

The signifiers of Islamophobic discourse are reliant on a Eurocentric understanding of values, so that those who identify with Islamophobia can draw in and on positive attributes, while dispelling negative attributes to Muslims. As a symbolic field of accumulation, Eurocentrism operates in such a way that individuals and groups can accumulate civilisational capital by laying claim to particular attributes believed to belong to the West, regardless of their skin colour, ethnic background, culture or religion, as long as they are not Muslim. This is because Muslims are understood within the ideological confines of Eurocentrism to be culturally antithetical to Western norms. Those who are unproblematically 'Western' have less discursive work to do than those whose heritage, ethnicity or skin colour mark them out as having originated from the non-West. For this latter group, Islamophobia provides a useful way of accumulating civilisational capital to stake their claim to Western Eurocentric space, and the right to decide who does and does not belong.

It is this fantasised right to decide that makes up the imperative of Islamophobia. Muslims are problematised within this discourse for the purpose of marking spatial boundaries and giving Eurocentric subjects dominion over them. By relegating Muslims to the position of local, national and civilisational object, Islamophobia promotes non-Muslim, Eurocentric subjects to the position of cultural managers. Islamophobia restores fantasised power to those who perceive Muslim cultural difference to be unacceptably changing a territory through an ideological process that first represents Muslims as making unacceptable demands of a particular territory, second, singles out a particular timeless value that is under threat, and third, reifies this value to an absolute. Through this process Muslims are put back in their place, while those participating experience a restoration of their cultural power to decide the values of a space.

POTENTIAL CRITICISMS

The theory advanced here describes a world in which some people receive 'natural' benefits by virtue of belonging unproblematically to Eurocentric culture. Accepting this theory means recognising that in a culturally racialised social system all non-Muslims receive unearned benefits. Some receive these benefits naturally, by belonging unproblematically to Eurocentric culture, being 'natural' citizens of Britain, and particularly being white. Others, whose skin colour and heritage marks them out as of immigrant descent have to articulate their belonging and mark themselves out explicitly as not Muslim by exercising cultural capital that often involves overtly Islamophobic discourse. As critical race scholars have argued, in a system of white supremacy whites develop defensive beliefs that attempt to explain their privileges as earned and legitimate. In a system of Eurocentric supremacy, natural Eurocentric subjects do the same, explaining their privileges as the result of socialisation in the culture of a 'free' society that values individualism, hard work and free expression.

Critics of this position may rebuke these claims by claiming I am making a fictitious distinction between Muslims and 'Westerners' real by reifying these categories. Some may even suggest that Muslims are themselves in the grip of Islamic supremacism or that Muslims' cultural practice is what holds them back from full participation in society, leading to self-segregation and ultimately violent extremism, which in turn colours the dominant group's view of them as unalterably 'other'.

Many of these are the same arguments made against any analysis that considers power relations to be systemic, and although ideological positions are rarely destabilised by rational arguments, I will answer each of the criticisms outlined.

First, on the reification of categories, there is a very sensible objection to be made to the use of terms such as 'Muslim', 'non-Muslim' and 'Westerner', and some may rightly point out that these terms not only have different meanings to different observers, but also are constructed categories in themselves. I agree that all social categories are constructed, and that the identity 'Muslim' will often mean very different things to those who consider themselves Muslim and those who mark others out as Muslim. I also agree with the point that 'non-Muslims' will rarely think of themselves in such terms. In fact, the identity 'non-Muslim' may seem an artificially constructed category within this analysis. I have used it not only to indicate the binary nature of the discourse of Islamophobia, but also to highlight the point that as a hegemonic ideology, those who naturally belong to Western culture view themselves as the universal, the norm that does not require articulation. A term such as 'non-Muslim' thus problematises this naturalisation of identity as the norm against which Muslims are considered aberrant. In addition it is important to remember that those who mark Muslims out as 'them' implicitly construct 'us'. It is the unarticulated nature of this 'us' that must be brought to the fore.

But further, these categories reinforce the distinctions that Islamophobia makes between people. Islamophobia works to sustain Eurocentric dominance by making the socially constructed categories of the discourse into social realities. Claiming that you do not consider yourself a 'non-Muslim' does not mean that you do not receive social, economic, political, cultural and psychological benefits from a systemic cultural racism that distributes these benefits according to such categories.

A corollary to this argument is that in my focus on cultural categories, other identifications are ignored, dismissed or their importance diluted. Although a consideration of Eurocentrism requires an inordinate focus on such constructions, at the expense of a consideration of the intersection of other identities, in seeking to understand Islamophobic discourse, analysts must approach it on its own terms. Islamophobia obliterates other identities in order to culturalise Muslims' religious identification as their primary and overriding identity. De-naturalising such constructions through critical analysis means attending to these arguments in order to destabilise their constructions. I have argued throughout this book that the culturalisation of Muslim interaction with society is a strategy of control that works to distribute privileges hierarchically. This does not mean that I consider these categories to be 'real' in any sense, or that I discount the actual, varied identifications of Muslims and non-Muslims.

In advancing this theoretical position, it is not my intention to ignore class and gender dimensions. Clearly differently positioned actors receive varying benefits. For example, it is usually low economic status Pakistani and Bangladeshi heritage Muslims who are targeted with the instruments of state Islamophobia. Men and women also receive different attention, with women usually considered to be damaging to internal integration and men considered a security risk. Similarly, middle-class professional Muslims who participate in wealth social exclusion and self-segregation are rarely targeted through state practices which aim to integrate them into British values. Nevertheless, while class and gender are important dimensions which condition how much Islamophobia individuals receive, the totalising nature of the discourse means that every Muslim, or individual identified as such, receives structural disadvantages in a Eurocentric system.

The same applies to non-Muslims, for whom class and racial distinctions are similarly relevant. The rank and file of the English Defence League, for example, are largely white working-class men who may not feel they receive any benefit from Eurocentric privilege. Yet the psychological advantages of being constructed as natural managers of particular local and national spaces means that they, as they constantly reiterate, have a right to be heard. They claim to be the voice of ordinary British people and they demand respect as such. As I argued in Chap. 4, an Islamic group which employed the same tactics and discourse as the EDL would be prohibited immediately as an extremist security threat. The EDL are correct in their assertions that they do not receive the same privileges as the elite, but despite all the condemnation from politicians and the media, the group has been permitted to voice its discontent in spectacular ways precisely because of Eurocentric privilege which assumes the EDL has a right to demonstrate, a privilege which has not been extended to many Muslim groups whose ideological position is considered distasteful.

On the second point, the position that Muslims are to blame for the discrimination they receive is a central trope of Islamophobia and turns on several arguments. I have discussed these in the preceding chapters, including the idea that Islamophobia is largely caused by Muslim terrorism (Chap. 6) and that excessive Muslim cultural difference makes them impossible to live alongside (Chap. 4). I want to attend here to the argument that Muslims are in the grip of their own cultural Islamic supremacism, leading them to demand special treatment that is unacceptable in a free society. An example often cited of this is the real and perceived demand that non-Muslims show deference to the Prophet by not depicting him, a central trope in both the Danish cartoons controversy and the January 2015 attacks on the *Charlie Hebdo* offices. Then Home Secretary Theresa May also alluded to this in her March 2015 speech on extremism, stating: 'in a pluralistic society like ours, there are responsibilities as well as rights. You don't only get the freedom to live how you choose to live. You have to respect other people's rights to do so too' (May 2015).

According to the analysis I have outlined, Islamic supremacism cannot exist in the same way that Eurocentric supremacism exists. This is because the latter relies on a 500 year system of domination which has accumulated wealth for its subjects through imperialist expansion and colonialist domination, created an epistemological hegemony that reified Western knowledge as the only true, rational knowledge, and has relied on a domination/subordination binary that has not only historically subjugated a large proportion of the 'Islamic world' (including the ancestors of today's Western Muslims, the vast majority of which are the descendants of post-1945 economic immigrants of former Western colonies) but continues to do so today through the neoliberal economic restructuring of the World Bank and the International Monetary Fund, as well as the wars of intervention and reconstruction that followed the September 11, 2001 attacks. Muslims, in the West and in the world, simply do not have the power to articulate a discourse of supremacism that is in any way comparable to Eurocentrism. There may well be individual Muslims, as well as Muslim societies and groups, who do claim that Islam is a superior social and cultural system, but this is not reinforced by the might of a global system boasting half a millennia of accumulated economic, political, epistemological, cultural and psychological privilege. Islamic supremacism, such as it exists, is an ethnocentrism and Muslims do not have the power to discipline non-Muslims in the ways I have discussed in this book.

Having said that, there is no theoretical reason why Muslims (as a socially constructed group) could not over a long period of time accumulate the wealth and power that would make this ethnocentrism universal in the Eurocentric sense, and thus become 'reverse-Islamophobic' towards Westerners. There is nothing intrinsic within Western culture that makes Eurocentrism inevitable, and any cultural group with a universalising mission could potentially accumulate advantages that allowed its particular culture to be articulated as both universal and superior. However, given the global reach of Eurocentric domination and the entrenched privileges that it has created for its social and cultural practices, this is unlikely. Islamic supremacism, thus, represents a particularistic position, while Eurocentrism is a global system of domination.

This project was initially conceived to focus exclusively on Islamophobia in the British context. As I explored these discourses further, however, it became obvious that although Islamophobic discourse was always wielded for particular purposes, in every case studied there were larger discourses at play. These broad civilisational themes emerged at every site studied, and intertwined with local and national narratives in ways that tied belonging to a much larger project of identity construction.

The understanding of Eurocentrism as the guiding narrative that gives shape to local and national Islamophobia, by positioning particular spaces as belonging to 'the West' and threatened by Muslims, is greatly indebted to the work of Ghassan Hage, who has interpreted these practices as nationalistic. The consistent return to Western values by differently situated speakers indicated that a larger discourse was being appealed to, and the recognition that this occurred in a number of European states precisely when Muslims were perceived to be more powerful than they should be led to the conceptualisation of Islamophobia as a form of Eurocentrism, articulated when the hegemonic understanding that 'the West' is the best is no longer taken for granted.

Charles Mills has argued that the modern world has been fundamentally shaped by European colonialism, and white supremacy as a system came into existence through European expansion and the historic domination of white Europe over non-white non-Europe (Mills 2003, 37–38).This understanding, that whiteness and Eurocentrism are fundamentally linked, has provided the conceptual framework for this analysis as inductive reasoning has produced research results that required explanation. In the light of the findings of the analyses across chapters, I have put forward a theory of Islamophobia that attempts to reconcile the local, national and civilisational spaces to which those employing the discourse appeal.

There is a further potential criticism that must be addressed, regarding the exclusive focus within this book on Islamophobic discourse, and the lack of engagement with discourses which seek to challenge the constructions that emerge. Peter Kolchin (2002, 162) has detailed this criticism with regard to CRT, arguing that a focus on image and representations makes it difficult to judge the prevalence of particular ideas, while quoting extensively from racist stereotypes tends to obscure the resistance of the opponents of such views. My focus throughout this book has been on trying to understand the nature and purpose of Islamophobic discourse. It may thus appear that the discourses of resistance, from those who seek to challenge these narratives within these discursive communities, have been omitted from the analysis.

In certain contexts, for example within the pages of *Dudley News* and on the EDL news website, there was very little challenge to the dominant discourse, and those that did remained within the discursive regime of Islamophobia (i.e. arguing that some Muslims are good, but all are potentially bad, and using the 'we are not against all Muslims, only extremists...' semantic move). What this suggests is that Islamophobia is a dominant discourse, and I have detailed how the discourse constrains the cognitive processes and social mind of those to whom it appeals.

Nevertheless, challenges to dominant discourses reveal a great deal about their nature and their ability to ideologically suture ruptures in their explanatory power. The experiential knowledge of those actors subjected to racialised discourses are of particular importance when adopting a CRT approach, and the viewpoints and experiences of Muslims would have added an extra dimension to this research, directing attention to the ways differently situated Muslims have understood and resisted their own objectification and potentially offering strategies for challenging and confronting Islamophobic discourse. Constraints of time and space have limited my ability to further pursue the way that challenges to Islamophobia and its dominant tropes are articulated by those objectified by the discourse, however this remains an important and fruitful area for further research.

The lack of attention to Muslims' own conceptualisation of how Islamophobia affects their lives has not been a deliberate attempt to exclude their perspectives. Much important work has been done in this area, and there are a number of directions that analyses which employ the methods and theoretical perspectives I have detailed here could potentially take. My focus has been on how and why non-Muslims employ Islamophobic discourse. As David Gillborn has noted, if those employing critical theoretical perspectives take seriously the importance of experiential knowledge, then the perspectives of white-identified people to help inform critical interventions must not be discounted (Gillborn 2008, 34). My own subjectivity as an uncomplicatedly white, and therefore Eurocentric identified researcher, has placed me in a position where, during my daily life, I am regularly subjected to many of the argumentative strategies and tropes that are central to Islamophobic discourse, spoken by fellow white-identified people who believe they are speaking to someone sympathetic with their views. As David Stovall has argued:

> Whites should be included in the focus on White privilege in that the responsibility in educating other Whites rests heavily with them. Their experiential knowledge of the construct enables them to unpack the intricate and subtle functions of White privilege and its various rationales. (Stovall 2006, 251–252)

My own experiential knowledge of the way Islamophobic discourse has an everyday and unconscious element has, in many ways, formed the rationale for this project as well as convincing me of its importance during the inevitable moments of doubt that come with the territory of any large research project. As such, this book may be seen in part as an attempt to unpack these common-sense and mundane Islamophobic discourses that non-Muslim identified people are subjected to. While it is not my intention to suggest that non-Muslims are somehow 'more hurt' by Islamophobia, that would be absurd, it is important to recognise that a *system* Islamophobia spans all social sites and encompasses all social actors, and that non-Muslim identified people are often seen as allies in Islamophobia. A central focus of this research has thus been to equip all actors to challenge articulations which claim to be rational and reasonable.

IMPLICATIONS: THE WASTE OF ISLAMOPHOBIA

In their book *White Racism* Feagin, Vera and Batur highlighted the waste of racism in terms of energy, a breakdown of human empathy and sacrifice of human talent (Feagin et al. 2001, 31). It is my position that Islamophobia should be resisted as a system of domination regardless of instrumental reasons for its opposition, however the colossal wastefulness of Islamophobia is simply too large to ignore.

Islamophobia has coloured the state's understanding of where to focus its attention to such an extent that it has been immensely wasteful of both human lives and state resources. The 'war on terror', which turned on Islamophobic constructions of Muslims as terrorists to be 'rooted out', oppressed Afghan women in desperate need of rescue, and the exportation of freedom through occupation, has been estimated to have directly led to the deaths of more than 350,000 people (Costs of War Project 2014) and cost more than $4.4 trillion (Crawford 2014). Similarly, British counterterrorism has pumped millions of pounds into counterterror programmes designed to disrupt a (highly contentious) 'conveyor belt of terror' (Moskalenko and McCauley 2009). The Islamophobic dimensions of these policies have included domestic surveillance programmes which focused their gaze on Muslim institutions, high-density Muslim communities, and Islamic university societies and charities (Erfan-Ghettani 2012; Spalek and Lambert 2008; Choudhury and Fenwick 2011; Ansari 2005; Fekete 2004), as well as racialised policing including 'shoot to kill' policies and increased stop and search of 'Muslim looking' individuals (Gillborn 2006, 320–323; Pantazis and Pemberton 2011; Poynting and Mason 2006, 375–376; Abbas 2013).

Based on Islamophobic understandings that culturalise politics and politicise culture, these practices have not only wasted lives, talent, time and resources, but there is strong evidence to suggest that they have also been largely counterproductive, failing to reach individuals most at risk of 'radicalisation', alienating large sections of the Muslim community and creating a widespread distrust of the state among both domestic and foreign Muslim populations (Thomas 2010, 52–58; Birt 2009; Choudhury and Fenwick 2011; Kundnani 2012; Pantazis and Pemberton 2008, 12–14).

But it is not just Muslim lives that are affected by the wastefulness of Islamophobia. The immense amount of energy invested in distrusting and fearing Muslims by those employing Islamophobic understandings, including the anti-Dudley mosque campaigners and the English Defence League, results not only in a breakdown of communal bonds and empathy, wasteful in itself, but a proliferation of perennially blocked identities. As Zeus Leonardo (2002, 31) has noted in relation to whiteness, the daily fears associated with the upkeep of this fragile construction mean that, as a performance, whiteness is always an inch away from being exposed as bogus. Constructed on the understanding that Muslim presence prevents a space being what it should be, contemporary Eurocentric identities are similarly built on shifting sands, and rely to a large extent on worry, anger and anxiety. The identity crises that result from conceptualising the world in this way can thus never be positively resolved and attending to the wastefulness of Islamophobia implies also the recognition that it is psychologically harmful to those employing it.

To interpret Islamophobia as a Eurocentric discourse of spatial dominance highlights its nature as a structural racism that serves to disadvantage Muslims in a number of ways, while conversely advantaging non-Muslims. To be a Muslim in the post-2001 period is to be held collectively responsible for society's gravest problems, relentlessly scrutinised for signs of extremism and anti-British or anti-Western sentiment, expected to consistently and monotonously condemn terrorism and extremism, to put the good of the nation above one's own cultural practices and to be deeply suspicious if perceived not to do so. What is being asked of Muslims in the contemporary climate is unjust and illegitimate. But more than this, it is impossible. Islamophobic discourse always implicitly or explicitly asserts that 'our' Western values are better, and they are proposed as the solution to all the problems that Muslims cause. The discourse asserts that if Muslims would practice their religion in a secular, liberal and invisible way, as 'we' practice ours, then the natural hostility of non-Muslims to their difference would dissolve. Couched in conditions that demand Muslims' first priority be respect for and recognition of Eurocentrism's implicit supremacy, Islamophobia informs Muslims that they will never be embraced in the nation or the 'civilisation' until they shed their cultural difference, secularise their religion and become like 'us'.

The problem with deploying universal values as weapons of control is that their very reification as non-negotiable and immutable diminishes their usefulness for the purposes they are being wielded. The consistent return to values as a salve to be applied to social conflict and excessive Muslim difference reveals something important about Islamophobia. It is understood that Eurocentric values are universal values, encompassing collective human aspirations to freedom, democratic representation, equality and tolerance. They are positioned as the starting point from which we are allowed to have differences, the glue that binds us, and as such are not open to debate; we must all accept these values as the expression of our sameness before we may assert our differences. Yet the sacrosanct positioning of such values as beyond challenge means that rather than being open to the scrutiny of alternative traditions, positions and understandings, Eurocentric values are increasingly wielded in a totalitarian manner that subverts contestation and reproduces difference as danger and threat.

Positioning such values as at the same time universal and immutable implies that one-way integrationis the only integration considered possible. Yet, as more Muslims are born and raised in Britain and the West, furnished with and expecting the same rights and entitlements, and interpreting their religious and cultural heritage in hybrid and novel ways, this understanding of integration is increasingly archaic. The recognition and respect demanded by Muslims, and by a progressive society in general, requires not the assimilation of Muslims who have shed their cultural baggage, but mutual integration that recognises diverse cultural rights and accords respect to all. It is this integration, and the attendant possibility that 'we' may be changed by 'them,' that Eurocentric Islamophobia fears most. And as a discourse of control it operates to prevent such change, and reinstate the dominance and might of the non-Muslim group.

CONCLUSION ✓ ᴵᴹᴾ

Recognising Islamophobia as an ideology of dominance that is wasteful of lives, talent and resources implies that, despite the scattered privileges associated with presenting oneself as a Eurocentric subject and thus laying claim to the benefits of Eurocentrism, the vast majority of people in Britain do not benefit from it. Sustained by a fear of loss, Islamophobia is an anxiety that saps the energy of those subscribing to its tenets as they try to maintain the way things are in the face of local, national and global change.

Islamophobia depends on the belief that Muslim participation in society is to be feared. If we were to remove this pillar and counter this idea, then Islamophobia would crumble. This is not an easy task. As an ideology, Islamophobia is not merely a collection of erroneous ideas that can be proved false, but a social narrative that provides its adherents with an explanation of how things are and how they should be. Within the ideology of Islamophobia, Muslims are blamed for society's problems, and the solution is considered to lie in the restoration of cultural control to non-Muslim managers whose values are considered better. While destabilising these narratives and the assertions on which they are based is important, it does little to destabilise the ideological Eurocentric supremacy on which Islamophobia is based and to which its adherents constantly turn in seeking justification.

How then to challenge Eurocentrism? As discussed above, the hegemonic articulation of Eurocentrism in the form of Islamophobia itself suggests that all is not well. When the politics of domination expressly articulates itself as such, it indicates that the dominated are not content to remain in their place. It is the interpretation of Muslim political action as indicative of a general Islamic cultural challenge to particular spaces that leads to the articulation of Islamophobia. In order to contest this ideologically, first the tendency to culturalise politics must be dismantled across society. Not only does this perspective encourage Islamophobia, but it also has been shown to be counterproductive and wasteful of state resources. Academic research in this area is crucial to destabilise the assumption that political positions are culturally determined.

Second, Muslim political perspectives must be heard. For too long the culturalisation of politics has rendered any Muslim political expression potentially risky. Controlling the boundaries of valid expression has had real-world effects on the communities targeted, causing distrust of each other, the government, police and security services, and wider society. As Arun Kundnani has discussed, it is the possibility rather than the fact of surveillance that is enough to pressure people into conformity and enforce a culture of self-censorship (Kundnani 2014, 281). The anxiety generated by state scrutiny and the policing of expression does not make for active and articulate Muslim citizens. By the same token, the fear of Muslim political activity experienced by the non-Muslim population has similarly erosive effects upon communities at all levels.

Finally, the sense of control that Islamophobia seeks to restore should be attended to. Islamophobia does not emerge from a vacuum and the need to fantasise dominance in order to feel worthy must be addressed. How can communities and individuals be empowered so they have no need to fantasise themselves as cultural managers in order to feel worthy? The crisis of dominance that is described in this book has found political expression on the world stage in recent months, as increasingly racist, sexist and Eurocentric positions are espoused by politicians and commentators who promise to restore the natural order of things. Just as the UK 'Brexit' referendum employed Islamophobic images of brown migrants invading the nation, so Donald Trump's election promises centred on forcing Muslim Americans to register with the government and preventing refugees entering the US from Muslim countries identified as 'dangerous'. As I write, President Trump has signed executive orders which will put his overtly Islamophobic promises into practice. For many across the world, the progressive gains of the last half a century have never seemed so fragile. Yet it is precisely at this moment in history that the work of disentangling the ideological narratives of us and them is most important.

The project of destabilising Eurocentrism requires a recognition that the spaces that Islamophobia seeks so desperately to protect are hybrid spaces, indebted to the 'others' who have not only created Europe's historical wealth but have also been central to the forging of its self-identity. This requires attending to the social fact of Islamophobia, revealing its discursive operations wherever they appear and destabilising the contestable assumptions upon which it relies. Further, it means supporting, intellectually and financially, those Muslims who speak up about and against Islamophobia as well as grassroots efforts to provide counter-narratives to the tendency to culturalise politics. Such work is crucial. As John Hobson has argued, the revelations of imperial racism were fundamentally important in catalysing decolonisation, and there is no reason to believe that the same strategies cannot be used to undermine the Eurocentrism of today (Hobson 2007, 114). This book represents a modest step in that direction, and aims to provide conceptual and analytical tools with which to challenge Islamophobic discourse and the Eurocentrism on which it relies.

But most importantly, an anti-Eurocentric policy must be prepared to relinquish control of culturally defined spaces. In a multiracial and multicultural society it is no longer feasible to assert the superiority of a Western subjectivity, without those historically and contemporarily objectified by this discourse protesting its supposedly unblemished record of progress. If the West has truly exported its positive qualities to the world, changing and influencing the cultures it came into contact with, it must now be willing to be changed. In Britain, this must start by recognising Islamophobia to be an articulation of Western supremacy, and admitting Muslims to the position of equal subjects with as legitimate a claim on the future of the nation as anyone else.

REFERENCES

Abbas, Madeline-Sophie. 2013. White Terror in the 'War on Terror'. *Critical Race and Whiteness Studies* 9 (1): 1–17.

Ansari, Fahad. 2005. British Anti-Terrorism: A Modern Day Witch-Hunt. *Islamic Human Rights Commission*. London: Islamic Human Rights Commission. http://www.ihrc.org.uk/file/2005BritishANtiTerrorism.pdf. Accessed 30 Dec 2010.

Birt, Yahya. 2009. Promoting Virulent Envy? *The RUSI Journal* 154 (4): 52–58.

Bonilla-Silva, Eduardo. 2001. *White Supremacy and Racism in the Post-Civil Rights Era*. London: Lynne Rienner.

Choudhury, Tufyal, and Helen Fenwick. 2011. The Impact of Counter-Terrorism Measures on Muslim Communities. *Equality and Human Rights Commission Research Report 72*. http://www.equalityhumanrights.com/uploaded_files/research/counter-terrorism_research_report_72.pdf. Accessed 5 Aug 2013.

Costs of War Project. 2014. Direct War Death in Afghanistan, Iraq, and Pakistan October 2001–April 2014. *Boston University*. http://www.costsofwar.org/sites/default/files/Direct War Death Toll in Iraq, Afghanistan and Pakistan since 2001 to April 2014 6 26.pdf. Accessed 27 Mar 2015.

Crawford, Neta. 2014. US Costs of Wars through 2014: $4.4 Trillion and Counting. *Boston University*. http://www.costsofwar.org/sites/default/files/articles/20/attachments/Costs of War Summary Crawford June 2014.pdf. Accessed 27 Mar 2015.

Erfan-Ghettani, Ryan. 2012. Strangers in Our Own Land. 23 March. *Institute of Race Relations*. http://www.irr.org.uk/news/strangers-in-our-own-land/.

Feagin, Joe R., Hernan Vera, and Pinar Batur. 2001. *White Racism*. New York: Routledge.

Fekete, Liz. 2004. Anti-Muslim Racism and the European Security State. *Race & Class* 46 (1): 3–29.

Gillborn, David. 2006. Rethinking White Supremacy. *Ethnicities* 6 (3): 318–340.

———. 2008. *Racism and Education: Coincidence or Conspiracy?*. London: Routledge.

Hobson, John M. 2007. Is Critical Theory Always for the White West and for Western Imperialism? Beyond Westphilian towards a Post-Racist Critical IR. *Review of International Studies* 33 (S1): 91–116.

Kolchin, Peter. 2002. Whiteness Studies: The New History of Race in America. *Journal of American History* 89 (1): 154–173.

Kundnani, Arun. 2012. Radicalisation: The Journey of a Concept. *Race & Class* 54 (2): 3–25.

———. 2014. *The Muslims Are Coming!*. London: Verso.

Leonardo, Zeus. 2002. The Souls of White Folk: Critical Pedagogy, Whiteness Studies, and Globalization Discourse. *Race, Ethnicity and Education* 5 (1): 37–41.

May, Theresa. 2015. Speech: A Stronger Britain, Built on Our Values (Delivered at Royal Institution of Chartered Surveyors, London). *Gov.uk*, 23 March.

https://www.gov.uk/government/speeches/a-stronger-britain-built-on-our-values. Accessed 28 Mar 2015.

Mills, Charles W. 2003. White Supremacy as a Sociopolitical System: A Philosophical Perspective. In *White Out: The Continuing Significance of Racism*, ed. Ashley Doane and Eduardo Bonilla-Silva, 35–48. London: Routledge.

Moskalenko, Sophia, and Clark McCauley. 2009. Measuring Political Mobilization: The Distinction Between Activism and Radicalism. *Terrorism and Political Violence* 21 (2): 239–260.

Pantazis, Christina, and Simon Pemberton. 2008. Trading Civil Liberties for Greater Security?: The Impact on Minority Communities. *Criminal Justice Matters* 73 (1): 12–14.

———. 2011. Restating the Case for The 'suspect Community': A Reply to Greer. *British Journal of Criminology* 51 (6): 1054–1062.

Poynting, Scott, and Victoria Mason. 2006. Tolerance, Freedom, Justice and Peace?: Britain, Australia and Anti-Muslim Racism since 11 September 2001. *Journal of Intercultural Studies* 27 (4): 365–391.

Spalek, Basia, and Robert Lambert. 2008. Muslim Communities, Counter-Terrorism and Counter-Radicalisation: A Critically Reflective Approach to Engagement. *International Journal of Law, Crime and Justice* 36 (4): 257–270.

Stovall, David. 2006. Forging Community in Race and Class: Critical Race Theory and the Quest for Social Justice in Education. *Race Ethnicity and Education* 9 (3): 243–259.

Thomas, Paul. 2010. Failed and Friendless: The UK's 'Preventing Violent Extremism' Programme. *The British Journal of Politics & International Relations* 12 (3): 442–458.

INDEX

© The Editor(s) (if applicable) and The Author(s) 2018
L.B. Jackson, *Islamophobia in Britain*,
DOI 10.1007/978-3-319-58350-1